D1393882

THE
BLUE CHAIR
JAM COOKBOOK

THE
BLUE CHAIR
JAM COOKBOOK

EDUCATION LIBRARY SERVICE 01606 275801	
RL	17-Sep-2012
	£ 12.50

RACHEL SAUNDERS

Photography by Sara Remington

**Andrews McMeel
Publishing, LLC**
Kansas City · Sydney · London

The Blue Chair Jam Cookbook text copyright © 2010 Rachel Saunders.
Photographs copyright © 2010 Sara Remington.

All rights reserved. Printed in China. No part of this book may be used or
reproduced in any manner whatsoever without written permission
except in the case of reprints in the context of reviews. For information, write
Andrews McMeel Publishing, LLC,
an Andrews McMeel Universal company
1130 Walnut Street
Kansas City, Missouri 64106.

10 11 12 13 14 SDB 10 9 8 7 6 5 4 3 2 1

ISBN-13: 978-0-7407-9143-7
ISBN-10: 0-7407-9143-5

Library of Congress Control Number: 2010921936

While every effort has been made to ensure the accuracy of the information
contained in this book, in no circumstances will the Author or Publisher be liable
or responsible for any loss or damage (including damage to property and/or
personal injury) arising from any error in or omission from the information
contained in this book, or from the failure of the reader to properly and
accurately follow any instructions contained in the book.

Design: Francesca Bautista
Food stylist: Ethel Brennan

www.andrewsmcmeel.com
www.bluechairfruit.com

ATTENTION: SCHOOLS AND BUSINESSES
Andrews McMeel books are available at quantity discounts with bulk purchase
for educational, business, or sales promotional use.
For information, please write to: Special Sales Department,
Andrews McMeel Publishing, LLC
1130 Walnut Street
Kansas City, Missouri 64106.

For Anne and Richard, who gave me my first stepstool so I could reach the kitchen counter.

And for Mark—I love you. I love you.

CONTENTS

PART I INTRODUCTION

THE ROOTS OF BLUE CHAIR FRUIT

The kitchen has always been my favorite room in the house and the market my favorite place outside. Some of my earliest memories revolve around food: strawberry picking; churning mocha ice cream on our back porch; making butter in the blender; and my favorite of all, the smell of fresh tomatoes in the yard. My mother taught me basic cooking when I was young and then set me free in the kitchen, where I eagerly began exploring. I started dreaming of California after receiving a San Francisco cookbook for Christmas one year. It was largely this book, which spoke of fruits I had never tasted and spices I had never heard of, that taught me to cook, always with my parents' encouragement.

I studied French and art in college, spending a year and a half in France and Tuscany by my early twenties. France was a delight: Meals were ritualized and structured, food was beautiful and fresh, and sweet things were always just sweet enough. The markets were awash with perfect, luscious fruit, much of which I had never seen before.

I moved to San Francisco upon receiving my degree, and shortly thereafter began working with food. I spent my off hours browsing at farmers' markets and reading cookbooks, always striving to learn more. The sheer numbers and beauty of the fruits available dazzled me. I tried to cook as many desserts as I could, but I found myself practically drowning in my creations. I couldn't possibly hope to eat them all! It was then that I decided to try my hand at jams.

My first batch of jam came from an excellent dessert cookbook, and it turned out well, but it was not exactly what I had envisioned. It was at that moment that I became hooked on jam making. Several years of intense experimentation ensued. I slaved away in my tiny kitchen, gradually developing my own techniques in my quest for perfect results. Over time, I grew to understand fruit. I also, through the course of these several years, formed my own vision of what the ideal textures were for different jams and marmalades.

After nearly a decade of work, I had finally reached the point where I felt I could create any jam or marmalade I desired. And my company, Blue Chair Fruit, was born.

For me, *blue chair* represents the nostalgic kitchen, brimming with comforting warmth and enticing smells and tastes. It is a natural extension of the farm and garden, a dynamic playground where there is always something new and delicious in season and where we can let our imaginations run wild. Above all, it is an *idea* of cooking—one in which inspiration is everywhere, waiting to be found. Aside from all the hard work involved in jam making, it is the sheer fun of it, and its rich rewards and sense of adventure, that inspired these pages. Few things match the satisfaction of gazing at a row of sparkling, brightly colored jars, just waiting to be shared with your family and friends, or the anticipation of trying that next idea or picking that next fruit from your backyard tree.

Turn to the preserving section of a midcentury cookbook and you will likely find recipes for a few simple preserves, perhaps one or two with a couple of interesting herbs or spices thrown in. You might be astonished by the extremely high quantity of sugar called for. And, once you select a recipe and begin making jam, the lack of clear directions may also amaze you. Something—you tell yourself after you have devoted a few hours, been splattered with blackberry juice, and are looking at a pile of dirty dishes and a few jars of leathery preserves—*something* was missing, but I'm just not sure what!

Preserving transforms raw ingredients—fruit, sugar, lemon—as much or as little as the individual cook desires. It is up to you, the jam maker, to determine the eventual texture, appearance, flavor, consistency, and complexity of each individual preserve. To do this with confidence, it is invaluable to have a clear understanding of both the technical and aesthetic possibilities of preserving.

The Blue Chair Jam Cookbook is a distillation of all I have learned about fruit in the past ten years. The recipes here represent my favorite ideas and techniques from each season. Every year, I make different jams and marmalades than the year before, because new ideas come to me all the time. The possibilities are endless and, once you have acquired the taste, it becomes difficult to resist making jam when the opportunity presents itself. Strawberries are an excellent example. This seemingly ordinary fruit can be transformed not only into delicious plain jam but also into something truly *extra*ordinary: combined with a whole host of other flavors, made into jelly, even incorporated into a marmalade. I am not a traditionalist when it comes to preserving, but I *am* a stickler for texture, balance, and appearance. The essential question is, does a preserve taste and look *great*? The answer to this question should always be yes.

Once you begin to explore the entire range of herbs, spices, spirits, liqueurs, and even extracts available, a whole new world reveals itself: One in which not merely a fruit but also a certain flavor that may seem to belong *with* that fruit may excite and inspire you. As you read through these pages, you will see preserves ranging from the most basic to the most complex, along with many suggestions for variations. I hope this approach will help you have fun making something exquisite, something more than the sum of its parts. And this, in a broader sense, is the joy of preserving and of cooking in general.

This book is about fruit, but in a very special context. Unlike fruit desserts, jams and marmalades are rarely eaten alone. Flavorless jam simply tastes sugary, and its personality fades away next to a slice of bread and butter or a cup of yogurt. Thus, using the absolute best fruit you can find is essential. The best fruit is what grows in your own backyard. My devotion to fresh, seasonal, local fruit informs every word of this book.

Great preserves stand out for their perfect balance of flavor, texture, and appearance. How do you achieve this balance? When making a jam or marmalade, even if you are following a preexisting recipe, nothing is more helpful or inspiring than understanding how to put your ideals into practice. Each batch of jam you make will differ slightly from the one that came before. Thus, a clear understanding of fruit, and of how it acts when cooked, will help you through the adventure of preserving.

chapter 1

JAMS, JELLIES & MARMALADES: GETTING THE MOST OUT OF FRUIT

DEFINING JAMS, JELLIES, MARMALADES & THEIR KIN

Although we have all tasted jams, jellies, and marmalades at one time or another, the question I am most often asked is simply: What is the difference between these three major types of preserves? The answer has nothing to do with the ingredients, although the one essential ingredient for all preserves is fruit. Instead, it concerns both the techniques used to prepare and cook the fruit and the texture of the resulting preserve. A jam is a fruit preserve consisting of pieces of fruit cooked with sugar until they thicken and partially break down. A jelly is an extracted fruit juice that has been combined with sugar, lemon juice, and (sometimes) added pectin and boiled until it sets. A marmalade is a jelly with clearly defined pieces of fruit suspended in it. Two other related types of preserves, butters and cheeses (or pastes), also exist. A fruit butter is a sweetened fruit puree cooked very slowly for a long time over low heat, generally resulting in a smoother texture than that of most jams. A fruit cheese or paste is a high-pectin fruit butter cooked until it has thickened and lost enough moisture to form a solid mass when cool.

Though they all begin with fruit, each type of preserve achieves its flavor differently. Both jams and marmalades have an intense taste, but they arrive at it in opposite ways. Good jams are cooked as quickly as possible with as little sugar as possible, so as best to capture the essence of the raw fruit; the idea is to take the fruit to its highest pinnacle of flavor and then immediately stop the cooking. Jellies and marmalades take the opposite approach, achieving their strength through *concentration*. A good jelly or marmalade, instead of quickly "flash-cooking" its ingredients, cooks them slowly over a very long period of time (with marmalade, often days) in order to draw out every last drop of flavor and pectin from the fruit. Jellies and marmalades, while they taste intensely of fruit, do not taste of *raw* fruit at all.

Though different fruits are perhaps more naturally suited to different preserving techniques, it is frequently a personal as much as a practical choice to make one type of preserve over another with a particular fruit. For example, rhubarb, which is most frequently associated with jam, may be used in both jellies and marmalades; and kumquats, which are most frequently associated with jellies and marmalades, may be used in jam.

UNDERSTANDING JAMS

Jam, no matter what the flavor, always reminds me of England. Jams as we know and think of them today have a special bond with that country. Many now-classic jam fruits, including damsons and wild blackberries, were first brought into wide use by the English, who still maintain a taste for these time-tested flavors. The word *jam* is unique to the English language and is British in origin. Its linguistic precursor, *marmalade*, has appeared in many different cultures and meant many different things over the centuries. In English, one often

thinks of marmalade as strictly a citrus preserve, but in other languages this word refers to fruit preserves of widely varying types.

The earliest fruit to be preserved was the quince, which was stored and cooked in honey in ancient Rome. From these early quince preserves, others followed, always using fruits, such as damsons or sour oranges, that were high in both pectin (a natural thickener) and acid (a natural preservative). The tradition of preserves made with low-pectin, low-acid fruits started much later. Fruits low in pectin and acid are not as naturally suited to long-term preservation, and they are often, unlike the earliest preserved fruits, excellent eaten raw.

Although there are many variations in technique, the basic idea and process of jam making remain the same, no matter what kind of jam you are creating. To make jam, raw fruit is combined *directly* with sugar and lemon juice and cooked until it thickens to a spreadable consistency.

Numerous factors affect the jam-making process, including the specific qualities of the fruit and your desired end result. Jam making may incorporate a wide range of techniques. Depending upon which jam you are preparing, you may alternately puree part of the fruit ahead of time, macerate it with sugar overnight to draw out its juice, extract some of its juice prior to cooking, cook it in stages, cook it over high heat, or cook it over low heat, to name just a few possibilities.

Jams should be spreadable and unified in texture. Although some jams may be "looser" than others, they should be neither watery nor overly firm. Jam's most important characteristic is its intensely fresh taste. Because a jam's fruit is cooked for a much shorter time than that of a jelly or marmalade, jams bring out the pure flavor of a fruit without dramatically altering it. The brief cooking time and uneven texture of jams make them the most rustic of preserves. When making jam, no matter what the fruit, your goal should always be to make the freshest-tasting, most balanced and flavorful, and best-textured jam possible.

THE BEAUTY OF JELLIES & MARMALADES

Jelly making transforms fruit, reducing it to a tiny quantity of very potent sweetened juice. The process concentrates the fruit's flavor dramatically, producing a result with a complex taste that may contrast sharply with its perfectly smooth texture. It is impossible to tell by simply looking at a jelly what fruit was used to make it. Jellies and marmalades are a labor of love, and they often require a large quantity of fruit. The effort of jelly and marmalade making is amply rewarded by the stunning end result.

The word *jelly* has acquired a negative connotation for many of us, because commercial jellies so frequently have a hard texture and have too often lost all taste of the fruits that were used to make them. But homemade jelly is a completely different story. Velvety and smooth, the jelly you make yourself will outshine nearly anything you might buy.

Similarly, it is difficult to find a really great store-bought marmalade, and people are often delighted and surprised upon sampling the marmalades in this book. Although I love bitter marmalade, marmalades need not be bitter if you do not want them to be. There are many milder marmalades to be made, which even the most determined marmalade hater may find delicious.

JELLY MAKING

To make jelly, fruit is simmered with water to extract its juice and then strained to make a perfectly clear liquid. This liquid is then cooked in small quantities with sugar and lemon juice until the setting point is reached. Because jellies rely on reaching the setting point, which can only be attained if the mixture has a high concentration of sugar, jellies often taste sweeter than jams. However, because of their smooth texture and concentrated flavor, you may use less, so a given volume of jelly usually lasts much longer than the identical volume of jam.

Things to Keep in Mind When Making Jelly

The most important thing to remember when making jelly is that in the initial stage, the fruit should be cooked for an extremely long time, long enough for *all* of its flavor and personality to leach into the juice. The entire character of the fruit is needed, including that of its skin, seeds, core, and rind. Thus, simply squeezing the juice from a raw fruit rarely works for jelly. If you shortchange this initial step, your juice will lack both pectin and flavor. You will know when the juice is ready because, even if you are using a low-pectin fruit, it will thicken to become noticeably more viscous than it was initially.

Take care to avoid adding either too much or too little water to the fruit for the initial cooking. Too much water will unnecessarily prolong the final cooking time, leading to an overcooked taste. Use the recipes here as a guide when you start cooking fruit. Then, if you feel at any stage of cooking that the juice is getting too thick or is cooking down too much, cautiously add a little more water. Factors that affect the quantity of water needed include the width and surface area of your pan, the water content and softness of the particular fruit, and the level of heat under your pot.

For jelly, it is best to strain the juice in two stages: first through a mesh strainer, to remove the bulk of the solids; then through a fine-mesh sieve, to remove any lingering solids clouding the juice. For the first straining, the fruit drains overnight to extract every last drop of juice. The second straining takes place the next day, after all the liquid has been extracted and the solids have been discarded. In the second straining, the liquid may be swirled or agitated to help the juice go through, but it should never be pressed through the sieve, as this will result in a cloudy mixture. Toward the end of each straining stage, the juice will start dripping much more slowly, and it is tempting at this point to continue with the recipe. However, these final drops of juice hold both the most pectin and the most flavor. Rushing this step can result in bland jelly that takes longer to set or jelly that may not set at all.

It is also important to remember that although you should usually add an ample amount of strained lemon juice to the mixture to tame the jelly's sweetness, jelly cooks down significantly during the final cooking stage. If too much lemon juice has been added, the result will be unpleasantly acidic.

Last, be sure to cook jellies only until they are just done, as overcooked jelly is unpalatable. Start out by testing your jelly frequently, beginning when its bubbles become smaller and it starts to turn syrupy. Then, as you become better acquainted with the jelly-making process, you will be able to test fewer times and closer to the setting point.

MARMALADE MAKING

Citrus Marmalades: The Classic Techniques
Although marmalade-making techniques may be applied to numerous different fruits, what we think of as "classic" marmalade today is always made from citrus. There are two different traditional processes for citrus marmalade making.

The first takes place over the course of a single day. It involves simmering the whole fruit for several hours until soft, and then cutting it open, scooping out the flesh, slicing the rind, and combining the fruit with sugar. This technique tends to result in coarse, bitter marmalade of varying quality; because the process is compressed into a single day, the fruit's flavor has little time to evenly distribute itself throughout the mixture. Also, because the fruit is sliced only after being cooked, it is often difficult to control the size and shape of the fruit slices.

The second, better, technique is traditionally a three-day process. This is because unlike jelly (for which the water becomes saturated with the fruit and the fruit loses all its character) or jam (for which little or no water is added and the only liquid comes from the fruit itself), marmalade contains a high proportion of both water and fruit solids. In order to make marmalade, three days are often needed for the flavor and pectin in these solids to leach enough into the water portion of the mixture for the marmalade to set and have a balanced flavor.

For the first day of this process, the fruit is sliced and soaked overnight with water at room temperature. On the second day, the mixture is cooked slowly until its volume has significantly reduced and the fruit is tender. On the third day, sugar and lemon juice are added and the mixture is cooked until done.

Marmalade Making Explored
Although classic English marmalade making typically involves this three-day process, numerous factors may affect which techniques are best applied for a specific marmalade. Marmalade making may involve a broad range of techniques. Factors affecting the citrus marmalade–making process may include:

> Physical Characteristics of Peel: Different citrus fruits possess skins of different permeability, thickness, toughness, and stringiness. These characteristics help determine how many times the fruit should be cooked, how thickly it should be sliced, and whether to remove part of its pith. Depending upon which techniques are called for, the process may take either two or three days to complete.

Strength of Flavor of Peel: Overly astringent peel may require preliminary blanching and/or partial removal of the fruit's pith; some old-fashioned recipes even call for removing the bitter membranes between the sections of fruit.

The Aesthetics of Marmalade

Marmalades are among the most satisfying and beautiful preserves to make. Their texture and appearance can vary widely. Although certain marmalades are less delicate than others, they all contain clearly defined pieces of fruit suspended in jelly.

There are many different approaches to marmalade in this book, each taken according to a particular vision of the perfect end result for that specific fruit or recipe. Below are descriptions of different types of marmalade and the processes used to make them. I have divided marmalades into the four broad categories listed below; many recipes fall somewhere in between.

Fine-Cut Marmalades: These are very delicately textured marmalades consisting of perfectly cooked jelly with a sprinkling of thin shreds of fruit throughout. Because the slices of fruit are so fine, and the jelly so soft and velvety, fine-cut marmalades may seem more like pure jellies at first glance. Slicing the fruit as thinly as possible gives the preserve a subtle elegance; although such slicing may result in marmalades having many shreds of fruit, their thinness prevents the marmalade from being overpowering. Marmalades in this category include Kumquat Marmalade (page 100), Citron Shred (page 305), Quince Marmalade (page 296), and Crabapple Marmalade (page 236).

Medium-Cut Marmalades: These marmalades are among the easiest to make. They consist of fruit (usually citrus) cut into medium-thick pieces, suspended in a jelly. The fruit is halved crosswise, quartered lengthwise, and then sliced crosswise, resulting in quarter-circle slices that may or may not remain completely intact during the cooking process. The flesh of the fruit is incorporated into the marmalade by virtue of being attached to the rind but requires no separate preparation. Depending on the fruit, medium-cut marmalades may take either two or three days to make. Examples include Meyer Lemon Marmalade with Mandarins & Lavender (page 104), Lemon Marmalade (page 54), Page Mandarin Marmalade (page 68), and Strawberry Blood Orange Marmalade with Rosemary (page 118).

Thick-Cut Marmalades: Thick-cut marmalades are most frequently found in Great Britain. They tend to be strong-flavored jellies, often incorporating fruit flesh, containing large chunks of bitter citrus rind. These marmalades are for true marmalade lovers, and they are best made using thick-skinned bitter fruits. They are usually made over three days in the traditional manner described at the start of this section; this approach maximizes flavor and pectin content. The proportion of jelly in such marmalades is extremely important because the chunks of fruit are so large; without ample jelly, the marmalade would be unspreadable. Thick-cut marmalades are extremely strong in flavor. Depending on the desired result and the fruit being used, the fruit may be blanched or not and may be sliced either before or after the initial cooking. Examples include Lemon & Pink Grapefruit Marmalade (page 61), English Marmalade (page 89), and English Three-Fruit Marmalade (page 92).

Marmalades Incorporating Fruit Flesh: These are marmalades that contain not only citrus rind or other clearly defined solids but also the soft flesh of fruit. This flesh is usually prepared (peeled, seeded, and/or chopped) separately from the rest of the solids and then recombined with them just prior to the final cooking. The fruit flesh tends to melt into the jelly portion of the marmalade, rendering it denser and more opaque than that of other marmalades. For this type of marmalade, it is important to carefully balance the different components, which may include freshly squeezed juice, cooked juice, sliced fruit, and/or multiple different fruits in addition to the soft fruit flesh. The citrus peel in such marmalades may be either thinly or coarsely cut, depending on the particular recipe. Examples include Early Girl Tomato Marmalade (page 276) and Yellow Grapefruit Marmalade (page 70).

Achieving a Perfect Texture in Marmalade

When making marmalade, you will need to decide not only how thick to slice or cut the fruit but also how to achieve the proper proportion of jelly to fruit pieces. For the proportion to be correct, it is almost always best to divide the raw fruit into two separate batches. One batch consists of the fruit slices to be included in the final marmalade. The other consists of larger pieces to be simmered for a long time with water and then discarded. The concentrated liquid resulting from this second batch is then added to the first batch, thinning it slightly to create a more balanced texture and intense flavor.

For marmalades consisting of more than one fruit, it is sometimes best to use only one of the fruits' solids in the final mixture. When deciding which fruit's solids to include in a particular marmalade, keep in mind that many fruits break down too much during cooking; only include fruits with firm structures. In any marmalade recipe, you may also tailor the texture to your liking by including more or fewer of the fruit solids, as long as the ratio of sugar to fruit remains unchanged.

Keep in Mind When Making Marmalade

Marmalade making shares many pitfalls with jelly making, but it also has some of its own. Perhaps the most important pitfall to avoid is adding too much water and overcooking the fruit solids. It is also important to plan well when making marmalade. For the marmalades in this book, adhering exactly to the time stated in each recipe is ideal. Although you may be able to take more time for certain marmalades, storing the mixture in the refrigerator between steps, this is often not a good idea because it can result in mushy solids that have steeped for too long in their liquid.

chapter 2

FRUIT: UNDERSTANDING THE ESSENTIAL INGREDIENT

WHERE AND HOW TO GET YOUR FRUIT

For both inspiration and quality, picking your own fruit or purchasing it at a farmers' market is essential. What could be more beautiful than a luscious, perfectly ripe fruit straight off the tree, or more satisfying than to open your cupboard, retrieve a jar of jewel-like jam, and instantly be transported back to the moment when you first laid eyes on that fruit? We often forget that preserving began with our desire to enjoy fruit all year round and with the necessity of planning for seasons when it was scarce. Preserving is by nature a local, sustainable enterprise.

The experience of choosing and preparing fruit will connect you deeply to both your ingredients and the preserving process and the closer you are to the source of your fruit, the more satisfying this process will be. There is something utterly timeless about picking fruit; it is a vital reminder of our past and of the seasons. It takes a surprisingly short time to gather fruit, and the rewards are enormous. One thing that always amazes me is the huge quantity of fruit found on even a smallish tree or bush in the right season. Fruits I love to pick include wild blueberries, lemons, apricots, plums, blackberries, limes, quinces, and apples. My picking completed, I eagerly hurry off to my kitchen to make preserves. Once you have experienced this strong connection to fruit, it is hard to resist!

The pleasure and sense of ownership that come from picking your own fruit are unparalleled, but foraging at your local farmers' market comes close. Local, small-scale farmers are not only the backbone of our ability to put quality food on the table but are also the guardians and promoters of our precious heirloom varieties. They hold the key to our culinary future. Ecologically minded farmers possess a profound understanding of the seasons and the land they farm. Speaking to and getting to know my local farmers has been a fundamental source of inspiration for me and visiting farms and markets remains a constant joy.

As you get to know local farmers, your understanding and appreciation not only of fruit but also of how fruit gets to you will grow. You may learn one year that the cherry crop has been washed off the trees and ruined by heavy rains, the next that the strawberries are especially good because of your region's dry spring weather. The world of a farmer, especially an organic farmer, is an ever-changing one, defined by constantly fluctuating variables. Visiting farms, a growing number of which now have pick-your-own options, is also an inspiring treat. No matter where you live, I urge you to explore your backyards, farms, and farmers' markets.

Because the most important part of any preserve is the fruit you use, I have included detailed fruit information both here and in Part III (page 316) to give an overview of fruit, details on individual fruits and flavors, and a clear understanding of how a fruit's specific qualities relate to the preserving process.

WHAT MAKES FRUIT GREAT

Great preserves begin with great fruit, but what does this actually mean, practically speaking? How should you assess a fruit, and how should this impact the jam-making process?

Thinking about fruit in terms of preserving is different, because the qualities that make a fruit ideal for preserves may or may not make it so for other uses. Knowing how a fruit's texture and flavor change when cooked at a high temperature, for example, will enable you to better understand how to use it in a preserve. Here are the main considerations:

Seasonality, Freshness & Ripeness

Always use sustainable, local, organic fruit. The best way to ensure a fruit's excellence is to be sure it has been raised well and has not traveled far.

Perfectly ripe fruit is ideal for jam making, as it contains more pectin and has a superior flavor and texture to either under- or overripe fruit. Preserving should never be seen as a way to use fruit that is past its prime. Assess freshness and ripeness by feeling and/or tasting the fruit. Understanding the seasons and knowing what grows in your area will help you weed out beautiful-looking fruits that may be either unripe or lacking in flavor.

Flavor, Sweetness & Perfume

Flavor is the single most important attribute of any fruit. Strong, vividly flavored fruit is ideal. However, many fruits that make great preserves may not be palatable in their raw state. Thus, other factors such as the fruit's origin, seasonality, aroma, freshness, and appearance come into play when assessing such fruit. Flavor is often concentrated in the skin, becoming more evenly distributed through cooking. When selecting fruit, remember that although cooking brings out flavors, a fruit that is flavorless to begin with will never make a great preserve.

Flavor can be influenced by the amount of water a plant has received. Some farmers overwater to swell their fruit and increase its weight, but this decreases flavor. Underwatering (or "dry-farming"), by contrast, often has the opposite effect; it intensifies flavor. Thus, when purchasing fruit, always try to sample first. Perfectly watered fruit should have a bright, clear flavor and firm texture.

Texture often plays a much bigger role than we realize in our perception of flavor. There are certain fruits whose flavor is largely due to their specific texture; when such fruits are heated, their texture changes and they become bland and uninteresting. Such fruits include loquats, Asian pears, and certain melons. These fruits, while tasty for eating out of hand, are not well suited to the high temperatures required for preserving.

Sweetness refers to the natural sugars in a fruit. While sweet fruit may be delicious for eating out of hand, overly sweet fruit sometimes yields a cloying, uninteresting preserve. Adding less sugar may help, but only to a point: A certain amount of sugar is necessary for the preserve to keep well and have a balanced flavor. Tarter fruit is thus generally best for preserving.

Perfume refers to the aromatic aspects of a fruit or herb, which can be difficult to capture in a preserve. To retain a fruit's perfume as much as possible, cook the preserve quickly and in small batches.

When using herbs as flavorings, it is generally best not to cook them, but instead to add and steep them in the mixture once the cooking has completed. A long-cooked herb lacks the fresh perfume of one that has been warmed only just long enough to release its aromas. Liquors, liqueurs, and spices, on the other hand, should often be added earlier in the cooking process.

Bitterness & Sourness

Bitterness and sourness are often distributed unevenly throughout a given fruit, and some fruits are much more bitter or sour than others.

Sour fruit has high acidity and an often overwhelmingly strong, pucker-inducing flavor. A too-sour fruit can be identified by the fact that no matter how much sugar is added to it, it leaves a strongly acidic feeling in the mouth and throat. However, most sour fruits are high in pectin as well as acid, and their ability to combine well with larger quantities of sugar makes them well suited to preserving. Fruits in this category include certain plums, red currants, cranberries, and the flesh of many citrus fruits.

Bitter fruit has a strong edge in its flavor. Depending upon the degree of bitterness and your personal taste, you may find this fruit to be either unpleasant or delicious. Bitterness is usually concentrated in the rind, skin, and cores. Underripe fruit is often undesirably bitter, and it may never ripen. For this reason, avoid any fruit that has been picked green.

Texture

Different textures of raw fruit yield widely varying results in jam. Cooking fruit usually breaks it down, but fruits break down to varying degrees. For example:

> Guavas, pears, black mulberries, quinces, citrus fruits, melons, and white cherries tend to break down very little

> Meaty stone fruits and firm-skinned berries tend to break down partially, but not completely

> Other stone fruits, other berries, and rhubarb tend to disintegrate more in the cooking process

> Other textural qualities to consider include fibrousness, the presence and size of seeds, the toughness of skin, graininess, and chewiness. Each fruit has a different balance of these characteristics.

HOW TO BALANCE A PRESERVE

Not every fruit is naturally suited to preserving, and even those that are often require a little finessing. Here are some common imbalances in fruits and ways to help compensate for them in the final product:

Fruit Lacks Pectin: There are many ways to compensate for the lack of pectin in a particular fruit. Always using high-quality fruit will help maximize whatever pectin the fruit naturally contains. However, there are additional steps you may take:

> To use a low-pectin fruit in a jelly or marmalade, cook the fruit for an extremely long time, until its juice has thickened and the fruit has lost everything but its fibers.

> Use a low-pectin fruit in combination with a high-pectin fruit. Remember when combining fruits that you are not only adding more pectin, but also adding a secondary flavor.

> To make a preserve with a low-pectin fruit without adding a second fruit, add commercial pectin.

Fruit Lacks Acid: The best way to solve this problem is to add lemon juice. Another way to boost acidity is to combine fruits, again being careful not to muddy flavors. Even when fruits are combined, however, you will almost always still need to add lemon juice.

Fruit Is Overly Sour or Bitter: Sometimes a fruit is so strong that the sugar added for jam making does not go far enough in countering its edge. If this happens, you may "rinse out" some of its flavor by blanching the fruit prior to cooking. You may also remove certain parts of the fruit, such as pith or cores, which contain the most bitterness.

Fruit Is Overly Sweet: The best way to use such fruits is to combine them with less sweet fruits to balance them. Adding extra lemon juice may not solve the problem of being too sweet, since it can result in an unpleasantly biting flavor.

Fruit Lacks Firmness: Many fruits disintegrate during cooking. There are different ways to control these changes and keep the fruit's original integrity:

> To minimize structural changes, minimize cooking time. Only doing small batches is essential, as is cooking in the proper type of pot. You may also sometimes cook the fruit in two stages.

> Incorporate the fruit's cooked juice into a jelly or marmalade rather than using it for a jam.

> If a fruit is particularly soft or likely to disintegrate during cooking, you may compensate by cutting the fruit into larger pieces. This will prevent it from dissolving completely into a puree.

Fruit Is Overly Firm: Generally speaking, the firmest fruits are best suited to jellies and marmalades. To prevent these preserves from becoming overly chunky, strain out some of the solids and cut the fruit into thin, small pieces. Keep a careful proportion of solids to jelly to help balance preserves made with very firmly structured fruits.

Flavor Lacks Complexity: To maximize flavor, be sure to avoid overcooking, and always add ample lemon juice for brightness. Combining fruits either with other fruits or with herbs or flavorings will also help to enhance the flavor.

chapter 3

PRESERVING:
PROCESS AND EQUIPMENT

SUGAR, ACID & PECTIN: THE THREE ESSENTIALS FOR PRESERVING

All preserves require a perfect balance of sugar, acid, and pectin. This balance varies according to each preserve's individual character. Sugar, acid, and pectin each play a different and essential role in the preserving process.

Sugar

Sugar counteracts the acidic taste fruits acquire when cooked. In addition to sweetening and preserving the cooked fruit, sugar acts as the primary thickener for preserves, preventing a watery texture. There is no such thing as a sugarless preserve; all preserves require some form of sugar to thicken them and make them palatable. Sugar substitutes are frequently used commercially for sugar-free preserves, but they give an inferior result. Brown sugars, unrefined sugars, and liquid sugars are not ideal either, as they tend to muddy the fruit's flavor and may adversely affect the preserve's texture. White cane sugar is best. Because it contains the fewest irregularities and impurities, it gives preserves a superb texture and lets the natural flavor of the fruit shine through.

When determining what quantity of sugar to use in a recipe, *always* base the amount of sugar on the total weight of raw *prepared* fruit being used; for example, 2 pounds sugar to every 4½ pounds pitted plums. Otherwise, due to the inexactitude of measuring fruit by volume, it will be impossible to ensure success.

With sugar, your own taste buds and prior experience should be your guides. Fruit, not sugar, should be the dominant flavor. Sweetness and sugariness are not the same, and an intensely fruity flavor is not the same as a sugary one. Keeping this in mind, always use the minimum amount of sugar required to achieve your preferred texture and flavor. Even the sweetest jellies should have a sugar-to-fruit ratio of no more than .75 to 1 to slightly higher than 1 to 1. Factors affecting the ideal quantity of sugar for a particular recipe include:

> Sweetness of Fruit: The sweetness of a fruit diminishes as the fruit's flavors become redistributed through cooking. The bitter skins and rinds of many fruits, such as plums and oranges, become much more dominant once the fruit is cooked.

> Type of Preserve and Desired Consistency: A high quantity of sugar is required to achieve the proper texture for a jelly or marmalade, regardless of the fruit's natural sweetness. This is because a fruit's natural sugars do not possess the same structure-forming qualities as cane sugar. For jam,

the quantity of sugar is generally lower than for jelly or marmalade. The quantity of sugar also varies according to the fruit type.

Desired Texture: There is a huge range in texture among jams. Texture is determined not only by fruit type but also by sugar content. If a jam is extremely low in sugar, other ways of thickening it must be found. For example, some of this book's stone fruit jams involve pureeing a portion of the fruit in order to help thicken them.

Sugar concentration strongly affects the cooking process: In general, the less sugar added, the slower, longer, and more careful the cooking must be. Using the proper type of pot (see page 25) reduces your risk of scorching the preserve, as do both scraping the bottom of the pan frequently and monitoring the heat closely. When making preserves with cooked juice, add only the minimum water necessary; this will help prevent the sickening flavor that can result from overcooking sugar. Making preserves in small, five- to twelve-jar batches is also essential to prevent both burning and an overcooked taste.

Acid

Though acid is present in all fruits to a varying degree, nearly every preserve requires freshly squeezed lemon juice, both to sharpen its flavor and to help give it the proper texture. Fruit with a medium to high amount of acid, such as red currants or lemons, is most naturally suited to jam making; it can tolerate a higher concentration of sugar, enabling the jam to thicken more easily. Once sugar has been added to the fruit, lemon juice brightens and balances the preserve's flavor. The amount of lemon juice needed for a given preserve is determined both by the amount of sugar that has been added and by the natural sweetness of the fruit.

Adding the right amount of lemon juice can be tricky. For best results, always add it to the room-temperature mixture just before the final cooking stage. Things taste sweeter when they are hot, so if you add lemon juice during the final cooking, you risk adding too much. Begin by cautiously adding a little less juice than you think you might need, and then slowly continue to add more, tasting as you go, until you can just taste the tartness and lemon flavor of the juice in the mixture. Do not overdo the lemon juice; too much will result in an overly acidic preserve and may ruin the preserve's texture.

Pectin

Pectin is a complex carbohydrate molecule found in all fruits. The pectin content of a given fruit type may vary widely, being affected by both ripeness and freshness. Pectin content changes over time but is at its peak in a perfectly ripe fruit that has just been picked. Fruits high in pectin tend to have stiff structures, such as skins, flesh, or rind, which do not easily break down in the cooking process. Certain fruits contain almost no pectin; others are high in it.

High-Pectin Fruits include citrus fruits, damsons, Concord grapes, persimmons, guavas, quinces, apples, red currants, white currants, and cranberries.

Medium-Pectin Fruits include sweet red cherries, plums (other than damsons), Pluots, plumcots, blueberries, cultivated blackberries and their relatives, and raspberries.

Medium-Low Pectin Fruits include Montmorency cherries, white cherries, nectarines, peaches, apricots, pears, and strawberries.

Low-Pectin Fruits include melons, figs, rhubarb, and mulberries.

Pectin requires sugar and acid to activate its structure-forming qualities, which are what enable preserves to thicken as they cool. High-pectin fruit requires more sugar than low-pectin fruit to activate its pectin. Lemon juice contains a small amount of pectin and can help boost the pectin level of your mixture slightly.

Rarely, you will need to use powdered pectin to achieve the right texture for a particular preserve. Use powdered pectin extremely sparingly and only if absolutely necessary. Otherwise, it can produce a stiff texture and chalky flavor. A good understanding of fruit will help you steer clear of powdered pectin as much as possible; fruit can almost always be manipulated to avoid it. However, some preserves simply could not exist without added pectin. These include jellies made solely with low-pectin fruits; marmalades whose liquid portion lacks pectin; and, rarely, jams made with low-pectin fruits. To use powdered pectin, whisk it very well into your sugar to evenly distribute the granules and prevent clumping, and then proceed with the rest of the recipe.

For preserving, just as important as understanding fruit is having a strong grasp of the overall preserving process. Having the proper equipment, knowing the stages of cooking, and being able to tell when a preserve is done cooking are each essential for success. The next section explores the preserving process in depth.

PROCESS & EQUIPMENT

The Pan & the Process

When you make preserves, your experience will be strongly influenced, if not defined, by one simple thing: the pan you use for the final cooking. This pan should ideally be a copper preserving pan, 11 inches wide at the base, 15 inches wide at the rim, and 5 inches high, with an 11- or 12-quart capacity. If such a pan is unavailable, use a wide pan of equivalent size and shape made of stainless-steel or another nonreactive metal. Never use an aluminum pan for preserving, because aluminum will react with the acid in the fruit, ruining the preserve's flavor and dulling its color.

You will need a very large pan to make a very small batch. In order for preserves to have a spreadable consistency when cool, a large quantity of moisture must be cooked out of them, and they must reach a very high temperature. The briefer the cooking, the more intact the fruit's original flavor will be. Because the moisture to be eliminated is directly proportional to the quantity of fruit used, a larger batch needs to be cooked for a much longer time. A wide pan is essential, as it allows a maximum of evaporation to occur in a minimum of time.

To prevent burning, the raw ingredients should be a few inches deep at the outset of the final cooking. If you are using a smaller pan than suggested, adjust the quantity of raw mixture accordingly; keep the ideal depth of fruit in mind, since you may need to cook off the preserve in two or more small batches instead of one big one.

Using the proper pan will not merely help you cook faster; it will help you cook better. The preserve mixture typically passes through several stages during cooking.

Stages of Cooking (illustrated on pages 28–33)

Initial Heating: The mixture heats up gradually, dissolving any undissolved sugar.

Initial Bubbling and Foaming: Once hot, the mixture starts either bubbling or foaming; if it foams, it may rise quite high in the pan. Having a pan with sloping sides helps minimize the risk of its boiling over.

Final Bubbling: As the volume of the mixture goes down and its moisture content decreases, smaller bubbles appear and the foam subsides. Depending upon how hot your stove is, you may need to decrease the heat at this point to prevent burning.

Final Phase: You will generally need to cook the mixture for a few minutes more once it has reached this stage, in order to eliminate the final bits of excess moisture and achieve a perfect texture.

Your choice of pan will have a profound effect on all these stages of cooking. If using a non-copper pan, be prepared to carefully monitor your heat and stir frequently to prevent sticking; copper is an extremely even heat conductor and tends to prevent scorching.

When Has a Preserve Finished Cooking?
A preserve may either set or thicken, depending upon its ingredients and the type of preserve it is.

A preserve "sets" when it reaches a high enough temperature to form a jelly when left to cool undisturbed. This temperature (220°F) can only be reached in mixtures containing a high proportion of sugar to moisture. Be careful to avoid cooking any preserve to a temperature higher than 220°F, since this will result in an irrevocably tough, leathery preserve.

Jellies and marmalades, because of their high pectin, sugar, and water contents, *must* reach the setting point, or they will end up a syrupy mess. However, many jams do not necessarily need to set; because their fruit tends to be less concentrated than a jelly's or a marmalade's, they require much less sugar to have a good flavor. Depending upon the type of fruit, quantity of sugar, and techniques employed, a jam may be more or less jelly-like.

Testing for Doneness (illustrated on pages 36–41)
When testing for doneness, remember that most preserves thicken significantly as they cool to room temperature.

STAGES OF COOKING: LOW-SUGAR JAM

Left: Initial Heating: The jam mixture (in this case, Early Girl Tomato & Damson Jam; page 280) heats up slowly, dissolving sugar. The mixture is stirred periodically and the heat is gradually increased to high as the sugar dissolves. *Above left:* Initial Bubbling and Foaming: Once hot, the mixture starts to foam. The tomato jam shown here rises moderately high in the pan; for foamier jams, such as apricot or plum, turning off the heat and skimming the foam partway through cooking helps prevent overflowing. *Above right:* Final Bubbling and Final Phase: As the volume and moisture content of the mixture decrease, the foam subsides. Stirring the mixture very frequently and reducing the heat slightly help prevent burning. The jam acquires a glossier look, the texture becomes more unified, and the color darkens. For testing for doneness, please see pages 36–37.

STAGES OF COOKING: HIGH-SUGAR JAM

Above left: Initial Heating: The jam mixture (in this case, My Raspberry Jam; page 234) heats up gradually over lowish heat, dissolving sugar. Because the fruit and sugar have not been macerating beforehand, the mixture is stirred constantly to prevent burning. The temperature is gradually inched up to high as the juice starts to run. *Above right:* Initial Bubbling and Foaming: Once hot, the jam starts to foam, rising quite high in the pan. The bubbles range from small to large, and the heat may need to be reduced slightly to prevent the jam from boiling over. *Right:* Final Bubbling and Final Phase: As the volume and moisture content of the mixture decrease, its bubbles become smaller and shinier and the foam starts to subside. Shiny foam may appear around the edges of the pan; this is often a sign of doneness. The color darkens slightly. Stirring the jam frequently helps prevent sticking. For testing for doneness, please see pages 38–39.

STAGES OF COOKING: MARMALADE

Cooking marmalade (here, Lemon & Pink Grapefruit Marmalade; page 61) is very similar to cooking jelly. *Left:* Initial Heating: The mixture is placed over high heat and is stirred periodically to help the sugar dissolve. *Above left:* Initial Bubbling and Foaming: The mixture reaches a rolling boil. Because of its high water content, it will bubble for several minutes before starting to foam. *Above right:* Final Bubbling and Final Phase: As the volume of the foaming mixture goes down and its moisture content decreases, its liquid portion darkens and its bubbles become smaller and shinier. The heat may need to be lowered slightly at this point to prevent burning. For testing for doneness, please see pages 40–41.

Testing for Doneness (illustrated on pages 36–41)

When testing for doneness, remember that most preserves thicken significantly as they cool to room temperature.

There are several ways to see if a preserve has finished cooking. For preserves that are cooked to reach the setting point, you may use a candy thermometer. However, I believe it is important to know what to actually *look* for to tell if a preserve is done, especially because not all preserves will reach the 220°F setting point. Thus, I prefer a combination of the freezer test and a visual examination of the preserve to test for doneness.

For the freezer test, place a few metal spoons (I suggest five in the recipes) on a saucer in the freezer before you start cooking the preserve. When you think the preserve might be ready, remove it from the heat, take a small representative half-spoonful (one containing both the liquidy and the more solid portions), and carefully transfer it onto one of the frozen spoons. If you are testing a jelly, marmalade, or high-sugar jam, it should resemble a shiny bead of liquid that is resisting the metal of the cold spoon slightly. If it is a low-sugar jam, it may not look as shiny, but it should look cohesive and not watery. Put the cold spoon back in the freezer for three to four minutes. Then, remove it from the freezer and carefully feel the underside of the spoon. It should be neither warm nor cold; if still warm, return it to the freezer for a moment. Tilt the spoon vertically to see if the preserve runs; depending on the individual preserve, it should run either slowly or not at all. If it has not yet reached the appropriate point, bring it back up to temperature, cook it for another three to four minutes, and test again.

Testing for doneness interrupts the heating process, so preserves should only be tested when you think they really are close to being done. Preserves change a lot as they cook. Here is what to look for:

> Bubbles and Foam: The fruit often foams a lot during the first stage of cooking; this foam eventually subsides by the time the preserve is done cooking. A preserve's bubbles become progressively less watery and more sugary as it cooks. Depending on the concentration of sugar, the bubbles may become progressively larger and more sputtering (low-sugar jams) or tiny and shiny (most jellies, marmalades, and high-sugar jams).

> Appearance: A finished preserve has a slight shine to it, because its concentration of sugar has increased so much during the cooking process. Additionally, the fruit will usually become suspended in the mixture rather than floating to the top; this is often a sign that the proper balance of moisture, acid, and pectin has been reached.

Ability to Sheet: You may test for doneness by dipping a metal spoon in the preserve and holding it perpendicular to the pot at a slight vertical angle while the preserve drips back into the pan. If the preserve is done, the drips will tend to run along the bottom edge of the spoon to collect into one big drip (this is known as "sheeting"). The final drips may tend to cling to the spoon and form little pearl-like drops. This test should always be done in combination with the freezer test, but it is nevertheless a useful way to gauge doneness without interrupting the cooking.

Ability to Set: While doing the freezer test, let the preserve in the pot sit still for a few minutes off the heat to see whether it starts to set. If, after a couple of minutes, the preserve has thickened slightly and started forming a skin across the top, it is likely done. If, however, little liquidy areas have formed on the surface and there is no skin forming, it is probably not ready quite yet.

Equipment

Having good equipment really eases the preserving process, not only producing a better result but also helping you cook your jams with more ease. Here are the essentials. For more information, see Sources (page 363).

A Preserving Pan (see page 25)

A Kitchen Scale: When making jam, one of the most important things you can do is to weigh your fruit and sugar. This is because, due to the chunkiness of raw fruit and the varying degrees to which water may evaporate during jelly making, it is impossible to ensure accuracy or good results unless you measure your prepared raw ingredients by weight rather than volume. For this purpose, a digital scale is ideal; it is most exact in its measurements and also takes up the least space in your kitchen!

A Good Stove: A gas stove is ideal for preserving. If working at home, you will probably need to use the highest heat possible; if using a commercial range, you may need to moderate the heat more. If you have an electric stove, be sure to clear an area nearby where you can put the jam pot to rest for a moment while you test for doneness or if you need to quickly lower the cooking temperature.

Knives: A very sharp chef's or other large knife and a very sharp paring knife will make preparing the fruit much easier.

TESTING FOR DONENESS: LOW-SUGAR JAMS

Above left and right: The Freezer Test: For this test, a small representative sample of the jam is transferred to a frozen spoon, then chilled rapidly to room temperature in the freezer. The left-hand photo shows an unsuccessful freezer test; though nearly ready, the jam is still slightly watery and runs quickly off the spoon. The right-hand photo shows a successful test of the same jam; the jam has been cooked a few more minutes and tested again. It is now cohesive and does not run easily off the spoon.

Right: Appearance and Ability to Set: The finished jam has a slight shine to it. During the second freezer test, the jam is left to rest for a few minutes off the heat. It forms a skin across the top and begins to thicken as it cools.

TESTING FOR DONENESS: HIGH-SUGAR JAMS

Bottom right: Ability to Sheet: For this preliminary test, a metal spoon is dipped into the simmering jam and held perpendicular to the pot at a slight vertical angle. In the left-hand photo, the jam is not quite done; it forms drips that are syrupy but still separate. In the right-hand photo, the jam is ready; after a few more minutes of cooking, its drops now run along the bottom edge of the spoon, collecting into one big drip. *Above left and right:* The Freezer Test: For this test, a small representative sample of the jam is transferred to a frozen spoon, then chilled rapidly to room temperature in the freezer. The photo at left shows an unsuccessful freezer test; the jam is still syrupy and runs quickly off the spoon. The photo at right shows a successful test of the same jam; the jam has been cooked further and tested again. It is now cohesive and its surface crinkles when nudged. *Top right:* Ability to Set: During the second freezer test, the jam is left to rest for a few minutes off the heat. It begins to form a skin across the top.

TESTING FOR DONENESS: MARMALADE

Above: The Freezer Test: For this test, a small representative sample of the marmalade is transferred to a frozen spoon, then chilled rapidly to room temperature in the freezer. When ready, it forms a jellylike mass with a soft texture. *Right:* Ability to Set: During the freezer test, the marmalade is left to rest for a few minutes off the heat. It rapidly begins to *set up*, or solidify into a jellylike mass; the first sign of this is the skin it forms across the top.

Other Essentials: Other very useful supplies include a large heatproof rubber spatula, heatproof gloves, two pint-size glass measuring pitchers, a fine-mesh sieve (preferably a chinois), a large heatproof colander or coarse-mesh sieve, a citrus juicer, a large stainless-steel spoon, several stainless-steel teaspoons, a potato masher, an oven thermometer, a mortar and pestle, a fine-mesh tea infuser, and a few nonreactive kettles or saucepans. You will also need jars (preferably no larger than 8 ounces) with self-sealing lids.

STERILIZATION & STORAGE

When making preserves, be sure to sterilize your jars and lids, unless you plan to eat your jam right away. Although jams and marmalades are unlikely to become contaminated with anything toxic, it is important to eliminate even the minutest risk.

There are many ways to sterilize jars, including putting them in a canning kettle or a sterilizing dishwasher, but my preferred way is in the oven. This method is easier than the other methods and, if you use an oven thermometer, is virtually foolproof. To sterilize jars and lids in the oven, first be sure they are perfectly clean. Place the clean jars upright with an equal number of clean unused lids on a baking sheet or sheet pan in a preheated 250°F oven. They should remain in the oven for a minimum of 30 minutes to ensure that they are heated through. Remove them from the oven right when you need to fill them. After you have filled them, leaving ¼ inch of room at the top, wipe the rims with a clean, damp cloth. Put the lids on, being careful to screw them on just until they are snug, and replace the jars in the oven for 15 minutes or so to ensure that they are completely sterilized. They will seal as they cool.

Sometimes the jars can become a little bit too hot when using this method, so before filling them, test their temperature first. Pour a little jam into one, and if it bubbles or boils in the jar, wait a few moments before filling the jars.

Upon removing your filled jars from the oven, place them 1 inch apart on a drying rack to set overnight at room temperature. Do not jiggle or disturb them during this time, as this may disrupt their ability to set correctly. As the preserves cool, you may hear a few little pops as the lids seal. Before putting your preserves away, be sure to feel the top of each lid to verify that it has sealed; it should be curving in very slightly in the middle. If any jars have not sealed, put them in the refrigerator for safekeeping.

To store sealed preserves, label and date them and keep them in a cool, dark place until you open them. After you open a jar, keep it in the refrigerator. You may also keep high-sugar preserves at room temperature, assuming you plan to eat them within a few weeks or so. Low-sugar preserves should always be refrigerated once opened, unless you plan to consume them right away.

part II

RECIPES

Fruit is inextricably bound to the seasons, and the pages that follow are structured around the year's natural cycles. There are three preserving seasons. The first starts at New Year's and stretches into March; the second goes from April to the end of July; and the third begins in August and ends in December. Within these, each month has its own fruits and personality.

For the recipes in this book, the ingredients are almost always measured after being fully prepared for cooking; the fruit is weighed after it has been seeded, stemmed, peeled, cored, chopped, or sliced. The exactitude of this method is essential for success.

Each recipe here comes with a suggested shelf life; however, no preserve will go bad if properly sterilized and sealed, and you may always keep your preserves for longer. As the color, flavor, and texture of different preserves may fade more or less quickly over time, each has its own ideal window for eating. The shelf lives here are meant as a guide.

A huge part of the joy of preserving is that of discovery; preserving is a way to explore fruit. Throughout these pages, you will thus see a wide array of different fruits, both commonplace and lesser known. To learn more about an individual fruit, please see Part III, Fruits for Preserving (page 316), where each fruit is illustrated and described in depth.

chapter 4

WINTER THROUGH
EARLY SPRING

Deepest winter fills me with joy, for it is at this time that the widest array of citrus fruits is in season. While it is true that many citrus trees bear fruit throughout the year, the rest do so only in winter. For three straight months, January through March, I cook nearly nothing but citrus, and there is very little else in backyards or at the market to distract me. My garden, except for its citrus trees, lies nearly dormant. Because I love marmalade, the cold months are always a special time for me.

In northern California, winter is the rainy season, so the days of sun when I go fruit picking are even more special. One of my favorite things of all is to spend a brisk winter day picking citrus fruit, after which my hair, clothes, and hands all smell of orange, lemon, or lime. Citrus picking can be a dangerous activity, as most citrus trees have sharp thorns, but I love the scratches, and the cool air and bright sun. To pick fruit is to engage with nature and what would it be without a little roughing-up?

Because citrus fruit keeps well and may stay ripe on the tree for several weeks, one has time to linger over it and give it more loving attention than many other fruits. I spent several weeks of my childhood in England, and in my mind's eye I always associate citrus marmalades with the cool wetness of that country. Making marmalade is not only timeless but also nostalgic. It is work, but utterly satisfying, the kind one always looks forward to. There is something extraordinarily grounding about setting to work on a pot of marmalade, and of waking to its bracingly bitter flavor each morning. It seems the very expression of winter itself.

BERGAMOT MARMALADE

Until I made this, I had never tasted a truly delicious bergamot marmalade, perhaps because bergamot can be difficult to work with. Its untamed flavor is grating and overpowering, a problem this recipe solves by double-blanching the fruit. This marmalade has become one of our most popular recipes, and everyone is always excited by its surprising flavor and delicate texture.

3 pounds bergamots, cut into eighths

2 pounds halved and seeded bergamots,

each half cut lengthwise into quarters and sliced very thinly crosswise

5 pounds white cane sugar

2 ounces strained freshly squeezed lemon juice

DAY 1

Place the bergamot eighths in a nonreactive saucepan where they will fit snugly in a single layer. Add enough cold water for the fruit to bob freely. Cover tightly and let rest overnight at room temperature.

DAY 2

Prepare the cooked bergamot juice: Bring the pan with the bergamot eighths to a boil over high heat, then decrease the heat to medium. Cook the fruit at a lively simmer, covered, for 2 to 3 hours, or until the bergamots are very soft and the liquid has become slightly syrupy. As the bergamots cook, press down on them gently with a spoon every 30 minutes or so, adding a little more water if necessary. The water level should stay consistently high enough for the fruit to remain submerged as it cooks.

When the bergamots have finished cooking, strain their juice by pouring the hot fruit and liquid into a medium strainer or colander suspended over a heatproof storage container or nonreactive saucepan. Cover the entire setup well with plastic wrap and let drip overnight at room temperature.

Meanwhile, prepare the sliced bergamot: Place the slices in a wide stainless-steel kettle and cover amply with cold water. Bring to a boil over high heat, then decrease the heat and simmer for 3 to 5 minutes. Drain, discarding the liquid. Repeat this process, then cover the blanched bergamot slices with 1 inch cold water. Bring to a boil over high heat, decrease the heat to medium, and cook at a lively simmer, covered, for 30 to 60 minutes, or until the fruit is very tender. As the fruit cooks, stir it gently every 15 minutes or so, adding a little more water if necessary. The water level should stay consistently high enough for the fruit to remain submerged as it cooks. Remove the pan from the heat, cover tightly, and let rest overnight at room temperature.

DAY 3

Place a saucer with five metal teaspoons in a flat place in your freezer for testing the marmalade later.

Remove the plastic wrap from the bergamot eighths and their juice and discard the bergamots. Strain the juice well through a very fine-mesh strainer to remove any lingering solids.

In a large mixing bowl, combine the sugar, lemon juice, cooked bergamot juice, and bergamot slices and their liquid, stirring well. Transfer the mixture to an 11- or 12-quart copper preserving pan or a wide nonreactive kettle.

Bring the marmalade mixture to a boil over high heat. Cook it at a rapid boil until the setting point is reached; this will take a minimum of 30 minutes, but may take longer depending on your individual stove and pan. Initially, the mixture will bubble gently for several minutes; then, as more moisture cooks out of it and its sugar concentration increases, it will begin foaming. Do not stir it at all during the initial bubbling; then, once it starts to foam, stir it gently every few minutes with a heatproof rubber spatula. As it gets close to being done, stir it every minute or two to prevent burning, decreasing the heat slightly if necessary. The marmalade is ready for testing when its color darkens slightly and its bubbles become very small.

To test the marmalade for doneness, remove it from the heat and carefully transfer a small representative half-spoonful to one of your frozen spoons. It should look slightly shiny and may have a few tiny bubbles scattered throughout. Replace the spoon in the freezer for 3 to 4 minutes, then remove and carefully feel the underside of the spoon. It should be neither warm nor cold; if still warm, return it to the freezer for a moment. Tilt the spoon vertically to see whether the marmalade runs; if it does not run, and if its top layer has thickened to a jelly consistency, it is done. If it runs, cook it for another few minutes, stirring, and test again as needed.

When the marmalade has finished cooking, turn off the heat but do not stir. Using a stainless-steel spoon, skim off any surface foam and discard. Pour the marmalade into sterilized jars and process according to the manufacturer's instructions or as directed on page 42.

Approximate Yield: **ten 8-ounce jars** *Shelf Life:* **1 year**

LEMON MARMALADES

Aside from Seville oranges, lemons are perhaps the best fruits for making marmalade. Like Sevilles, they are tart with bitter rind, and their flavor holds up well when cooked. Plain lemon marmalade is hard to improve upon, though lemons also combine well with guava, pear, strawberry, lime, grapefruit, bergamot, orange, and more. Aside from their high pectin content, lemons have the advantage of being an excellent background flavor for these other fruits, providing tartness without always being the dominant flavor. Depending on the individual recipe, the lemon pieces may either remain in the mixture or be strained from it after the initial cooking.

When making marmalade with lemons, it is often best to blanch the fruit slices for a few minutes at the beginning of the recipe; this eliminates some of the bitterness in the rind and tenderizes the fruit. Lemons make a very pretty marmalade. The thickness of the slices may vary, depending on your desired end result.

LEMON MARMALADE

2½ pounds lemons (preferably Lisbon), cut into eighths

2 pounds seeded lemons, halved crosswise,

each half cut lengthwise into quarters and sliced crosswise medium-thin

4¼ pounds white cane sugar

1 to 2 extra lemons, to make 2 ounces strained freshly squeezed juice

DAY 1

Place the lemon eighths in a nonreactive saucepan where they will fit snugly in a single layer. Add enough cold water for the fruit to bob freely. Cover tightly and let rest overnight at room temperature.

DAY 2

Prepare the cooked lemon juice: Bring the pan with the lemon eighths to a boil over high heat, then decrease the heat to medium. Cook the fruit at a lively simmer, covered, for 2 to 3 hours, or until the lemons are very soft and the liquid has become slightly syrupy. As the lemons cook, press down on them gently with a spoon every 30 minutes or so, adding a little more water if necessary. The water level should stay consistently high enough for the fruit to remain submerged as it cooks.

When the lemons are finished cooking, strain their juice by pouring the hot fruit and liquid into a medium strainer or colander suspended over a heatproof storage container or nonreactive saucepan. Cover the entire setup well with plastic wrap and let drip overnight at room temperature.

Meanwhile, prepare the sliced lemons: Place the slices in a wide stainless-steel kettle and cover amply with cold water. Bring to a boil over high heat, then decrease the heat and simmer for 5 minutes. Drain, discarding the liquid. Return the lemon slices to the kettle and cover with 1 inch cold water. Bring

to a boil over high heat, decrease the heat to medium, and cook at a lively simmer, covered, for 30 to 40 minutes, or until the fruit is very tender. As the fruit cooks, stir it gently every 15 minutes or so, adding a little more water if necessary. The water level should stay consistently high enough for the fruit to remain submerged as it cooks. Remove the pan from the heat, cover tightly, and let rest overnight at room temperature.

DAY 3

Place a saucer with five metal teaspoons in a flat place in your freezer for testing the marmalade later.

Remove the plastic wrap from the lemon eighths and their juice and discard the lemons. Strain the juice well through a very fine-mesh strainer to remove any lingering solids.

In a large mixing bowl, combine the sugar, cooked lemon juice, fresh lemon juice, and lemon slices and their liquid, stirring well. Transfer the mixture to an 11- or 12-quart copper preserving pan or a wide nonreactive kettle.

Bring the mixture to a boil over high heat. Cook at a rapid boil until the setting point is reached; this will take a minimum of 25 minutes, but may take longer depending on your individual stove and pan. Initially, the mixture will bubble gently for several minutes;

then, as more moisture cooks out of it and its sugar concentration increases, it will begin foaming. Do not stir it at all during the initial bubbling; then, once it starts to foam, stir it gently every few minutes with a heatproof rubber spatula. As it gets close to being done, stir it slowly every minute or two to prevent burning, decreasing the heat a tiny bit if necessary. The marmalade is ready for testing when its color darkens slightly and its bubbles become very small.

To test the marmalade for doneness, remove it from the heat and carefully transfer a small representative half-spoonful to one of your frozen spoons. It should look shiny, with tiny bubbles throughout. Replace the spoon in the freezer for 3 to 4 minutes, then re-move and carefully feel the underside of the spoon. It should be neither warm nor cold; if still warm, re-turn it to the freezer for a moment. Tilt the spoon vertically to see whether the marmalade runs; if it does not run, and if its top layer has thickened to a jelly consistency, it is done. If it runs, cook it for another few minutes, stirring, and test again as needed.

When the marmalade has finished cooking, turn off the heat but do not stir. Using a stainless-steel spoon, skim off any surface foam and discard. Pour the marmalade into sterilized jars and process according to the manufacturer's instructions or as directed on page 42.

Approximate Yield: ten 8-ounce jars *Shelf Life:* 2 years

ITALIAN LEMON MARMALADE

One recent winter, I came across some lovely Sorrento lemons, which I used to make this excellent marmalade. It has a perfectly clear lemon taste, laced with the potent flavor of limoncello liqueur.

2 pounds Sorrento or other thin-skinned tart lemons, cut into eighths

2 pounds Sorrento lemons, halved crosswise,

each half cut lengthwise into quarters and sliced crosswise medium-thin

4 pounds white cane sugar

6½ ounces limoncello

2½ ounces strained freshly squeezed Eureka or Lisbon lemon juice

DAY 1

Place the lemon eighths in a nonreactive saucepan where they will fit snugly in a single layer. Add enough cold water for the fruit to bob freely. Cover tightly and let rest overnight at room temperature.

DAY 2

Prepare the cooked lemon juice: Bring the pan with the lemon eighths to a boil over high heat, then decrease the heat to medium. Cook the fruit at a lively simmer, covered, for 2 to 3 hours, or until the lemons are very soft and the liquid has become slightly syrupy. As the lemons cook, press down on them gently with a spoon every 30 minutes or so, adding a little more water if necessary. The water level should stay consistently high enough for the fruit to remain submerged as it cooks.

When the lemons are finished cooking, strain their juice by pouring the hot fruit and liquid into a medium strainer or colander suspended over a heatproof storage container or nonreactive saucepan. Cover the entire setup well with plastic wrap and let drip overnight at room temperature.

Meanwhile, prepare the sliced lemons: Place the slices in a wide stainless-steel kettle and cover with

1-inch cold water, pressing down on the fruit to be sure the water level is correct. Bring to a boil over high heat, decrease the heat to medium, and cook uncovered at a lively simmer for 20 to 30 minutes, or until the fruit is very tender and the liquid has reduced significantly. Remove the pan from the heat, cover tightly, and let rest overnight at room temperature.

DAY 3

Place a saucer with five metal teaspoons in a flat place in your freezer for testing the marmalade later.

Remove the plastic wrap from the lemon eighths and their juice and discard the lemons. Strain the juice well through a very fine-mesh strainer to remove any lingering solids.

In a large mixing bowl, combine the sugar, cooked lemon juice, limoncello, fresh lemon juice, and lemon slices and their liquid, stirring well. Transfer the mixture to an 11- or 12-quart copper preserving pan or a wide nonreactive kettle.

Bring the mixture to a boil over high heat. Cook at a rapid boil over high heat until the setting point is reached; this will take a minimum of 30 minutes, but may take longer depending upon your individual stove and pan. Initially, the mixture will bubble gently for several minutes; then, as more moisture cooks out of it and its sugar concentration increases, it will begin foaming. Do not stir it at all during the initial bubbling; then, once it starts to foam, stir it gently every few minutes with a heatproof rubber spatula. As it gets close to being done, stir it slowly every minute or two to prevent burning, decreasing the heat a tiny bit if necessary. The marmalade is ready for testing when its color darkens slightly and its bubbles become very small.

To test the marmalade for doneness, remove it from the heat and carefully transfer a small representative half-spoonful to one of your frozen spoons. It should look shiny, with tiny bubbles throughout. Replace the spoon in the freezer for 3 to 4 minutes, then re-move and carefully feel the underside of the spoon. It should be neither warm nor cold; if still warm, re-turn it to the freezer for a moment. Tilt the spoon ver-tically to see whether the marmalade runs; if it does not run, and if its top layer has thickened to a jelly consistency, it is done. If it runs, cook it for another few minutes, stirring, and test again as needed.

When the marmalade has finished cooking, turn off the heat but do not stir. Using a stainless-steel spoon, skim off any surface foam and discard. Let the marmalade rest for 10 minutes off the heat, then fill 1 jar. Wait a few moments to see if the rinds seem to be floating to the top; if so, let the marmalade rest for another 5 minutes. If not, quickly pour the marmalade into the remaining jars. Process accord-ing to the manufacturer's instructions or as directed on page 42.

Approximate Yield: eleven 8-ounce jars *Shelf Life:* 2 years

LEMON & PINK GRAPEFRUIT
MARMALADE

This is the perfect everyday marmalade: coarsely cut grapefruit and thinly sliced lemon suspended in a sparkling citrus jelly. The grapefruit is blanched twice and the lemons once, rinsing out some of their bitterness and balancing their flavors. It is tart yet not astringent, delicate but full of fruit, flavorful yet not overpowering.

1 pound lemons (preferably Lisbon), cut into eighths

1 pound seeded lemons, halved crosswise,

each half cut lengthwise into quarters and sliced thinly crosswise

3¾ pounds pink grapefruits

5 pounds white cane sugar

2 or 3 extra lemons, to make 5 ounces strained freshly squeezed lemon juice

DAY 1

Place the lemon eighths in a nonreactive saucepan where they will fit snugly in a single layer. Add enough cold water for the fruit to bob freely. Cover tightly and let rest overnight at room temperature.

DAY 2

Prepare the cooked lemon juice: Bring the pan with the lemon eighths to a boil over high heat, then decrease the heat to medium. Cook the fruit at a lively simmer, covered, for 2 to 3 hours, or until the lemons are very soft and the liquid has become slightly syrupy. As the lemons cook, press down on them gently with a spoon every 30 minutes or so, adding a little more water if necessary. The water level should stay consistently high enough for the fruit to remain submerged as it cooks.

When the lemons are finished cooking, strain their juice by pouring the hot fruit and liquid into a medium strainer or colander suspended over a heatproof storage container or nonreactive saucepan. Cover the entire setup well with plastic wrap and let drip overnight at room temperature.

Meanwhile, prepare the sliced lemons: Place the slices in a wide stainless-steel kettle and cover amply with cold water. Bring to a boil over high heat, then decrease the heat and simmer for 5 minutes. Drain, discarding the liquid. Return the lemon slices to the kettle and cover with 1 inch cold water. Bring to a boil over high heat, decrease the heat to medium, and cook at a lively simmer, covered, for 30 to 40 minutes, or until the fruit is very tender. As the fruit cooks, stir it gently every 15 minutes or so, adding a little more water if necessary. The water level should stay consistently high enough for the fruit to remain submerged as it cooks. Remove the pan from the heat, cover tightly, and let rest overnight at room temperature.

Last, prepare the grapefruits: Cut them in half, squeeze the halves, and strain their juice. Cover the juice and place it in the refrigerator. Put the juiced grapefruit halves in a large nonreactive kettle and cover them amply with cold water. Bring to a boil over high heat, then decrease the heat to medium and cook at a lively simmer for 5 minutes. Drain,

discarding the liquid. Repeat this process, then return the blanched grapefruit halves to the kettle and add cold water to cover. Bring the halves to a boil over high heat, then decrease the heat to medium-low and cook, covered, at a lively simmer for 1 to 2 hours, or until the fruit is easily pierced with a skewer. As the grapefruit cooks, press down on it gently with a spoon every 30 minutes, adding more water if necessary. The water level should stay consistently high enough for the fruit to remain submerged as it cooks. When the grapefruit is tender, remove the pan from the heat, cover tightly, and let rest overnight at room temperature.

DAY 3

Place a saucer with five metal teaspoons in a flat place in your freezer for testing the marmalade later.

Remove the plastic wrap from the lemon eighths and their juice and discard the lemons. Strain the juice well through a very fine-mesh strainer to remove any lingering solids.

Prepare the grapefruit: Remove the grapefruit halves from their kettle, reserving the cooking liquid. Over a large bowl, use a soup spoon to scoop the flesh from each grapefruit half. Then, take each half and, cradling it in one hand, use the spoon to gently scrape its interior of excess pith and fibers. Repeat with the rest of the halves, going around each one two or three times until its interior is smooth and its rind is a uniform thickness. Cut each grapefruit half into 5 equal strips, then cut each strip crosswise into thick slices and reserve. Strain the scraped pith and fibers, along with the mushy interiors of the grapefruits, back into the cooking liquid, letting them drip for several minutes. Discard the solids. Pour the liquid through a fine-mesh strainer.

In a large mixing bowl, combine the sugar, strained grapefruit cooking liquid, reserved fresh grapefruit juice, reserved grapefruit rinds, cooked lemon juice, fresh lemon juice, and lemon slices and their liquid, stirring well. Transfer the mixture to an 11- or 12-quart copper preserving pan or a wide nonreactive kettle.

Bring the mixture to a boil over high heat. Cook at a rapid boil until the setting point is reached; this will take a minimum of 30 minutes, but may take longer depending on your individual stove and pan. Initially, the mixture will bubble gently for several minutes; then, as more moisture cooks out of it and its sugar concentration increases, it will begin foaming. Do not stir it at all during the initial bubbling; then, once it starts to foam, stir it gently every few minutes with a heatproof rubber spatula. As it gets close to being done, stir it slowly every minute or two to prevent burning, decreasing the heat a tiny bit if necessary. The marmalade is ready for testing when its color darkens slightly and its bubbles become very small.

To test the marmalade for doneness, remove it from the heat and carefully transfer a small representative half-spoonful to one of your frozen spoons. It should look shiny, with tiny bubbles throughout. Replace the spoon in the freezer for 3 to 4 minutes, then remove and carefully feel the underside of the spoon. It should be neither warm nor cold; if still warm, return it to the freezer for a moment. Tilt the spoon vertically to see whether the marmalade runs; if it does not run, and if its top layer has thickened to a jelly consistency, it is done. If it runs, cook it for another few minutes, stirring, and test again as needed.

When the marmalade has finished cooking, turn off the heat but do not stir. Using a stainless-steel spoon, skim off any surface foam and discard. Pour the marmalade into sterilized jars and process according to the manufacturer's instructions or as directed on page 42.

Approximate Yield: eleven 8-ounce jars *Shelf Life:* 2 years

WHITE GUAVA-MEYER LEMON MARMALADE

This marmalade boasts both an aromatic tropical flavor and a very tart bite, without a trace of bitterness. It has been known to convert even the most skeptical of marmalade eaters.

2¼ pounds perfectly ripe white guavas, cut into eighths

1½ pounds seeded Meyer lemons, halved crosswise,

each half cut lengthwise into quarters and sliced crosswise medium-thin

2 pounds 11 ounces white cane sugar

2 to 3 ounces strained freshly squeezed Eureka or Lisbon lemon juice

DAY 1

First, prepare the guava juice: Place the guava eighths in a medium nonreactive kettle and cover with enough cold water for the fruit to bob freely. Bring to a boil over high heat, then decrease the heat to a simmer. Cover and cook the fruit for 2 to 3 hours, or until the guavas are very soft and the liquid has become syrupy. As the guavas cook, stir them every 20 to 30 minutes, adding more water if necessary. The level of water should stay consistently high enough for the fruit to remain submerged as it cooks.

Strain the guava juice by pouring the hot fruit and liquid into a medium-fine-mesh strainer suspended over a heatproof storage container or nonreactive saucepan. Cover the entire setup well with plastic wrap and place in the refrigerator to drip overnight.

While the guavas are cooking, place the lemon slices in a separate nonreactive saucepan and cover with enough water to reach 1 inch above the tops. Cover tightly and let rest overnight at room temperature.

DAY 2

Place a saucer with five metal teaspoons in a flat place in your freezer for testing the marmalade later.

Bring the pan with the lemon slices to a boil over high heat, then decrease the heat to medium, and cook, uncovered, at a lively simmer for 20 to 30 minutes, or until the fruit is tender.

While the lemon slices are cooking, remove the plastic wrap from the guavas and their juice and discard the guavas. Strain the juice well through a very fine-mesh strainer to remove any lingering solids.

When the lemon slices are ready, place them with their liquid into a large mixing bowl with the sugar, cooked guava juice, and 2 ounces lemon juice. Stir well to combine, then taste, and slowly add a little more lemon juice if necessary. You should be able to taste the lemon juice, but it should not be overpowering. Keep adding lemon juice only until you are just able to detect its tartness in the mixture. Transfer the mixture to an 11- or 12-quart copper preserving pan or a wide nonreactive kettle.

Bring the mixture to a boil over high heat. Cook at a rapid boil until the setting point is reached; this will take a minimum of 35 minutes, but may take longer depending on your individual stove and pan. Initially, the mixture will bubble gently for several minutes; then, as more moisture cooks out of it and its sugar concentration increases, it will begin foaming. Do not stir it at all during the initial bubbling; then, once it starts to foam, stir it gently every few minutes with a heatproof rubber spatula. As it gets close to being done, stir it slowly every minute or two to prevent burning, decreasing the heat a tiny bit if necessary. The marmalade is ready for testing when its color darkens slightly and its bubbles become very small.

To test the marmalade for doneness, remove it from the heat and carefully transfer a small representative half-spoonful to one of your frozen spoons. It should look shiny, with tiny bubbles throughout. Replace the spoon in the freezer for 3 to 4 minutes, then re-move and carefully feel the underside of the spoon. It should be neither warm nor cold; if still warm, re-turn it to the freezer for a moment. Tilt the spoon ver-tically to see whether the marmalade runs; if it does not run, and if its top layer has thickened to a jelly consistency, it is done. If it runs, cook it for another few minutes, stirring, and test again as needed.

When the marmalade is ready, turn off the heat but do not stir. Using a stainless-steel spoon, skim off any surface foam and discard. Pour the marmalade into sterilized jars and process according to the man-ufacturer's instructions or as directed on page 42.

Variation:
LIME & GUAVA MARMALADE
This is a very tart and exceptionally delicious marma-lade in its own right. To make this version, replace the Meyer lemons with an equal quantity of ripe yellow Bearss (Persian) limes, and use only 1 ounce lemon juice. Proceed with the rest of the recipe as directed.

Approximate Yield: seven 8-ounce jars   *Shelf Life:* 1 year

PAGE MANDARIN
MARMALADE

Among mandarins, Pages are particularly well suited to marmalade making; unlike numerous other varieties, their skin adheres closely to their flesh, making them much easier to prepare. Their rind is delicious and makes a sweet, orangey marmalade. I have used lime juice, rather than lemon, in this recipe because limes and mandarins are such natural partners.

2 pounds Page mandarins, quartered

2 pounds Page mandarins, halved crosswise and seeded if necessary,
each half cut lengthwise into quarters and sliced crosswise medium-thin

3 pounds 7 ounces white cane sugar

5 ounces strained freshly squeezed lime juice

DAY 1

Place the quartered mandarins in a nonreactive saucepan where they will fit snugly in a single layer. Add enough cold water for the fruit to bob freely. Cover tightly and let rest overnight at room temperature.

In a separate nonreactive saucepan, place the sliced mandarins with enough water to cover the tops by 1 inch. Cover tightly and let rest overnight at room temperature.

DAY 2

Prepare the mandarin juice: Bring the pan with the mandarin quarters to a boil over high heat, then decrease the heat to medium. Cook the fruit at a lively simmer, covered, for 2 to 3 hours, or until the mandarins are very soft and the liquid has become slightly syrupy. As the mandarins cook, press down on them gently with a spoon every 30 minutes or so, adding a little more water if necessary. The water level should stay consistently high enough for the fruit to remain submerged as it cooks.

When the mandarins are finished cooking, strain their juice by pouring the hot fruit and liquid into a medium strainer or colander suspended over a heat-proof storage container or nonreactive saucepan. Cover the entire setup well with plastic wrap and let drip overnight at room temperature.

Meanwhile, prepare the sliced mandarins: Bring the pan with the mandarin slices to a boil over high heat, then decrease the heat to medium and cook, covered, at a lively simmer for 1 ½ to 2 hours, or until the rinds are tender. As the fruit cooks, stir it gently every 30 minutes or so, adding a little more water if necessary. The water level should stay consistently high enough for the fruit to remain submerged as it cooks. When the mandarins have finished cooking, remove the pan from the heat, cover tightly, and let rest overnight at room temperature.

DAY 3

Place a saucer with five metal teaspoons in a flat place in your freezer for testing the marmalade later.

Remove the plastic wrap from the mandarin eighths and their juice and discard the mandarins. Strain the juice well through a very fine-mesh strainer to remove any lingering solids.

In a large mixing bowl, combine the sugar, cooked mandarin juice, fresh lime juice, and mandarin slices and their liquid, stirring well. Transfer the mixture to an 11- or 12-quart copper preserving pan or a wide nonreactive kettle.

Bring the mixture to a boil over high heat. Cook at a rapid boil until the setting point is reached; this will take a minimum of 30 minutes, but may take longer depending on your individual stove and pan. Initially, the mixture will bubble gently for several minutes; then, as more moisture cooks out of it and its sugar concentration increases, it will begin foaming. Do not stir it at all during the initial bubbling; then, once it starts to foam, stir it gently every few minutes with a heatproof rubber spatula. As it gets close to being done, stir it slowly every minute or two to prevent burning, decreasing the heat a tiny bit if necessary. The marmalade is ready for testing when its color darkens slightly and its bubbles become very small.

To test the marmalade for doneness, remove it from the heat and carefully transfer a small representative half-spoonful to one of your frozen spoons. It should look shiny, with tiny bubbles throughout. Replace the spoon in the freezer for 3 to 4 minutes, then remove and carefully feel the underside of the spoon. It should be neither warm nor cold; if still warm, return it to the freezer for a moment. Tilt the spoon vertically to see whether the marmalade runs; if it does not run, and if its top layer has thickened to a jelly consistency, it is done. If it runs, cook it for another few minutes, stirring, and test again as needed.

When the marmalade has finished cooking, turn off the heat but do not stir. Using a stainless-steel spoon, skim off any surface foam and discard. Pour the marmalade into sterilized jars and process according to the manufacturer's instructions or as directed on page 42.

Approximate Yield: nine to ten 8-ounce jars *Shelf Life:* 2 years

YELLOW GRAPEFRUIT
MARMALADE

This classic bitter English marmalade is a refreshing change from traditional Seville orange marmalade, its closest cousin. Because it contains both the flesh and rinds of the fruit, its flavor is extra-strong and delicious. Use any high-quality seedless grapefruit for this recipe.

3¼ pounds yellow grapefruits, halved crosswise and juiced, juice reserved

1¾ pounds yellow grapefruits, halved crosswise,

juiced and juice reserved, then cut into medium chunks

5 pounds white cane sugar

5½ ounces strained freshly squeezed lemon juice

DAY 1

Combine the juice from the two quantities of grapefruits. Strain the juice, cover, and refrigerate for later.

Place the grapefruit halves in a large stainless-steel kettle and cover amply with cold water. Bring to a boil over high heat, then decrease the heat to medium and cook at a lively simmer for 5 minutes. Drain, discarding the liquid. Repeat this process, then return the blanched grapefruit halves to the kettle and add cold water to cover. Bring the halves to a boil over high heat, then decrease the heat to medium-low, and cook, covered, at a lively simmer for 1 to 2 hours, or until the fruit is easily pierced with a skewer. As the grapefruit cooks, press down on it gently with a spoon every 30 minutes, adding more water if necessary. The water level should stay consistently high enough for the fruit to remain submerged as it cooks. When the grapefruit is tender, remove the pan from the heat, cover tightly, and let rest overnight at room temperature.

Meanwhile, place the grapefruit chunks in a large nonreactive saucepan. Add enough cold water to cover the grapefruit by 1 inch. Bring to a boil over high heat, then decrease the heat to medium. Cook the fruit at a lively simmer, covered, for 3 to 4 hours, or until the grapefruit is very soft and the liquid has become slightly syrupy. As the chunks cook, press down on them gently with a spoon every 30 minutes or so, adding a little more water when necessary. The water level should stay consistently high enough for the fruit to remain submerged as it cooks.

When the grapefruit chunks have finished cooking, strain their juice by pouring the hot fruit and liquid into a medium strainer or colander suspended over a heatproof storage container or nonreactive saucepan. Cover the entire setup well with plastic wrap and let drip overnight at room temperature.

DAY 2

Place a saucer with five metal teaspoons in a flat place in your freezer for testing the marmalade later.

Remove the plastic wrap from the grapefruit chunks and their juice and discard the chunks. Strain the juice well through a very fine-mesh strainer to remove any lingering solids.

Remove the grapefruit halves from their kettle, reserving the cooking liquid. Over a large bowl, use a soup spoon to scoop the flesh from each grapefruit half. Then, take one of the halves and, cradling it in one hand, use the spoon to gently scrape its interior of excess pith and fibers. Repeat with the rest of the halves, going around each one two or three times until its interior is smooth and its rind a uniform thickness. Cut each grapefruit half into 5 equal strips, then cut each strip crosswise into thin slices and reserve. Coarsely chop the scraped pith and fibers, along with the mushy interiors of the grapefruits, and return them to the cooking liquid.

In a large mixing bowl, combine the sugar, cooked grapefruit juice, reserved fresh grapefruit juice, lemon juice, sliced grapefruit rinds, and grapefruit cooking liquid and solids, stirring well. Transfer the mixture to an 11- or 12-quart copper preserving pan or a wide nonreactive kettle.

Bring the mixture to a boil over high heat. Cook at a rapid boil until the setting point is reached; this will take a minimum of 35 minutes, but may take longer depending on your individual stove and pan. Initially, the mixture will bubble gently for several minutes; then, as more moisture cooks out of it and its sugar concentration increases, it will begin foaming somewhat. Do not stir it at all during the initial bubbling; then, once it starts to foam, stir it gently every few minutes with a heatproof rubber spatula. As it gets close to being done, stir it slowly every minute or two to prevent burning, decreasing the heat a tiny bit if necessary. The marmalade is ready for testing when it has been foaming for several minutes and its color darkens.

To test the marmalade for doneness, remove it from the heat and carefully transfer a small representative half-spoonful to one of your frozen spoons. Replace the spoon in the freezer for 3 to 4 minutes, then remove and carefully feel the underside of the spoon. It should be neither warm nor cold; if still warm, return it to the freezer for a moment. Tilt the spoon vertically to see whether the marmalade runs; if it does not run, and if it has thickened to a spreadable consistency, it is done. If it runs, cook it for another few minutes, stirring, and test again as needed.

When the marmalade has finished cooking, turn off the heat but do not stir. Using a stainless-steel spoon, skim off any surface foam and discard. Pour the marmalade into sterilized jars and process according to the manufacturer's instructions or as directed on page 42.

Approximate Yield: ten 8-ounce jars *Shelf Life:* 2 years

SILVER THREE-FRUIT MARMALADE

Three-fruit marmalades, generally containing oranges, lemons, and grapefruits, are relatively common in the British Isles; but for this marmalade I turned to the other side of the channel. In Paris, one of my most beloved tea shops makes a delicious black tea scented with lemon, lime, and bergamot, and there I found my inspiration. This marmalade's delicate texture and exquisitely balanced flavor have made it a personal favorite, and a favorite among my marmalade-loving clients. I hope you will love it, too.

1 pound limes (preferably yellow Persian Bearss), cut into eighths

¾ pound lemons (preferably Lisbon), cut into eighths

1¼ pounds bergamots, cut into eighths

1 pound limes, halved crosswise,

each half cut lengthwise into quarters and sliced very thinly crosswise

1 pound seeded lemons, halved crosswise,

each half cut lengthwise into quarters and sliced very thinly crosswise

5 pounds white cane sugar

1 to 2 extra lemons, to make 2 ounces strained freshly squeezed juice

DAY 1

Place the lime, lemon, and bergamot eighths in a nonreactive saucepan where they will fit snugly in a single layer. Add enough cold water for the fruit to bob freely. Cover tightly and let rest overnight at room temperature.

DAY 2

Prepare the citrus juice: Bring the pan with the citrus eighths to a boil over high heat, then decrease the heat to medium. Cook the fruit at a lively simmer, covered, for 2 to 3 hours, or until the fruit is very soft and the liquid has become slightly syrupy. As the fruit cooks, press down on it gently with a spoon every 30 minutes or so, adding a little more water if necessary. The water level should stay consistently high enough for the fruit to remain submerged as it cooks.

When the citrus fruit has finished cooking, strain its juice by pouring the hot fruit and liquid into a medium strainer or colander suspended over a heatproof storage container or nonreactive saucepan. Cover the entire setup with plastic wrap and let drip overnight at room temperature.

Meanwhile, prepare the thinly sliced limes and lemons: Place the slices in a wide stainless-steel kettle and cover amply with cold water. Bring to a boil over high heat, then decrease the heat and simmer for 5 minutes. Drain, discarding the liquid. Return the slices to the kettle and add cold water just to cover. Bring to a boil over high heat, then decrease the heat to medium, and cook, covered, at a lively simmer for 20 to 30 minutes, or until the fruit is very tender. Remove the pan from the heat, cover tightly, and let rest overnight at room temperature.

DAY 3

Place a saucer with five metal teaspoons in a flat place in your freezer for testing the marmalade later.

Remove the plastic wrap from the citrus eighths and their juice and discard the solids. Strain the juice well through a very fine-mesh strainer.

In a large mixing bowl, combine the sugar, cooked citrus juice, fresh lemon juice, and sliced fruit and its liquid. Transfer the mixture to an 11- or 12-quart copper preserving pan or a wide nonreactive kettle.

Bring the mixture to a boil over high heat. Cook at a rapid boil until the setting point is reached; this will take a minimum of 25 minutes, but may take longer depending on your individual stove and pan. Initially, the mixture will bubble gently for several minutes; then, as more moisture cooks out of it and its sugar concentration increases, it will begin foaming. Do not stir it at all during the initial bubbling; then, once it starts to foam, stir it gently every few minutes with a heatproof rubber spatula. As it gets close to being done, stir it slowly every minute or two to prevent burning, decreasing the heat a tiny bit if necessary. The marmalade is ready for testing when its color darkens slightly and its bubbles become very small.

To test the marmalade for doneness, remove it from the heat and carefully transfer a small representative half-spoonful to one of your frozen spoons. It should look shiny, with tiny bubbles throughout. Replace the spoon in the freezer for 3 to 4 minutes, then remove and carefully feel the underside of the spoon. It should be neither warm nor cold; if still warm, return it to the freezer for a moment. Tilt the spoon vertically to see whether the marmalade runs; if it does not run, and if its top layer has thickened to a jelly consistency, it is done. If it runs, cook it for another few minutes, stirring, and test again as needed.

When the marmalade has finished cooking, turn off the heat but do not stir. Using a stainless-steel spoon, skim off any surface foam and discard. Pour the marmalade into sterilized jars and process according to the manufacturer's instructions or as directed on page 42.

Approximate Yield: ten 8-ounce jars *Shelf Life:* 2 years

ORANGE MARMALADES

For me, nothing could possibly be better than a really good orange marmalade, slathered on some thickly buttered brown bread or baguette and accompanied by a mug of rich malty black tea. Orange marmalade is one of my favorite foods, and few things make me happier than spending an afternoon in a Seville orange tree, happily plucking fruit while surrounded by the unmistakable Seville orange fragrance. For orange marmalade, Seville oranges are the classic ingredient. After breakfasting on some really top-notch Seville marmalade, I am ready to face the day with bells on.

Seville orange marmalade can take many forms, depending on your taste. It may be thick cut or fine cut, dark or light, plain or spiced. I have included a variety of my favorite recipes here, each with different proportions and techniques. For a flavor that is balanced yet retains adequate bitterness, it is sometimes best to blanch the rinds before making them into marmalade; otherwise, the rind may be so bitter it hurts your teeth. When seeding the oranges, always work over a bowl to catch the juice. The juice may then be strained and saved; it is excellent in savory dishes in place of lemon juice, and it adds a special sourness to citrus desserts.

Though nothing can match the special bitter flavor of Seville oranges, extremely delicious marmalades, including several of my favorites, are also made with sweet Valencia and blood oranges. Unlike most Seville marmalades, sweet orange marmalades are often beautiful to look at as well as to eat, because the orange slices tend to stay more intact and the jelly portion is clearer. Orange marmalades made with sweet oranges have a much lighter flavor than those made with Sevilles, though the process for making them is similar. Sweet orange marmalades also have the distinct advantage of being able to be made year-round, because many varieties bear fruit throughout the year.

BITTER ORANGE
& CINNAMON MARMALADE

For this excellent Seville marmalade, I turned to the classic Spanish flavor combination of orange and cinnamon. The oranges are thinly sliced, and the jelly portion of the mixture contains just a little lemon to lighten the flavor. Ceylon cinnamon is best for this recipe; its peppery quality is the perfect partner for these bitter oranges.

1¼ pounds Seville oranges, cut into eighths

¾ pound lemons (preferably Lisbon), cut into eighths

2¾ pounds seeded Seville or other sour oranges, halved crosswise,

each half cut lengthwise into quarters and sliced thinly crosswise

4 pounds white cane sugar

3 to 4 extra Seville oranges, to make 6 ounces strained freshly squeezed juice

3 or 4 (3-inch) cinnamon sticks

DAY 1

Prepare the cooked citrus juice: Place the orange and lemon eighths in a large nonreactive saucepan. Add enough cold water to cover the fruit by 1 inch. Bring the fruit to a boil over high heat, then decrease the heat to medium. Cook at a lively simmer, covered, for 3 hours, or until the fruit is very soft and the liquid has become slightly syrupy. As the oranges and lemons cook, press down on them gently with a spoon every 30 minutes or so, adding a little more water if necessary. The water level should stay consistently high enough for the fruit to remain submerged as it cooks.

When the oranges and lemons are finished cooking, strain their juice by pouring the hot fruit and liquid into a medium strainer or colander suspended over a heatproof storage container or nonreactive saucepan. Cover the entire setup well with plastic wrap and let drip overnight at room temperature.

Meanwhile, prepare the thinly sliced oranges: Place the slices in a wide stainless-steel kettle and cover amply with cold water. Bring to a boil over high heat, then decrease the heat and cook at a lively simmer for 5 minutes. Drain, discarding the liquid. Return the orange slices to the kettle and cover with 1 inch cold water. Bring to a boil over high heat, then decrease the heat to medium and cook, covered, at a lively simmer for 2 hours, or until the fruit is very tender. As the fruit cooks, stir it gently every 30 minutes or so, adding a little more water if necessary. The water level should stay consistently high enough for the fruit to remain submerged as it cooks. Remove the pan from the heat, cover tightly, and let rest overnight at room temperature.

DAY 2

Place a saucer with five metal teaspoons in a flat place in your freezer for testing the marmalade later.

Remove the plastic wrap from the orange and lemon eighths and their juice and discard the fruit. Strain the juice well through a very fine-mesh strainer to remove any lingering solids.

In a large mixing bowl, combine the sugar, cooked citrus juice, fresh orange juice, cinnamon sticks, and orange slices and their liquid, stirring well. Transfer the mixture to an 11- or 12-quart copper preserving pan or a wide nonreactive kettle.

Bring the mixture to a boil over high heat. Cook at a rapid boil over high heat until the setting point is reached; this will take a minimum of 20 minutes, but may take longer depending on your individual stove and pan. Initially, the mixture will bubble gently for several minutes; then, as more moisture cooks out of it and its sugar concentration increases, it will start to foam. Do not stir it at all during the initial bubbling; then, once it starts to foam, stir it gently every few minutes with a heatproof rubber spatula. As it gets close to being done, stir it slowly every minute or two to prevent burning, decreasing the

heat a tiny bit if necessary. The marmalade is ready for testing when its color darkens and its bubbles become very small.

To test the marmalade for doneness, remove it from the heat and carefully transfer a small representative half-spoonful to one of your frozen spoons. It should look shiny, with tiny bubbles throughout. Replace the spoon in the freezer for 3 to 4 minutes, then remove and carefully feel the underside of the spoon. It should be neither warm nor cold; if still warm, return it to the freezer for a moment. Tilt the spoon vertically to see whether the marmalade runs; if it does not run, and if its top layer has thickened to a jelly consistency, it is done. If it runs, cook it for another few minutes, stirring, and test again as needed.

When the marmalade has finished cooking, turn off the heat but do not stir. Remove the cinnamon sticks. Using a stainless-steel spoon, skim off any surface foam and discard. Pour the marmalade into sterilized jars and process according to the manufacturer's instructions or as directed on page 42.

Approximate Yield: **twelve 8-ounce jars** *Shelf Life:* **2 years**

SEVILLE ORANGE MARMALADE WITH RUM, VANILLA & PILONCILLO

This bitter orange marmalade has a subtle and very special mix of flavors. Piloncillo, the hard raw cane sugar common in Mexico, lends its exotic edge to the oranges, which are then gently buoyed by rum and vanilla. This is a fine-cut Seville marmalade for a chilly winter's morning.

3 pounds 3 ounces Seville oranges, cut into eighths

2 pounds seeded Seville oranges, halved crosswise,

each half cut lengthwise into quarters and sliced crosswise as thinly as possible

5 pounds 3 ounces white cane sugar

3½ ounces strained freshly squeezed lemon juice

Several gratings of piloncillo

A scant ½ ounce vanilla extract (preferably Mexican)

1½ ounces amber or dark rum

DAY 1

Place the orange eighths in a nonreactive kettle where they will fit snugly in a single layer. Add enough cold water for the fruit to bob freely. Cover tightly and let rest overnight at room temperature.

DAY 2

Bring the pan with the orange eighths to a boil, then decrease the heat to a lively simmer. Cook the orange eighths, covered, for 3 hours, or until they are very soft and their liquid has become slightly syrupy. As the fruit cooks, stir it gently every 30 minutes or so, adding a little more water if necessary. The water level should stay consistently high enough for the fruit to remain submerged as it cooks.

When the orange eighths have finished cooking, strain their juice by pouring the hot fruit and liquid into a medium strainer or colander suspended over a heatproof storage container or nonreactive sauce-pan. Cover the entire setup well with plastic wrap and let drip overnight at room temperature.

Meanwhile, prepare the thinly sliced oranges: Place the slices in a wide stainless-steel kettle and cover amply with cold water. Bring to a boil over high heat, then decrease the heat and simmer for 5 minutes. Drain, discarding the liquid. Return the orange slices to the kettle and add enough cold water to cover them by 1 inch. Bring to a boil over high heat, then decrease the heat to medium and cook, covered, at a lively simmer for 2 hours, or until the fruit is very tender. As the fruit cooks, stir it gently every 30 minutes or so, adding a little more water if necessary. The water level should stay consistently high enough for the fruit to remain submerged as it cooks. Remove the pan from the heat, cover tightly, and let rest overnight at room temperature.

DAY 3

Place a saucer with five metal teaspoons in a flat place in your freezer for testing the marmalade later.

Remove the plastic wrap from the orange eighths and their juice and discard the oranges. Strain the juice well through a very fine-mesh strainer to remove any lingering solids.

In a large mixing bowl, combine the sugar, cooked orange juice, fresh lemon juice, and orange slices and their liquid, stirring well. Transfer the mixture to an 11- or 12-quart copper preserving pan or a wide nonreactive kettle.

Bring the mixture to a boil over high heat, then stir in a small handful of grated piloncillo. Continue adding piloncillo until the mixture darkens perceptibly. Carefully taste the marmalade and add a tiny bit more piloncillo if necessary; the flavor should be subtle.

Cook the mixture for 5 minutes more, then stir in the vanilla. Continue cooking the marmalade at a rapid boil over high heat until the setting point is reached; this will take a minimum of 20 minutes, but may take longer depending on your individual stove and pan. Initially, the mixture will bubble gently for several minutes; then, as more moisture cooks out of it and its sugar concentration increases, it will start to foam. Do not stir it at all during the initial bubbling; then, once it starts to foam, stir it gently every few minutes with a heatproof rubber spatula. As it gets close to being done, stir it slowly every minute or two to prevent burning, decreasing the heat a tiny bit if necessary. When nearly done, stir in the rum. The marmalade is ready for testing when its color darkens slightly and its bubbles become very small.

To test the marmalade for doneness, remove it from the heat and carefully transfer a small representative half-spoonful to one of your frozen spoons. It should look shiny, with tiny bubbles throughout. Replace the spoon in the freezer for 3 to 4 minutes, then remove and carefully feel the underside of the spoon. It should be neither warm nor cold; if still warm, return it to the freezer for a moment. Tilt the spoon vertically to see whether the marmalade runs; if it does not run, and if its top layer has thickened to a jelly consistency, it is done. If it runs, cook it for another few minutes, stirring, and test again as needed.

When the marmalade has finished cooking, turn off the heat but do not stir. Using a stainless-steel spoon, skim off any surface foam and discard. Pour the marmalade into sterilized jars and process according to the manufacturer's instructions or as directed on page 42.

Variation:
SEVILLE ORANGE MARMALADE WITH
VANILLA & MUSCOVADO
Muscovado sugar has a milder flavor than piloncillo and is often easier to find. For this version, omit the piloncillo, and use only a few drops of vanilla and a small splash of rum. Add 2¼ ounces dark muscovado sugar to the marmalade mixture before the start of the final cooking. Proceed with the rest of the recipe as directed.

Approximate Yield: ten to eleven 8-ounce jars *Shelf Life:* 2 years

SOUR ORANGE & LEMON MARMALADE

In this marmalade, the bold winter combination of sour oranges and lemons makes for a refreshing flavor. This is a British-style marmalade, meant for morning toast and tea.

¾ pound lemons, cut into eighths
1¼ pounds seeded lemons (preferably Lisbon), halved crosswise,
each half cut lengthwise into quarters and sliced thickly crosswise
3 pounds seeded Seville or other sour oranges, halved crosswise
5 pounds white cane sugar
5 ounces strained freshly squeezed lemon juice

DAY 1

Place the lemon eighths in a nonreactive saucepan where they will fit snugly in a single layer. Add enough cold water for the fruit to bob freely. Cover tightly and let rest overnight at room temperature.

DAY 2

Prepare the cooked lemon juice: Bring the pan with the lemon eighths to a boil over high heat, then decrease the heat to medium. Cook the fruit at a lively simmer, covered, for 2 to 3 hours, or until the lemons are very soft and the liquid has become slightly syrupy. As the lemons cook, press down on them gently with a spoon every 30 minutes or so, adding a little more water if necessary. The water level should stay consistently high enough for the fruit to remain submerged as it cooks.

When the lemons are finished cooking, strain their juice by pouring the hot fruit and liquid into a medium strainer or colander suspended over a heatproof storage container or nonreactive saucepan. Cover the entire setup well with plastic wrap and let drip overnight at room temperature.

Meanwhile, prepare the sliced lemons: Place the slices in a wide stainless-steel kettle and cover amply with cold water. Bring to a boil over high heat, then decrease the heat and simmer for 5 minutes. Drain, discarding the liquid. Return the lemon slices to the kettle and add enough cold water to cover them by 1 inch. Bring to a boil over high heat, then decrease the heat to medium and cook at a lively simmer, covered, for 30 to 40 minutes, or until the fruit is very tender. As the fruit cooks, stir it gently every 15 minutes or so, adding a little more water if necessary. The water level should stay consistently high enough for the fruit to remain submerged as it cooks. Remove the pan from the heat, cover tightly, and let rest overnight at room temperature.

Last, prepare the orange slices: Juice the orange halves, cover the juice, and refrigerate overnight. Quarter each orange half lengthwise and slice the quarters thickly crosswise. Place the slices in a stainless-steel kettle and cover amply with cold water. Bring to a boil over high heat, then decrease the heat and simmer for 5 minutes. Drain, discarding the liquid. Return the orange slices to the kettle and cover with 2 inches cold water. Bring to a boil over high heat, then decrease the heat to medium and cook, covered, at a lively simmer for 1 to 2 hours, or until the fruit is very tender. As the fruit cooks, stir it gently every 30 minutes or so, adding a little more water if necessary. The water level should stay consistently high enough for the fruit to remain submerged as it cooks. When the slices are ready, remove the pan from the heat, cover tightly, and let rest overnight at room temperature.

DAY 3

Place a saucer with five metal teaspoons in a flat place in your freezer for testing the marmalade later.

Remove the plastic wrap from the lemon eighths and their juice and discard the lemons. Strain the juice well through a very fine-mesh strainer to remove any lingering solids.

In a large mixing bowl, combine the sugar, cooked lemon juice, fresh lemon and orange juices, and lemon and orange slices and their liquid, stirring well. Transfer the mixture to an 11- or 12-quart copper preserving pan or a wide nonreactive kettle.

Bring the mixture to a boil over high heat. Cook at a rapid boil until the setting point is reached; this will take a minimum of 25 minutes, but may take longer depending upon your individual stove and pan.

Initially, the mixture will bubble gently for several minutes; then, as more moisture cooks out of it and its sugar concentration increases, it will begin foaming. Do not stir it at all during the initial bubbling; then, once it starts to foam, stir it gently every few minutes with a heatproof rubber spatula. As it gets close to being done, stir it slowly every minute or two to prevent burning, decreasing the heat a tiny bit if necessary. The marmalade is ready for testing when its color darkens slightly and its bubbles become very small.

To test the marmalade for doneness, remove it from the heat and carefully transfer a small representative half-spoonful to one of your frozen spoons. It should look shiny, with tiny bubbles throughout. Replace the spoon in the freezer for 3 to 4 minutes, then remove and carefully feel the underside of the spoon. It should be neither warm nor cold; if still warm, return it to the freezer for a moment. Tilt the spoon vertically to see whether the marmalade runs; if it does not run, and if its top layer has thickened to a jelly consistency, it is done. If it runs, cook it for another few minutes, stirring, and test again as needed.

When the marmalade has finished cooking, turn off the heat but do not stir. Using a stainless-steel spoon, skim off any surface foam and discard. Pour the marmalade into sterilized jars and process according to the manufacturer's instructions or as directed on page 42.

Approximate Yield: ten 8-ounce jars *Shelf Life:* 2 years

ENGLISH MARMALADE

If you are a die-hard marmalade lover whose vision of marmalade resembles an ultra-thick-cut, treacly preserve redolent of wintry spice, this is the marmalade for you. Nothing quite matches its dark and very bitter flavor.

1½ pounds Seville oranges, cut into eighths

2½ pounds seeded Seville oranges, halved crosswise,
each half cut lengthwise into quarters and sliced thickly crosswise

2¼ pounds white cane sugar

2¼ pounds light brown cane sugar

4 star anise

Generous splash of bourbon

DAY 1

Place the orange eighths in a nonreactive kettle where they will fit snugly in a single layer. Add enough cold water for the fruit to bob freely. Cover tightly and let rest overnight at room temperature.

Place the orange slices in a second large nonreactive kettle and add water to cover the tops of the fruit by 2 inches. Cover the kettle tightly and let rest overnight at room temperature.

DAY 2

Bring both kettles to a boil, then decrease the heat to a lively simmer.

Cook the orange eighths, covered, for 3 hours, or until they are very soft and their liquid has become slightly syrupy.

Cook the orange slices, covered, for 2 to 3 hours, or until the rinds are very tender. As the fruit cooks, stir it gently every 30 minutes or so, adding a little more water if necessary. The water level should stay consistently high enough in both pans for the fruit to remain submerged as it cooks.

When the orange eighths have finished cooking, strain their juice by pouring the hot fruit and liquid into a medium strainer or colander suspended over a heatproof storage container or nonreactive saucepan. Cover the entire setup well with plastic wrap and let drip overnight at room temperature. When the orange slices have finished cooking, cover them tightly and let rest overnight at room temperature.

DAY 3

Place a saucer with five metal teaspoons in a flat place in your freezer for testing the marmalade later.

Remove the plastic wrap from the orange eighths and their juice and discard the oranges. Strain the juice well through a very fine-mesh strainer to remove any lingering solids.

In a large mixing bowl, combine the sugars, cooked orange juice, star anise, and orange slices and their liquid, stirring well. Transfer the mixture to an 11- or 12-quart copper preserving pan or a wide nonreactive kettle.

Bring the mixture to a boil over high heat. Cook at a rapid boil until the setting point is reached; this will take a minimum of 30 to 45 minutes, but may take longer depending on your individual stove and pan. Initially, the mixture will bubble gently for several minutes; then, as more moisture cooks out of it and its sugar concentration increases, it will begin foaming somewhat. Do not stir it at all during the initial bubbling; then, once it starts to foam, stir it gently every few minutes with a heatproof rubber spatula. After several minutes of foaming, stir in the bourbon. As the marmalade gets close to being done, stir it slowly every minute or two to prevent burning, decreasing the heat a tiny bit if necessary. The marmalade is ready for testing when its color darkens slightly and its bubbles become very small.

To test the marmalade for doneness, remove it from the heat and carefully transfer a small representative half-spoonful to one of your frozen spoons. It should look shiny, with tiny bubbles throughout. Replace the spoon in the freezer for 3 to 4 minutes, then remove and carefully feel the underside of the spoon. It should be neither warm nor cold; if still warm, return it to the freezer for a moment. Tilt the spoon vertically to see whether the marmalade runs; if it is reluctant to run, and if its top layer has thickened to a jelly consistency, it is done. If it runs, cook it for another few minutes, stirring, and test again as needed. Be careful not to overcook the marmalade, as it may continue to thicken slightly after it cools.

When the marmalade has finished cooking, turn off the heat but do not stir. Using a stainless-steel spoon, skim off any surface foam and discard. Remove the star anise. Pour the marmalade into sterilized jars and process according to the manufacturer's instructions or as directed on page 42.

Variations:

ENGLISH MARMALADE WITH CASSIA
Omit the star anise, instead adding 2 or 3 sticks cassia cinnamon to the mixture at the start of the final cooking. Proceed with the rest of the recipe as directed.

SEVILLE ORANGE MARMALADE WITH COFFEE AND CARDAMOM
This is an even more richly flavored marmalade than the original; the effect of the coffee is to deepen the flavor, adding another layer of bitterness. For this version, omit the bourbon and star anise. Crush 2 tablespoons green cardamom pods lightly in a mortar to release their seeds. Divide the crushed cardamom and ½ cup best regular coffee beans equally between two large mesh stainless-steel tea infusers with firm latches and add them to the marmalade at the start of the final cooking. Press down on the infusers to be sure they are submerged, then proceed with the rest of the recipe as directed.

Approximate Yield: **eight 8-ounce jars** *Shelf Life:* **2 years**

ENGLISH THREE-FRUIT MARMALADE

The very strong and delicious classic British trio of grapefruit, lemon, and Seville orange here is brought up a notch with the barest hint of gin, which perfectly draws all the flavors together. The secret to this marmalade is to prepare each fruit separately and to cut it into extremely thick pieces; this approach produces both the cleanest flavor and the most fun marmalade to eat.

2 pounds pink grapefruits, halved crosswise

1½ pounds Seville oranges, halved crosswise

1½ pounds lemons (preferably Lisbon), halved crosswise,
each half cut into quarters lengthwise and thickly sliced

5 pounds white cane sugar

1 to 2 extra lemons, to make 5 ounces strained freshly squeezed juice

2 ounces plus 1 teaspoon gin, such as Hendrick's

DAY 1

First, prepare the grapefruits: Squeeze and strain the grapefruit juice. Cover the juice and place it in the refrigerator. Put the juiced grapefruit halves in a medium stainless-steel kettle and cover amply with cold water. Bring to a boil over high heat, then decrease the heat to medium and cook at a lively simmer for 5 minutes. Drain, discarding the liquid. Repeat this process, then return the blanched grapefruit halves to the kettle and cover with enough cold water for the fruit to bob freely. Bring the halves to a boil over high heat, then decrease the heat to medium-low and cook, covered, at a lively simmer for 1 to 2 hours, or until the fruit is easily pierced with a skewer. As the grapefruit cooks, press down on it gently with a spoon every 30 minutes or so, adding more water if necessary. The water level should stay consistently high enough for the fruit to float freely as it cooks. When the grapefruit is tender, remove the pan from the heat, cover tightly, and let rest overnight at room temperature.

Meanwhile, prepare the orange slices: Juice the orange halves, strain the juice, and add it to the reserved grapefruit juice. Cover the orange-grapefruit juice and refrigerate it overnight. Quarter each orange half lengthwise and slice the quarters thickly crosswise. Place the slices in a stainless-steel kettle and cover amply with cold water. Bring to a boil over high heat, then decrease the heat and simmer for 5 minutes. Drain, discarding the liquid. Return the orange slices to the kettle and cover with 1 inch cold water. Bring to a boil over high heat, then decrease the heat to medium and cook, covered, at a lively simmer for 1 to 2 hours, or until the fruit is very tender. As the fruit cooks, stir it gently every 30 minutes or so, adding a little more water if necessary. The water level should stay consistently high enough for the fruit to remain submerged as it cooks. When the slices are ready, remove the pan from the heat, cover tightly, and let rest overnight at room temperature.

Last, prepare the sliced lemons: Place the slices in a stainless-steel kettle and cover amply with cold water. Bring to a boil over high heat, then decrease the heat and simmer for 5 minutes. Drain, discarding the liquid. Return the lemon slices to the kettle and cover with 1 inch cold water, pressing down on the fruit to be sure the water level is correct. Bring to a boil over high heat, then decrease the heat to medium and cook at a lively simmer for 30 to 40 minutes, or until the fruit is very tender. Remove the pan from the heat, cover tightly, and let rest overnight at room temperature.

DAY 2

Place a saucer with five metal teaspoons in a flat place in your freezer for testing the marmalade later.

Prepare the grapefruit: Remove the grapefruit halves from their kettle, reserving the cooking liquid. Over a large bowl, use a soup spoon to scoop the flesh from each grapefruit half. Then, take each half and, cradling it in one hand, use the spoon to gently scrape its interior of excess pith and fibers. Repeat with the rest of the halves, going around each one two or three times until its interior is smooth and its rind is a uniform thickness. Cut each grapefruit half into 5 equal strips, then cut each strip crosswise into thick slices and reserve. Strain the scraped pith and fibers, along with the mushy interiors of the grapefruits, back into the cooking liquid, letting them drip for several minutes. Discard the remaining solids. Pour the liquid through a fine-mesh strainer.

In a large mixing bowl, combine the sugar, strained grapefruit cooking liquid, fresh grapefruit-orange juice, grapefruit rinds, fresh lemon juice, 2 ounces gin, and lemon and orange slices and their liquid, stirring well. Transfer the mixture to an 11- or 12-quart copper preserving pan or a wide nonreactive kettle.

Bring the mixture to a boil over high heat. Cook at a rapid boil until the setting point is reached; this will take a minimum of 25 minutes, but may take longer depending on your individual stove and pan. Initially, the mixture will bubble gently for several minutes; then, as more moisture cooks out of it and its sugar concentration increases, it will begin foaming. Do not stir it at all during the initial bubbling; then, once it starts to foam, stir it gently every few minutes with a heatproof rubber spatula. As it gets close to being done, stir it slowly every minute or two to prevent burning, decreasing the heat a tiny bit if necessary. The marmalade is ready for testing when its color darkens slightly and its bubbles become very small.

To test the marmalade for doneness, remove it from the heat and carefully transfer a small representative half-spoonful to one of your frozen spoons. It should look shiny, with tiny bubbles throughout. Replace the spoon in the freezer for 3 to 4 minutes, then remove and carefully feel the underside of the spoon. It should be neither warm nor cold; if still warm, return it to the freezer for a moment. Tilt the spoon vertically to see whether the marmalade runs; if it does not run, and if its top layer has thickened to a jelly consistency, it is done. If it runs, cook it for another few minutes, stirring, and test again as needed.

When the marmalade has finished cooking, turn off the heat but do not stir. Using a stainless-steel spoon, skim off any surface foam and discard. Stir in the remaining teaspoon of gin. Pour the marmalade into sterilized jars and process according to the manufacturer's instructions or as directed on page 42.

Approximate Yield: ten 8-ounce jars *Shelf Life:* 2 years

ORANGE-KUMQUAT MARMALADE WITH CARDAMOM

A perfectly clear jelly with orange slices and kumquat quarters suspended in it, this Valencia marmalade has everything: visual beauty, a hauntingly exotic flavor, and a perfect melt-in-your-mouth texture. I particularly enjoy it as a filling for tarts, where its cardamom flavor adds an intriguing and unexpected twist.

¾ pound seeded and quartered kumquats

1½ pounds seeded Valencia oranges, halved crosswise,
each half quartered lengthwise and sliced crosswise medium-thin

1½ pounds Valencia oranges, cut into eighths

½ pound kumquats, halved

3 pounds 14 ounces white cane sugar

3 ounces strained freshly squeezed lemon juice

1½ tablespoons green cardamom pods, crushed lightly in a mortar to release their seeds

A few drops of orange flower water

DAY 1

Place the kumquat quarters and orange slices in a medium nonreactive saucepan. Add enough cold water to cover the fruit by 1 inch. Cover tightly and let rest overnight at room temperature.

In a separate saucepan, combine the orange eighths and the halved kumquats. Add enough cold water for the fruit to bob freely. Cover tightly and let rest overnight at room temperature.

DAY 2

Prepare the cooked citrus juice: Bring the pan with the orange eighths and kumquat halves to a boil over high heat, then decrease the heat to medium. Cook the fruit at a lively simmer, covered, for 3 hours, or until the oranges are very soft and the liquid has become slightly syrupy. As the fruit cooks, press down on it gently with a spoon every 30 minutes or so,

adding a little more water if necessary. The water level should stay consistently high enough for the fruit to remain submerged as it cooks.

When the fruit has finished cooking, strain its juice by pouring the hot fruit and liquid into a medium strainer or colander suspended over a heatproof storage container or nonreactive saucepan. Cover the entire setup well with plastic wrap and let drip overnight at room temperature.

Meanwhile, prepare the kumquat quarters and orange slices: Bring the pan with them to a boil over high heat, then decrease the heat and cook, covered, for 45 to 60 minutes, or until the orange rinds are tender. As the fruit cooks, press down on it gently with a spoon every 20 minutes or so, adding a little more water if necessary. The water level should stay consistently high enough for the fruit to remain submerged as it cooks. Remove the kumquats and oranges from the heat, cover tightly, and let rest overnight at room temperature.

DAY 3
Place a saucer with five metal teaspoons in a flat place in your freezer for testing the marmalade later.

Remove the plastic wrap from the orange eighths and kumquat halves and their juice and discard the fruit. Strain the juice well through a very fine-mesh strainer to remove any lingering solids.

Place the sugar in an 11- or 12-quart copper preserving pan or a wide nonreactive kettle. Gradually stir in the cooked citrus juice, fresh lemon juice, and kumquat quarters and orange slices and their liquid. Place the cardamom into a fine-mesh stainless-steel tea infuser with a firm latch and add it to the mixture, pressing down on it to be sure it is submerged.

Bring the mixture to a boil over high heat. Cook at a rapid boil until the setting point is reached; this will take a minimum of 45 minutes, but may take longer depending on your individual stove and pan. Initially, the mixture will bubble gently for several minutes; then, as more moisture cooks out of it and its sugar concentration increases, it will begin foaming. Do not stir it at all during the initial bubbling; then, once it starts to foam, stir it gently every few minutes or so with a heatproof rubber spatula. As it gets close to being done, stir it slowly every minute or two to prevent burning. The marmalade is ready for testing when its color darkens slightly and its bubbles become very small.

To test the marmalade for doneness, remove it from the heat and carefully transfer a small representative half-spoonful to one of your frozen spoons. It should look shiny, with tiny bubbles throughout. Replace the spoon in the freezer for 3 to 4 minutes, then remove and carefully feel the underside of the spoon. It should be neither warm nor cold; if still warm, return it to the freezer for a moment. Tilt the spoon vertically to see whether the marmalade runs; if it does not run, and if its top layer has thickened to a jelly consistency, it is done. If it runs, cook it for another few minutes, stirring, and test again as needed.

When the marmalade has finished cooking, turn off the heat but do not stir. Remove the tea infuser. Using a stainless-steel spoon, skim off any surface foam and discard. Stir in the orange flower water. Pour the marmalade into sterilized jars and process according to the manufacturer's instructions or as directed on page 42.

Variation:
SEVILLE ORANGE & KUMQUAT MARMALADE WITH CARDAMOM
In this variation, the flavor of the Seville oranges dominates. To make this marmalade with Sevilles, replace the Valencia slices with Seville slices. On day 2, blanch the slices for 5 minutes and drain, then cover with 1 inch cold water and simmer, covered, for 2 hours or until tender. Meanwhile, cook the kumquat quarters as directed above, adjusting the amount of water accordingly. Replace the Valencia eighths with 1½ pounds Seville eighths, and use 2 ounces lemon juice rather than 3 ounces. Proceed with the rest of the recipe as directed.

Approximate Yield: **eleven 8-ounce jars** *Shelf Life:* **2 years**

LEMON-KUMQUAT
MARMALADE

This tart marmalade perfectly showcases the visual beauty and bright flavor of lemons and kumquats. For this recipe, the lemon slices are not blanched beforehand and are sliced a little more thinly than usual, resulting in a very clear jelly with an equally clear flavor.

1¼ pounds seeded lemons (preferably Lisbon), halved crosswise,
each half cut lengthwise into quarters and sliced thinly crosswise

1 pound seeded and quartered kumquats

½ pound lemons, cut into eighths

1 pound kumquats, halved

3 pounds 6 ounces white cane sugar

1 to 2 extra lemons, to make 3½ ounces strained freshly squeezed juice

DAY 1

Place the lemon slices and kumquat quarters in a medium nonreactive saucepan. Cover with 1 inch cold water. Cover tightly and let rest overnight at room temperature.

In a separate saucepan, combine the lemon eighths and kumquat halves. Add enough cold water for the fruit to bob freely. Cover tightly and let rest overnight at room temperature.

DAY 2

Prepare the cooked citrus juice: Bring the pan with the lemon eighths and kumquat halves to a boil over high heat, then decrease the heat to medium. Cook the fruit at a lively simmer, covered, for 3 hours, or until the lemons are very soft and the liquid has become slightly syrupy. As the fruit cooks, press down on it gently with a spoon every 30 minutes or so, adding a little more water if necessary. The water level should stay consistently high enough for the fruit to remain submerged as it cooks.

When the fruit is finished cooking, strain its juice by pouring the hot fruit and liquid into a medium strainer or colander suspended over a heatproof storage container or nonreactive saucepan. Cover the entire setup well with plastic wrap and let drip overnight at room temperature.

Meanwhile, prepare the lemon slices and kumquat quarters: Bring the pan with them to a boil over high heat, then decrease the heat and cook, covered, for 45 to 60 minutes, or until the fruit is tender. As the fruit cooks, press down on it gently with a spoon every 20 minutes or so, adding a little more water if necessary. The water level should stay consistently high enough for the fruit to remain submerged as it cooks. Remove the fruit from the heat, cover tightly, and let rest overnight at room temperature.

DAY 3

Place a saucer with five metal teaspoons in a flat place in your freezer for testing the marmalade later.

Remove the plastic wrap from the drained fruit and its juice and discard the fruit. Strain the juice well through a very fine-mesh strainer to remove any lingering solids.

In a large mixing bowl, combine the sugar, cooked citrus juice, fresh lemon juice, and lemon slices and kumquat quarters and their liquid, stirring well. Transfer the mixture to an 11- or 12-quart copper preserving pan or a wide nonreactive kettle.

Bring the mixture to a boil over high heat. Cook at a rapid boil until the setting point is reached; this will take a minimum of 45 minutes, but may take longer depending on your individual stove and pan. Initially, the mixture will bubble gently for several minutes; then, as more moisture cooks out of it and its sugar concentration increases, it will begin foaming. Do not stir it at all during the initial bubbling; then, once it starts to foam, stir it gently every few minutes with a heatproof rubber spatula. As it gets close to being done, stir it slowly every minute or two to prevent burning. The marmalade is ready for testing when its color darkens slightly and its bubbles become very small.

To test the marmalade for doneness, remove it from the heat and carefully transfer a small representative half-spoonful to one of your frozen spoons. It should look shiny, with tiny bubbles throughout. Replace the spoon in the freezer for 3 to 4 minutes, then remove and carefully feel the underside of the spoon. It should be neither warm nor cold; if still warm, return it to the freezer for a moment. Tilt the spoon vertically to see whether the marmalade runs; if it does not run, and if its top layer has thickened to a jelly consistency, it is done. If it runs, cook it for another few minutes, stirring, and test again as needed.

When the marmalade has finished cooking, turn off the heat but do not stir. Using a stainless-steel spoon, skim off any surface foam and discard. Let the marmalade rest for 10 minutes off the heat, then fill 1 jar. Wait a few moments to see if the rinds seem to be floating to the top; if so, let the marmalade rest for another 5 minutes. If not, quickly pour the marmalade into the remaining jars and process according to the manufacturer's instructions or as directed on page 42.

Approximate Yield: eleven to twelve 8-ounce jars *Shelf Life:* 2 years

KUMQUAT MARMALADE

This lovely marmalade is actually a Meyer lemon–kumquat jelly with fine shreds of kumquat scattered throughout. Kumquats have an exceptionally long growing season, and this marmalade is one I like to make in March, when not many other fruits are in season.

2 pounds 10 ounces Meyer lemons, cut into eighths

1 pound kumquats, halved

1 pound 3 ounces seeded kumquats, halved crosswise,

each half cut lengthwise into quarters and sliced thinly crosswise

5¼ pounds white cane sugar

5 ounces strained freshly squeezed lemon juice

DAY 1

Place the lemon eighths and kumquat halves in a nonreactive saucepan where they will fit snugly in a single layer. Add enough cold water for the fruit to bob freely. Cover tightly and let rest overnight at room temperature.

In a separate saucepan, place the sliced kumquats with enough cold water to cover by 1 inch. Cover tightly and let rest overnight at room temperature.

DAY 2

Prepare the cooked lemon-kumquat juice: Bring the pan with the lemon eighths and kumquat halves to a boil over high heat, then decrease the heat to medium. Cook the fruit at a lively simmer, covered, for 2 to 3 hours, or until the fruit is very soft and the liquid has become slightly syrupy. As the fruit cooks, press down on it gently with a spoon every 30 minutes or so, adding a little more water when necessary. The water level should stay consistently high enough for the fruit to remain submerged as it cooks.

When the lemons and kumquats are finished cooking, strain their juice by pouring the hot fruit and liquid into a medium strainer or colander suspended over a heatproof storage container or nonreactive saucepan. Cover the entire setup well with plastic wrap and let drip overnight at room temperature.

Meanwhile, prepare the sliced kumquats: Bring the pan with the slices to a boil over high heat, then decrease the heat to medium, and cook, uncovered, at a lively simmer for 30 to 40 minutes, or until the fruit is very tender and the liquid has reduced significantly. Remove the pan from the heat, cover tightly, and let rest overnight at room temperature.

DAY 3

Place a saucer with five metal teaspoons in a flat place in your freezer for testing the marmalade later.

Remove the plastic wrap from the drained fruit pieces and their juice and discard the fruit. Strain the juice well through a very fine-mesh strainer to remove any lingering solids.

In a large mixing bowl, combine the sugar, cooked lemon-kumquat juice, fresh lemon juice, and kumquat slices and their liquid, stirring well. Transfer the mixture to an 11- or 12-quart copper preserving pan or a wide nonreactive kettle.

Bring the mixture to a boil over high heat. Cook at a rapid boil until the setting point is reached; this will take a minimum of 35 minutes, but may take longer depending on your individual stove and pan. Initially, the mixture will bubble gently for several minutes; then, as more moisture cooks out of it and its sugar concentration increases, it will begin foaming. Do not stir it at all during the initial bubbling; then, once it starts to foam, stir it gently every few minutes with a heatproof rubber spatula. As it gets close to being done, stir it slowly every minute or two to prevent burning, decreasing the heat a tiny bit if necessary. The marmalade is ready for testing when its color darkens slightly and its bubbles become very small.

To test the marmalade for doneness, remove it from the heat and carefully transfer a small representative half-spoonful to one of your frozen spoons. It should look shiny, with tiny bubbles throughout. Replace the spoon in the freezer for 3 to 4 minutes, then remove and carefully feel the underside of the spoon. It should be neither warm nor cold; if still warm, return it to the freezer for a moment. Tilt the spoon vertically to see whether the marmalade runs; if it does not run, and if its top layer has thickened to a jelly consistency, it is done. If it runs, cook it for another few minutes, stirring, and test again as needed.

When the marmalade has finished cooking, turn off the heat but do not stir. Using a stainless-steel spoon, skim off any surface foam and discard. Let the marmalade rest for 10 minutes off the heat, then fill 1 jar. Wait a few moments to see if the rinds seem to be floating to the top; if so, let the marmalade rest for another 5 minutes. If not, quickly pour the marmalade into the remaining jars and process according to the manufacturer's instructions or as directed on page 42.

Approximate Yield: ten to eleven 8-ounce jars   *Shelf Life:* 2 years

MEYER LEMON MARMALADE
WITH MANDARINS & LAVENDER

I much prefer this marmalade to plain Meyer lemon marmalade, which to me always seems somewhat one-dimensional. Here, Meyer lemons are the dominant flavor but are set off by spring mandarins and a touch of herby lavender.

2 pounds 5 ounces Gold Nugget or other flavorful mandarins, cut into eighths

1 pound 5 ounces seeded Meyer lemons, halved crosswise,

each half cut lengthwise into quarters and sliced thinly crosswise

1 (8-inch) sprig lavender

2½ pounds white cane sugar

2 to 3 ounces strained freshly squeezed Eureka or Lisbon lemon juice

DAY 1

Place the mandarin eighths in a nonreactive sauce-pan where they will fit snugly in a single layer. Add enough cold water for the fruit to bob freely. Cover tightly and let rest overnight at room temperature.

DAY 2

Prepare the cooked mandarin juice: Bring the pan with the mandarin eighths to a boil over high heat, then decrease the heat to medium. Cook the fruit at a lively simmer, covered, for 2 to 3 hours, or until the mandarins are very soft and the liquid has become slightly syrupy. As the mandarins cook, press down on them gently with a spoon every 30 minutes or so, adding a little more water if necessary. The water level should stay consistently high enough for the fruit to remain submerged as it cooks.

When the mandarins are finished cooking, strain their juice by pouring the hot fruit and liquid into a medium strainer or colander suspended over a heat-proof storage container or nonreactive saucepan. Cover the entire setup well with plastic wrap and let drip overnight at room temperature.

Meanwhile, place the lemon slices in a wide stainless-steel kettle and cover with 1 inch cold water. Cover tightly and let rest overnight at room temperature.

DAY 3

Place a saucer with five metal teaspoons in a flat place in your freezer for testing the jam later. Rinse the lavender well under cold water, pat dry between two clean kitchen towels, and set aside.

Remove the plastic wrap from the mandarin eighths and their juice and discard the mandarins. Strain the juice well through a very fine-mesh strainer to re-move any lingering solids.

Bring the lemon slices to a boil over high heat, then decrease the heat to medium and cook at a lively simmer, uncovered, for 20 to 30 minutes, or until the fruit is tender. As the fruit cooks, stir it gently every 10 minutes or so, adding a little more water if necessary. The water level should stay consistently high enough for the fruit to remain submerged as it cooks.

In a large mixing bowl, combine the sugar, cooked mandarin juice, 2 ounces fresh lemon juice, and lemon slices and their liquid, stirring well. Taste the mixture and add a dash more lemon juice if necessary. You should be able to taste the lemon juice, but it should not be overpowering. Transfer the mixture to an 11- or 12-quart copper preserving pan or a wide nonreactive kettle.

Bring the mixture to a boil over high heat. Cook at a rapid boil until the setting point is reached; this will take a minimum of 30 minutes, but may take longer depending on your individual stove and pan. Initially, the mixture will bubble gently for several minutes; then, as more moisture cooks out of it and its sugar concentration increases, it will begin foaming. Do not stir it at all during the initial bubbling; then, once it starts to foam, stir it gently every few minutes with a heatproof rubber spatula. As it gets close to being done, stir it slowly every minute or two to prevent burning, decreasing the heat a tiny bit if necessary. The marmalade is ready for testing when its color darkens slightly and its bubbles become very small.

To test the marmalade for doneness, remove it from the heat and carefully transfer a small representative half-spoonful to one of your frozen spoons. It should look shiny, with tiny bubbles throughout. Replace the spoon in the freezer for 3 to 4 minutes, then remove and carefully feel the underside of the spoon. It should be neither warm nor cold; if still warm, return it to the freezer for a moment. Tilt the spoon vertically to see whether the marmalade runs; if it does not run, and if its top layer has thickened to a jelly consistency, it is done. If it runs, cook it for another few minutes, stirring, and test again as needed.

When the marmalade has finished cooking, turn off the heat but do not stir. Using a stainless-steel spoon, skim off any surface foam and discard. Place the lavender sprig into the mixture and let steep for a few minutes off the heat. Carefully taste the marmalade and either remove the lavender or leave it for another minute or two, keeping in mind that its flavor will be slightly weaker once the marmalade has cooled. Using tongs, discard the lavender. Pour the marmalade into sterilized jars and process according to the manufacturer's instructions or as directed on page 42.

Approximate Yield: eight to nine 8-ounce jars *Shelf Life:* 1 year

chapter 5

LATE SPRING
THROUGH MIDSUMMER

Nothing brings out my fanciful side like the start of summer. What could be more exciting, after months of nearly nothing but citrus, than the first full flush of summer fruit? What could be more luscious than a kitchen brimming with flats of beautiful berries or more satisfying than a sunny afternoon spent in the bramble patch?

Summer fruits have a directness and simplicity about them that delights almost everyone. Berries, peaches, apricots, cherries, and all the other fruits of this time of year just beg to be eaten, and quickly, for they do not keep well. Nothing can match the brightness of a perfectly ripe peach or apricot or a raspberry just plucked from the bush. Summer is an incomparably vibrant time for fruit, and when I think of the jammiest fruits, my mind invariably turns to this time of year.

The rush of summer's bounty is dramatic, made all the more so by its rapidity; the season for many varieties is short, and there are so many different fruits available that one struggles to enjoy them all. Everything about these fruits, from their brief season to their lush flavor, reminds one of summer's fleeting nature. A perfect berry or peach always seems unique, more perfect than any to come. To pick berries is to realize not only their beauty but also their fragility, for a berry's glow starts to fade the moment it is plucked. Likewise, picking peaches or plums always fills me with awe at how much energy has gone into each individual piece of delicate fruit; each one seems like a small miracle. Summer is an embarrassment of riches, each more enthralling than the next. Yet her time upon the stage is fleeting and is over before we know it. The cooler days of autumn lie just ahead.

RHUBARB-ROSE CONSERVE
WITH CHERRIES

This is a jam for the first few weeks of spring, when fresh cherries have not yet appeared at market.

2½ pounds trimmed rhubarb stalks, cut into 3- to 4-inch lengths

2½ pounds white cane sugar

5 ounces strained freshly squeezed lemon juice

1¾ pounds chopped dried cherries

Several drops of rose water

DAY 1

Place the rhubarb in a large glass or hard plastic storage container and pour the sugar over it, shaking to combine. Drizzle the lemon juice over the fruit, cover tightly, and let macerate for 24 hours at room temperature. For this, a slightly warm location, such as the top of a gas stove not in use, is best; the warmth will help the rhubarb release its juices.

DAY 2

Place a saucer with five metal teaspoons in a flat place in your freezer for testing the jam later.

Transfer the rhubarb mixture to an 11- or 12-quart copper preserving pan or a wide nonreactive kettle, stirring well to dissolve the sugar. Stir in the cherries. Bring the mixture to a boil over high heat, stirring occasionally with a large heatproof rubber spatula. Boil, stirring frequently and decreasing the heat slightly if the conserve starts to stick, until thickened, about 20 minutes. For the last 5 to 10 minutes of cooking, you will need to stir the conserve nearly constantly to keep it from sticking.

When the conserve has thickened, test it for doneness. To test, carefully transfer a small representative half-spoonful of conserve to one of your frozen spoons. Replace the spoon in the freezer for 3 to 4 minutes, then remove and carefully feel the underside of the spoon. It should be neither warm nor cold; if still warm, return it to the freezer for a moment. Tilt the spoon vertically to see how quickly the conserve runs; if it runs slowly, and if it has thickened to a gloppy consistency, it is done. If it runs very quickly or appears watery, cook it for another few minutes, stirring, and test again as needed.

Turn off the heat but do not stir. Using a stainless-steel spoon, skim any foam from the surface of the conserve. Stir in a few drops of rose water, carefully taste, then stir in a few drops more if necessary, keeping in mind that the rose flavor will be slightly milder once the jam has cooled. Pour the conserve into sterilized jars and process according to the manufacturer's instructions or as directed on page 42.

Approximate Yield: six to seven 8-ounce jars   *Shelf Life:* 8 months

RHUBARB JAM

One thing that always mystifies me is the difficulty of finding rhubarb cooked on its own; we always seem to succumb to the temptation to combine it with something else. Yet rhubarb's unique flavor and texture set it apart from other early summer ingredients, and a really perfect plain rhubarb jam is hard to beat.

4 pounds trimmed rhubarb stalks, cut into 3- to 4-inch lengths
2¾ pounds white cane sugar
3 ounces strained freshly squeezed lemon juice

DAY 1

Place the rhubarb in a large glass or hard plastic storage container and pour the sugar over it, shaking to combine. Pour the lemon juice over the fruit, cover tightly, and let macerate for 24 hours at room temperature. For this, a slightly warm location, such as the top of a gas stove not in use, is best; the warmth will help the rhubarb release its juices.

DAY 2

Place a saucer with five metal teaspoons in a flat place in your freezer for testing the jam later.

Transfer the rhubarb mixture to an 11- or 12-quart copper preserving pan or a wide nonreactive kettle, stirring well to dissolve the sugar. Bring the mixture to a boil over high heat, stirring occasionally with a large heatproof rubber spatula. Boil, stirring frequently and gradually decreasing the heat if the jam starts to stick, until thickened and no longer watery, about 20 minutes. For the last 5 to 10 minutes of cooking, you will need to stir the jam nearly constantly to keep it from sticking.

When the jam has thickened, test it for doneness. To test, carefully transfer a small representative half-spoonful of jam to one of your frozen spoons. Replace the spoon in the freezer for 3 to 4 minutes, then remove and carefully feel the underside of the spoon. It should be neither warm nor cold; if still warm, return it to the freezer for a moment. Tilt the spoon vertically to see how quickly the jam runs; if it runs slowly, and if it has thickened to a gloppy consistency, it is done. If it runs very quickly or appears watery, cook it for another few minutes, stirring, and test again as needed. This jam, while spreadable, has a relatively loose texture.

Turn off the heat but do not stir. Using a stainless-steel spoon, skim any foam from the surface of the jam. Pour the jam into sterilized jars and process according to the manufacturer's instructions or as directed on page 42.

Approximate Yield: **six to seven 8-ounce jars** *Shelf Life:* **6 months**

STRAWBERRY JAMS

Strawberry jam is perhaps the most "basic" jam, yet it is also the easiest to ruin. Nothing is more satisfying than a candy-like batch of this childhood favorite, yet truly great strawberry jam is nearly impossible to find; it is almost always either too gummy, cloyingly sweet, not sweet enough, or overcooked. Through the years, I have seen numerous different recipes for this jam, most of which complicate the process unnecessarily. Making great strawberry jam is not difficult, as long as you keep a few simple things in mind.

For strawberry jam, use the absolute freshest, most flavorful unsprayed berries you can find; if possible, start making your jam immediately upon returning home with your berries. Strawberries require ample sugar in order to shine; however, because they also lack acidity, a large quantity of fresh lemon juice is needed to balance the jam's sweetness. Strawberry jam may have a somewhat looser texture than many jams, though it will still be spreadable; this is necessary to stay true to the fruit and prevent overcooking. Leave the berries whole, being sure to discard any blemished ones. To make a beautiful clear jam, be sure to skim the foam from the jam extremely thoroughly. Last, always cook strawberry jam in tiny batches to avoid overcooking; the secret to great strawberry jam lies in its freshness of flavor.

In addition to the simplest classic strawberry jam, there are endless possible flavor combinations. I have included several of my favorites here. Strawberries combine exceptionally well with other fruits, and they have a very long growing season, so you will find many recipes for them throughout this book.

STRAWBERRY-ROSE GERANIUM JAM

This lovely jam is the embodiment of late spring; rather than the leaves, this recipe uses the beautiful pale pink blossoms of the rose geranium plant, which starts to flower in late April and early May. What I especially love about this jam is the lightness of its floral flavor. The leaves make a delicious flavoring themselves, but the blossoms are a different animal altogether; they are much smoother, lighter, and less peppery than the leaves. My favorite berries for this recipe are Chandlers; their brightness lends itself perfectly to this springy jam.

4 pounds hulled large strawberries

2½ pounds white cane sugar

7 ounces strained freshly squeezed lemon juice

10 heads rose geranium blossoms

DAY 1

Place the strawberries in a glass or hard plastic storage container and add the sugar and lemon juice. Shake the container slightly to evenly distribute the sugar, cover tightly, and let macerate in the refrigerator for 24 hours.

DAY 2

Place a saucer with five metal teaspoons in a flat place in your freezer for testing the jam later.

Remove the strawberry mixture from the refrigerator. Rinse the rose geranium heads under cold running water and pat them dry between two clean kitchen towels. Gently pull the blossoms into pieces and add them to the strawberries, discarding the stems.

Transfer the strawberry mixture to an 11- or 12-quart copper preserving pan or a wide nonreactive kettle, stirring to dissolve the sugar. Bring the mixture to a boil over high heat, stirring frequently with a heat-proof rubber spatula.

Boil vigorously, gently scraping the bottom of the pan often with your spatula to be sure the mixture is not sticking. If it does begin to stick, decrease the heat slightly, being sure the jam continues to cook at a rapid boil. Continue to cook, stirring and scraping the bottom frequently, until the foam subsides, the mixture acquires a darker, shinier look, and the berries appear softened and saturated with liquid, about 20 minutes total.

At this point, remove the jam from the heat and let rest for 2 to 3 minutes, skimming any white foam from the surface of the jam. Lower the heat to medium-high, return the pan to the heat, and continue to cook, stirring, for 3 to 5 minutes more to rid the jam of any lingering excess moisture.

When the jam appears shiny and thickened, remove it from the heat and test for doneness, using a metal spoon to carefully scrape all the white foam off the top of the mixture while you test. Do not stir. To test for doneness, carefully transfer a small

representative half-spoonful of jam to one of your frozen spoons. Replace the spoon in the freezer for 3 to 4 minutes, then remove and carefully feel the underside of the spoon. It should be neither warm nor cold; if still warm, return it to the freezer for a moment. Tilt the spoon vertically to see how quickly the jam runs; if it runs slowly, and if it has thickened to a gloppy consistency, it is done. If it runs very

quickly or appears watery, cook it for another couple of minutes, stirring, and test again as needed.

When the jam is ready, stir it to evenly distribute the berries, then pour the jam into sterilized jars and process according to the manufacturer's instructions or as directed on page 42.

Approximate Yield: six to seven 8-ounce jars *Shelf Life:* 6 to 8 months

STRAWBERRY-
BLOOD ORANGE MARMALADE
WITH ROSEMARY

This excellent marmalade is gorgeous to behold, with its strips of orange rind shimmering in brick red jelly. The different ingredients come together perfectly into an exquisitely rich bouquet. It is a breathtaking use for early-season strawberries and is extremely versatile; breakfast toast, lunch sandwiches, tart fillings, and after-dinner cheese are but a few of its many delectable uses.

2¼ pounds hulled strawberries

1½ pounds seeded Moro blood oranges, halved crosswise,

each half cut into quarters lengthwise and sliced crosswise medium-thin

2 (8-inch) sprigs rosemary

2 pounds 10 ounces white cane sugar

2 to 4 ounces strained freshly squeezed lemon juice

DAY 1

First, prepare the strawberry juice: Place the strawberries in a medium stainless-steel kettle and add enough cold water to just cover the tops of the fruit. Bring to a boil over high heat, then decrease the heat to a simmer. Cover and cook the fruit for 1 to 1½ hours, or until the berries are brown and shapeless and the liquid has become syrupy.

Strain the strawberry juice by pouring the hot fruit and liquid into a medium-fine-mesh strainer suspended over a heatproof storage container or nonreactive saucepan. Cover the entire setup well with plastic wrap and place in the refrigerator to drip overnight.

While the strawberries are cooking, place the orange slices in a separate nonreactive saucepan with water to reach 1 inch above the tops. Cover tightly and let rest overnight at room temperature.

DAY 2

Place a saucer with five metal teaspoons in a flat place in your freezer for testing the marmalade later. Rinse the rosemary well under cold water, pat it dry between two clean kitchen towels, and set aside.

Bring the pan with the orange slices to a boil over high heat, decrease the heat to medium, and cook, covered, at a lively simmer for 30 to 60 minutes, or until the fruit is very tender. If necessary, add a little more water during the cooking; the fruit should remain submerged throughout the cooking process.

While the orange slices are cooking, remove the plastic wrap from the strawberries and their juice and discard the berries. Strain the juice well through a very fine-mesh strainer to remove any lingering solids.

When the orange slices are ready, place them in a large mixing bowl with the sugar, cooked strawberry juice, and 2 ounces lemon juice, stirring well. Taste, and slowly add a little more lemon juice if necessary. You should be able to taste the lemon juice, but it should not be overpowering. Keep adding lemon juice only until you are just able to detect its tartness in the mixture. Transfer the mixture to an 11- or 12-quart copper preserving pan or a wide nonreactive kettle.

Bring the mixture to a boil over high heat. Cook at a rapid boil until the setting point is reached; this will take a minimum of 35 minutes, but may take longer depending on your individual stove and pan. Initially, the mixture will bubble gently for several minutes; then, as more moisture cooks out of it and its sugar concentration increases, it will begin foaming. Do not stir it at all during the initial bubbling; then, once it starts to foam, stir it gently every few minutes with a heatproof rubber spatula. As it gets close to being done, stir it slowly every minute or two to prevent burning, decreasing the heat a tiny bit if necessary. The marmalade is ready for testing when its color darkens and its bubbles become very small.

To test the marmalade for doneness, remove it from the heat and carefully transfer a small representative half-spoonful to one of your frozen spoons. It should look shiny, with tiny bubbles throughout. Replace the spoon in the freezer for 3 to 4 minutes, then remove and carefully feel the underside of the spoon. It should be neither warm nor cold; if still warm, return it to the freezer for a moment. Tilt the spoon vertically to see whether the marmalade runs; if it does not run, and if its top layer has thickened to a jelly consistency, it is done. If it runs, cook it for another few minutes, stirring, and test again as needed.

When the marmalade has finished cooking, turn off the heat but do not stir. Using a stainless-steel spoon, skim off any surface foam and discard. Place the rosemary into the mixture and let steep for a few minutes off the heat. Stir and carefully taste the marmalade. Remove the sprigs or leave them in for another minute or two, keeping in mind that their flavor will be slightly milder once the marmalade has cooled. Using tongs, discard the rosemary. Pour the marmalade into sterilized jars and process according to the manufacturer's instructions or as directed on page 42.

Approximate Yield: six to seven 8-ounce jars *Shelf Life:* 1 year

CHERRY JAMS

Of all spring and summer jams, cherry jam has perhaps the most complex flavor. An acquaintance recently told me of her young daughter's first experience with cherries; as she put one in her mouth and bit down, her eyes opened wide with wonder. The rush of flavors in that one small bite was unlike anything she had tasted before. There is truly nothing to match the extraordinary beauty and intensity of this gorgeous fruit.

Cherries have long been used throughout Europe to flavor a wide variety of liqueurs and spirits, each with its own distinct personality. Some of these, such as kirsch, include whole cherry pits; to make others, such as maraschino, the pits are cracked prior to the beginning of the process to expose the tiny kernels inside. The flavor of these kernels is quite distinct from those of other stone fruits. While apricot or peach kernels taste mostly of almond, cherry kernels have a deeper flavor, which is utterly and mysteriously cherry. As you will see throughout this chapter, there are numerous different possibilities for cherry jam. Cherries do not break down to the same degree as other stone fruits when heated; thus, in order not to become overly chunky, they often demand a somewhat marmalade-like approach.

FIRST-OF-THE-SEASON
RED CHERRY JAM

Each year, the arrival of summer's first cherries inspires and delights me. I especially look forward to the Burlats and Brooks, which to me are everything early-season cherries should be: bright red, firm in texture, and bursting with tart, almondy flavor. This jam, flavored with cherry kernels and maraschino, perfectly captures them at their peak.

3 pounds plus 1 pound pitted flavorful tart red cherries (such as Burlat or Brooks), pits reserved

1¾ pounds plus 7 ounces white cane sugar

5¾ ounces strained freshly squeezed lemon juice

3 to 4 tablespoons maraschino liqueur

Place the cherry pits on the floor between two old, clean cloths and, using a hammer, tap them through the top cloth until they crack. Carefully remove the tiny almond-like kernel from each pit until you have enough kernels to make 1½ tablespoons coarsely chopped. Discard the shells and remaining pits. Place the chopped kernels into a fine-mesh stainless-steel tea infuser with a firm latch and set aside.

Place a saucer with five metal teaspoons in a flat place in your freezer for testing the jam later.

Combine 3 pounds of the cherries with 1¾ pounds of the sugar in a large heatproof mixing bowl. In a glass measuring cup, combine the lemon juice with the maraschino and set aside.

Place the remaining 1 pound of cherries and 7 ounces of sugar, along with 2 ounces of water, in an 11- or 12-quart copper preserving pan or a wide nonreactive kettle. Cook over low heat, stirring constantly with a heatproof rubber spatula and inching the heat gradually up to medium, until the mixture boils, then cook 7 minutes more, or until the cherries have shriv-

eled and the liquid has become thick and syrupy. Immediately pour the hot cherries into a metal strainer over the bowl with the raw cherries and sugar, pressing down on the cooked fruit and draining until every last drop of liquid goes through. Discard the cooked cherries. Add half the lemon juice mixture to the uncooked cherry mixture, stir well to combine, and transfer the mixture back to your copper preserving pan. Place the mesh tea infuser into the mixture, pressing down on it to be sure it is submerged.

Bring the mixture to a boil over medium heat, gradually increasing the heat to high. Boil rapidly, stirring every minute or two with a heatproof rubber spatula, for 10 to 15 minutes. Monitor the heat closely as you stir; if the jam begins to stick, decrease the heat slightly. Between stirrings, use a stainless-steel spoon to skim the foam carefully off the top of the mixture. After 10 to 15 minutes, remove from the heat. Do not stir. Let the mixture rest for a moment, then carefully scrape all the white foam off the top of the mixture and discard. When you have removed every last bit of white, stir in the remaining half of the lemon juice mixture. Return the jam to the stove over medium-high heat and continue to cook, stirring frequently. If necessary, gradually lower the heat to prevent scorching.

After 5 more minutes, your jam should be close to ready. To test for doneness, remove the jam from the heat. Do not stir. Carefully transfer a small representative half-spoonful of jam to one of your frozen spoons. Replace the spoon in the freezer for 3 to 4 minutes, then remove and carefully feel the underside of the spoon. It should be neither warm nor cold; if still warm, return it to the freezer for a moment. Tilt the spoon vertically to see whether the jam runs; if it is reluctant to run, and if it has thickened to a near-jelly consistency, it is done. If it runs very quickly, cook it for another few minutes, stirring, and test again as needed.

While your jam sample is cooling, remove the mesh tea infuser and use a stainless-steel spoon to skim any foam from the surface of the jam. When the jam is ready, pour it into sterilized jars and process according to the manufacturer's instructions or as directed on page 42.

Approximate Yield: **five 8-ounce jars** *Shelf Life:* **1 year**

RHUBARB
& RED CHERRY JAM

An exciting and delicious marriage of flavors that, though less well known than strawberry-rhubarb, should not be overlooked. This soft jam makes a luscious and elegant accompaniment to yogurt, both for breakfast and as a lovely light springtime dessert.

2½ pounds trimmed rhubarb stalks, cut into 3-inch lengths
2½ pounds white cane sugar
5 ounces strained freshly squeezed lemon juice
1¾ pounds unpitted Burlat or Bing cherries or other flavorful sweet red cherries
A few drops of kirsch (optional)

Place a saucer with five metal teaspoons in a flat place in your freezer for testing the jam later.

Place the rhubarb, sugar, and lemon juice in an 11- or 12-quart copper preserving pan or a wide nonreactive kettle and stir to combine. Place the pan over medium-low heat and cook, stirring, until juice begins to run from the rhubarb. Increase the heat to high and continue to cook, stirring frequently, until the mixture reaches a boil. Lower the heat slightly and boil for a few minutes, until the rhubarb begins to soften but still holds its shape; by this time, there should be ample liquid in the pan.

Remove the pan from the heat and, using a slotted spoon, transfer the rhubarb pieces to a heatproof bowl, leaving as much liquid as possible in the pan. Position a fine-mesh stainless-steel strainer over the rhubarb and set aside.

Place the cherries into the rhubarb liquid in the pan and set over high heat. Cook, stirring frequently, until the mixture reaches a boil; then decrease the heat slightly and continue to cook, stirring from time to time. Cook until the cherries have shriveled and the foam turns a dark rose color, 5 to 8 minutes. Remove the pan from the heat.

Using a slotted spoon, transfer the cherries from their liquid to the strainer above the reserved rhubarb pieces. Press down on the cherries to get every last drop of juice from them, then discard the cherries.

Add the cooked rhubarb pieces and cherry liquid back into the remaining liquid in the pan. Place the pan over high heat and cook, stirring frequently and lowering the heat gradually to medium, until the jam has thickened and the rhubarb has lost most of its shape, 10 to 15 minutes. As you cook, skim as much of the white foam as possible from the surface of the jam.

To test the jam for doneness, carefully transfer a small representative half-spoonful of jam to one of your frozen spoons. Replace the spoon in the freezer for 3 to 4 minutes, then remove and carefully feel the underside of the spoon. It should be neither warm nor cold; if still warm, return it to the freezer for a moment. Nudge the jam gently with your finger; if it is cohesive when you nudge it, it is either done or nearly done. Tilt the spoon vertically to see how quickly the jam runs; if it is reluctant to run, and if it has thickened to a gloppy consistency, it is done. If it runs very quickly, cook it for another few minutes, stirring, and test again as needed.

Turn off the heat but do not stir. Using a stainless-steel spoon, skim all the remaining foam from the surface of the jam. Stir in a few drops of kirsch, if using. Pour the jam into sterilized jars and process according to the manufacturer's instructions or as directed on page 42.

Approximate Yield: four to five 8-ounce jars *Shelf Life:* 1 year

BRANDIED RED CHERRY CONSERVE

Even at the very beginning of summer, I keep the cooler months in the back of my mind, always trying to stash away a few wintry jams when the occasion presents itself. Cherries are particularly suited to spice, and this is one preserve I love to make in mid-May, when the first flush of summer cherries arrives. Its flavor is very concentrated, almost like mincemeat's, and it makes a staggeringly good holiday pie filling. This recipe may be varied any number of ways: Use a different combination of dried and candied fruits, or replace the plum brandy with plain brandy or cognac. But the combination of citron, cloves, and plum brandy is my favorite: Christmas in a jar.

3 pounds pitted sweet red cherries

1¼ pounds white cane sugar

3 ounces strained freshly squeezed lemon juice

2 ounces dried currants

½ pound chopped candied citron (see page 314)

2½ ounces slivovitz or other dry plum brandy

3 to 4 drops almond extract

3 cloves

Place a saucer with five metal teaspoons in a flat place in your freezer for testing the conserve later.

Combine 1½ pounds of the cherries with 10 ounces of the sugar and 1½ ounces of the lemon juice in an 11- or 12-quart copper preserving pan or a wide nonreactive kettle. Bring the mixture to a boil over high heat, stirring frequently, and cook until the cherries have softened, about 5 minutes. Turn off the heat and let the cherries rest for 5 minutes. Put them through the fine holes of a food mill, scraping any fruit that will not go through back into the resulting puree.

In a large mixing bowl, combine the cherry puree with the remaining cherries, sugar, and lemon juice,

and the currants, citron, brandy, and almond extract, stirring well to combine. Let the mixture macerate at room temperature for 45 minutes, stirring occasionally.

After 45 minutes, transfer the mixture back to your preserving pan. Put the cloves into a fine-mesh stainless-steel tea infuser with a firm latch and add it to the mixture, pressing down on it to be sure it is submerged. Bring the mixture to a boil over high heat, stirring often.

Boil vigorously, gently scraping the bottom of the pan with your spatula every minute or two to be sure the mixture is not sticking. Continue to cook, monitoring the heat closely, until the conserve acquires a darker, shinier look, about 20 minutes. At this point, remove

the pan from the heat, discarding any cherry pits that may have found their way into the mixture, and test the conserve for doneness. While you are testing, use a metal spoon to carefully scrape all the stiff white foam from the top of the mixture and discard.

To test the conserve for doneness, carefully transfer a small representative half-spoonful of conserve to one of your frozen spoons. Replace the spoon in the freezer for 3 to 4 minutes, then remove and carefully feel the underside of the spoon. It should be neither warm nor cold; if still warm, return it to the freezer for a moment. Tilt the spoon vertically to see how quickly the conserve runs; if it runs slowly, and if it has thickened to a gloppy consistency, it is done. If it appears watery, cook it for another couple of minutes, stirring, and test again as needed. When the conserve is ready, remove the mesh tea infuser. Stir the conserve briefly to evenly distribute the cherries, then pour it into sterilized jars and process according to the manufacturer's instructions or as directed on page 42.

Approximate Yield: six 8-ounce jars *Shelf Life:* 8 to 10 months

KUMQUAT JAMS
AND MARMALADES

The unmistakable flavor of kumquats is an essential component of many of early spring's best jams and marmalades, among them the three that follow. Although kumquats are delicious paired with citrus, they are perhaps best showcased in jams, where their distinctive flavor can play off of another type of fruit—in this case, cherries, strawberries, or rhubarb. When used in this way, kumquats need not be precooked; their thin skins allow them to cook through quite quickly, and the faint crunch that remains after cooking provides a welcome contrast to the softness of the other fruits. In addition, the relatively low moisture content of kumquats shortens the cooking time slightly, helping to preserve the brightness and structural integrity of the companion fruit. These three very different jams each benefit from the sparkling flavor and high pectin content of kumquats. They are among the brightest and most unusual of spring preserves.

RED CHERRY JAM
WITH KUMQUATS & BAY

Bay leaf is tragically underemployed in today's kitchens, but its unique flavor lends itself well to a surprisingly wide range of culinary uses. In Europe, bay leaf and orange flower water were commonly used for centuries to add what was considered an almondy flavor to creams and other desserts.

3 pounds unpitted sweet red cherries

1 pound seeded kumquats, sliced crosswise into very thin rounds

2 pounds white cane sugar

3½ ounces strained freshly squeezed lemon juice

2 large bay leaves

Place a saucer with five metal teaspoons in a flat place in your freezer for testing the jam later.

In a large mixing bowl, combine the cherries, kumquat rounds, sugar, and lemon juice, stirring well to combine. Let the mixture macerate at room temperature for 45 minutes, stirring occasionally.

After 45 minutes, transfer the mixture to an 11- or 12-quart copper preserving pan or a wide nonreactive kettle. Add the bay leaves. Place the pan over medium-low heat and cook, stirring constantly with a heatproof rubber spatula. After a few minutes, when the mixture begins foaming a little around the edges, gradually raise the heat to high, stirring often.

Boil vigorously, gently scraping the bottom of the pan with your spatula every minute or two to be sure the mixture is not sticking. If it begins to stick, decrease the heat slightly, being sure the jam remains at a rapid boil. Continue to cook, stirring and scraping frequently, until the mixture acquires a darker, shinier look, about 15 minutes total. At this point, remove

the pan from the heat and let the jam rest for 1 to 2 minutes, discarding any cherry pits that may have found their way into the mixture. Return the jam to the heat and cook for 1 to 2 minutes more, then test it for doneness. While you are testing, use a metal spoon to carefully scrape all the white foam from the top of the mixture and discard.

To test the jam for doneness, carefully transfer a small representative half-spoonful of jam to one of your frozen spoons. Replace the spoon in the freezer for 3 to 4 minutes, then remove and carefully feel the underside of the spoon. It should be neither warm nor cold; if still warm, return it to the freezer for a moment. Tilt the spoon vertically to see how quickly the jam runs; if it runs slowly or not at all, and if it has thickened to a gloppy consistency, it is done. If it runs very quickly or appears watery, cook it for another couple of minutes, stirring, and test again as needed. When the jam is ready, stir it briefly to evenly distribute the cherries, then pour it into sterilized jars and process according to the manufacturer's instructions or as directed on page 42.

Approximate Yield: seven 8-ounce jars *Shelf Life:* 8 to 10 months

STRAWBERRY-KUMQUAT JAM

This jam is a spring celebration in your mouth. The bright flavor and slight crunch of barely cooked kumquats, the loveliness of whole strawberries, and the fresh acidity of lemon come together into a vivid ensemble that is a delight both to make and to eat.

2½ pounds hulled large strawberries

1½ pounds seeded tart kumquats, sliced crosswise into very thin rounds

2 pounds 10 ounces white cane sugar

5½ ounces strained freshly squeezed lemon juice

Place a saucer with five metal teaspoons in a flat place in your freezer for testing the jam later.

Combine all the ingredients in an 11- or 12-quart copper preserving pan or a wide nonreactive kettle. Place the pan over medium-low heat and cook, stirring constantly with a heatproof rubber spatula. After a few minutes, as the juice starts to run and the mixture begins foaming a little around the edges, gradually raise the heat to high, stirring often.

Boil vigorously, gently scraping the bottom of the pan every minute or two with your spatula to be sure the mixture is not sticking. If it begins to stick, decrease the heat slightly, being sure the jam continues to cook at a rapid boil. Continue to cook, stirring and scraping frequently, until the foam subsides, the mixture acquires a darker, shinier look, and the berries appear softened and saturated with liquid, about 20 minutes total.

At this point, remove the jam from the heat and test it for doneness, using a metal spoon to carefully scrape all the white foam from the top of the mixture while you test. Do not stir. To test for doneness, carefully transfer a small representative half-spoonful of jam to one of your frozen spoons. Replace the spoon in the freezer for 3 to 4 minutes, then remove and carefully feel the underside of the spoon. It should be neither warm nor cold; if still warm, return it to the freezer for a moment. Tilt the spoon vertically to see how quickly the jam runs; if it runs slowly, and if it has thickened to a gloppy consistency, it is done. If it runs very quickly or appears watery, cook it for another couple of minutes, stirring, and test again as needed. When the jam is ready, stir it briefly to evenly distribute the berries, then pour into sterilized jars and process according to the manufacturer's instructions or as directed on page 42.

Approximate Yield: seven to eight 8-ounce jars *Shelf Life:* 8 to 10 months

RHUBARB-KUMQUAT JAM

This is a very lovely and subtly floral jam, lightly perfumed with orange flower water. The jam cooks quite quickly because of the kumquats' low moisture content. This, plus the macerating of the rhubarb, allows the rhubarb to keep much of its shape, lending the jam a beautiful texture, a pale rosy color, and a very fresh flavor.

3½ pounds trimmed rose-colored rhubarb stalks, cut into 2-inch lengths

2 pounds 14 ounces white cane sugar

5 ounces strained freshly squeezed lemon juice

¾ pound seeded tart kumquats, sliced crosswise into very thin rounds

2 to 3 drops of orange flower water

DAY 1

Place the rhubarb in a large glass or hard plastic storage container and pour the sugar over it, shaking to combine. Drizzle the lemon juice over the mixture, then cover tightly and let macerate for 24 hours at room temperature. For this, a slightly warm location, such as the top of a gas stove not in use, is best; the warmth will help the rhubarb release its juices.

DAY 2

Place a saucer with five metal teaspoons in a flat place in your freezer for testing the jam later.

Transfer the rhubarb mixture to an 11- or 12-quart copper preserving pan or a wide nonreactive kettle. Add the kumquats, stirring well to dissolve the sugar. Bring the mixture to a boil over high heat, stirring occasionally with a large heatproof rubber spatula. Boil, stirring frequently and gradually decreasing the heat if the jam starts to stick, until thickened and no longer watery, 15 to 20 minutes. For the last 5 to 10 minutes of cooking, stir the jam nearly constantly to keep it from sticking.

When the jam has thickened, test it for doneness. To test, carefully transfer a small representative half-spoonful of jam to one of your frozen spoons. Replace the spoon in the freezer for 3 to 4 minutes, then remove and carefully feel the underside of the spoon. It should be neither warm nor cold; if still warm, return it to the freezer for a moment. Tilt the spoon vertically to see how quickly the jam runs; if it runs slowly, and if it has thickened to a gloppy consistency, it is done. If it runs very quickly or appears watery, cook it for another few minutes, stirring, and test again as needed.

Turn off the heat but do not stir. Using a stainless-steel spoon, skim any foam from the surface of the jam. Add the orange flower water, stirring well. Pour the jam into sterilized jars and process according to the manufacturer's instructions or as directed on page 42.

Approximate Yield: **nine 8-ounce jars** *Shelf Life:* **1 year**

APRIUM JAMS

Apriums, a cross between plums and apricots, are among the first stone fruits of summer, and for me their greatly anticipated appearance at market is one of the brightest moments of the year. Though somewhat similar to apricots, there is a richness and subtly different flavor to Apriums which sets them apart. I have included four recipes for them here, each with its own distinct personality. My preferred variety for these jams is the Honey Rich, which to me perfectly embodies the essence of early summer.

APRIUM JAM

In this exotic and subtly perfumed jam, orange flower, honey, and almond form a delicate backdrop for the robust flavor of the Apriums. The fruit is partially pureed, making a smooth jam punctuated by larger pieces of fruit.

2¼ pounds pitted and quartered Apriums

1¼ pounds plus 12 ounces white cane sugar

2 to 4 ounces strained freshly squeezed lemon juice

2¼ pounds pitted and halved Apriums

½ to 1 teaspoon pure almond extract

½ to ¾ ounce orange flower water

1 to 1½ ounces orange blossom honey

DAY 1

Combine the quartered Apriums with 1¼ pounds of the sugar and 1 ounce of the lemon juice in a large heatproof glass or hard plastic storage container. Combine the halved Apriums with the remaining 12 ounces of sugar and 1 ounce of lemon juice in a medium stainless-steel kettle. Press a sheet of plastic wrap directly onto the surface of each Aprium mixture, smoothing well to minimize air bubbles (this will help keep the fruit from browning as it sits). Cover both mixtures tightly with lids and let macerate in the refrigerator for 24 hours.

DAY 2

Place a saucer with five metal spoons in a flat place in your freezer for testing the jam later.

Remove both containers of Apriums from the refrigerator. Heat the Aprium halves over medium-high heat, stirring often, until they soften, 5 to 10 minutes. Remove them from the heat, put them through the fine holes of a food mill, and add them to the Aprium quarters. Scrape any solids that will not go through the food mill back into the rest of the fruit, breaking up the chunks as you go.

Taste the jam mixture and slowly add 1 to 2 ounces more lemon juice if necessary. You should be able to taste the lemon juice, but it should not be overpowering. Keep adding lemon juice until you are just able to detect its tartness in the mixture. Add ½ teaspoon almond extract, ½ ounce orange flower water, and 1 ounce orange blossom honey, stirring well to combine. Taste one final time and cautiously adjust the flavorings if necessary; the flavors should be subtle. Transfer the mixture to an 11- or 12-quart copper preserving pan or a wide nonreactive kettle.

Bring the jam mixture to a boil over high heat, stirring frequently with a large heatproof rubber spatula. Boil, stirring frequently, for 4 minutes. Remove from the heat and, using a large stainless-steel spoon, skim the stiff foam from the top of the mixture and discard. Return the jam to a boil, then decrease the heat slightly. Continue to cook, monitoring the heat closely, until the jam thickens, 30 to 45 minutes. Scrape the bottom of the pan often with your spatula, and reduce the heat gradually as more and more moisture cooks out of the jam. For the last 10 to 15 minutes of cooking, stir the jam slowly and steadily to keep it from scorching.

When the jam seems ready, test it for doneness. To test, carefully transfer a small representative half-spoonful of jam to one of your frozen spoons. Replace the spoon in the freezer for 3 to 4 minutes, then remove and carefully feel the underside of the spoon. It should be neither warm nor cold; if still warm, return it to the freezer for a moment. Tilt the spoon vertically to see how quickly the jam runs; if it is reluctant to run, and it seems thick and gloppy, it is done. If it runs very quickly, cook it for another few minutes, stirring, and test again as needed.

Turn off the heat but do not stir. Using a stainless-steel spoon, skim all the remaining foam from the surface of the jam. Pour the jam into sterilized jars and process according to the manufacturer's instructions or as directed on page 42.

Approximate Yield: five to six 8-ounce jars   *Shelf Life:* 8 months

APRIUM JAM
WITH GREEN ALMONDS

This extremely vivid jam is ever so slightly more tart than the preceding recipe, and the green almonds make it the embodiment of springtime. For an excellent plain Aprium jam, you may omit the almonds.

2¼ pounds pitted Apriums, cut into eighths

1¼ pounds plus 12 ounces white cane sugar

2¼ pounds pitted and halved Apriums, pits reserved

½ pound unshelled green almonds

1 to 4 ounces strained freshly squeezed lemon juice

DAY 1

Combine the Aprium eighths with 1¼ pounds of the sugar in a large heatproof glass or hard plastic storage container. Combine the Aprium halves with the remaining 12 ounces of sugar in a medium stainless-steel kettle. Press a sheet of plastic wrap directly onto the surface of each Aprium mixture, smoothing well to minimize air bubbles (this will help keep the fruit from browning as it sits). Cover both mixtures tightly with lids and let macerate in the refrigerator for 24 hours.

DAY 2

Place a saucer with five metal spoons in a flat place in your freezer for testing the jam later.

Shell the green almonds: Using a paring knife, carefully cut a slit down one side of each almond shell, open the almond, and remove its inner nut. Discard the shells. Using your fingers or a small paring knife, carefully remove the thin outer skin of each almond. (If your almonds are very soft and jelly-like, you may omit this step.) Set the almonds aside.

Place 10 Aprium pits, or more to taste, on the floor between two old, clean cloths and, using a ham-

mer, tap them through the top cloth until they crack. Carefully remove the almond-like kernel from each pit, discarding the shells. Chop the kernels coarsely, place them in a fine-mesh stainless-steel tea infuser with a firm latch, and set aside.

Remove both sets of Apriums from the refrigerator. Heat the Aprium halves over medium-high heat, stirring often, until they soften, 5 to 10 minutes. Remove them from the heat, put them through the fine holes of a food mill, and add them to the Aprium eighths. Scrape any solids that will not go through the food mill back into the rest of the fruit, breaking up the chunks as you go.

Add 1 ounce of the lemon juice. Taste and slowly add more lemon juice if necessary. You should be able to taste the lemon juice, but it should not be overpowering. Keep adding lemon juice until you are just able to detect its tartness in the mixture. Transfer the mixture to an 11- or 12-quart copper preserving pan or a wide nonreactive kettle. Place the tea infuser into the mixture, pressing down on it to be sure it is submerged.

Bring the jam mixture to a boil over high heat, stirring frequently with a large heatproof rubber spatula. Boil, stirring frequently, for 4 minutes. Remove from the heat and, using a large stainless-steel spoon, skim the stiff foam from the top of the mixture and discard. Return the jam to a boil, then decrease the heat slightly. Continue to cook, monitoring the heat closely, until the jam thickens, 30 to 45 minutes. Scrape the bottom of the pan often with your spatula, and decrease the heat gradually as more and more moisture cooks out of the jam. For the last 10 to 15 minutes of cooking, stir the jam slowly and steadily to keep it from scorching. When the jam is nearly ready, stir in the green almonds.

When the jam seems ready, test it for doneness. To test, remove it from the heat and carefully transfer a small representative half-spoonful of jam to one of your frozen spoons. Replace the spoon in the freezer for 3 to 4 minutes, then remove and carefully feel the underside of the spoon. It should be neither warm nor cold; if still warm, return it to the freezer for a moment. Tilt the spoon vertically to see how quickly the jam runs; if it is reluctant to run, and it seems thick and gloppy, it is done. If it runs very quickly, cook it for another few minutes, stirring, and test again as needed.

When the jam has finished cooking, turn off the heat but do not stir. Remove the tea infuser. Using a stainless-steel spoon, skim all the remaining foam from the surface of the jam. Pour the jam into sterilized jars and process according to the manufacturer's instructions or as directed on page 42.

Approximate Yield: six to seven 8-ounce jars   *Shelf Life:* 8 months

APRIUM-ORANGE JAM

This jam's flavor and aroma are reminiscent of a glass of the most perfect fresh orange juice. Yet it is so much fuller, so much deeper, and so much rounder than a pure orange could ever be. The bright richness of Apriums makes this jam shine. Like all Aprium jams, it is a superb orange color. The orange slices in it make it extra-fun to eat.

1 pound seeded Valencia oranges, halved crosswise,
each half cut into quarters lengthwise and sliced crosswise medium-thin
2¾ pounds pitted and quartered Apriums
3 pounds 5 ounces white cane sugar
7 ounces strained freshly squeezed lemon juice

DAY 1

First, prepare the orange slices: Place the slices in a wide stainless-steel kettle and cover amply with cold water. Bring to a boil over high heat, boil for 1 minute, and drain, discarding the liquid. Return the slices to the kettle and cover with 1 inch cold water. Bring to a boil over high heat, then decrease the heat to medium, and cook, covered, at a lively simmer for 45 minutes, or until the fruit is very tender.

When the oranges are finished cooking, combine them with the Aprium quarters, sugar, and lemon juice in a hard plastic or glass storage container. Stir well, cover tightly, and let macerate in the refrigerator overnight.

DAY 2

Place a saucer with five metal teaspoons in a flat place in your freezer for testing the jam later.

Remove the Aprium mixture from the refrigerator and transfer it to an 11- or 12-quart copper preserving pan or a wide nonreactive kettle, stirring well to incorporate any undissolved sugar.

Bring the jam mixture to a boil over high heat, stirring frequently with a large heatproof rubber spatula. Boil, stirring frequently, for 4 minutes. Remove from the heat and, using a large stainless-steel spoon, skim the stiff foam from the top of the mixture and discard. Return the jam to a boil, then decrease the heat slightly. Continue to cook, monitoring the heat closely, until the jam thickens, 25 to 35 minutes. Scrape the bottom of the pan often with your spatula, and decrease the heat gradually as more and more moisture cooks out of the jam. For the last 10 to 15 minutes of cooking, stir the jam slowly and steadily to keep it from scorching.

When the jam seems ready, test it for doneness. To test, carefully transfer a small representative half-spoonful of jam to one of your frozen spoons. Replace the spoon in the freezer for 3 to 4 minutes, then remove and carefully feel the underside of the spoon. It should be neither warm nor cold; if still warm, return it to the freezer for a moment. Tilt the spoon vertically to see how quickly the jam runs; if it is reluctant to run, and has formed a skin across the top, it is ready. If it runs, cook it for another few minutes, stirring, and test again as needed.

Turn off the heat but do not stir. Using a stainless-steel spoon, skim all the remaining foam from the surface of the jam. Pour the jam into sterilized jars and process according to the manufacturer's instructions or as directed on page 42.

Approximate Yield: eight 8-ounce jars *Shelf Life:* 1 year

APRIUM & CANDIED GINGER JAM

Apriums and ginger are natural partners, and this barely sweet jam puts the sharpness of the ginger front and center. This is both delicious and exciting to make: Its electrifying orange color, velvet texture, and spicy ginger flavor will wow you. A scant amount of vanilla provides a touch of softness, drawing everything together into a scrumptious whole.

5 pounds pitted and quartered Apriums

2 pounds white cane sugar

7 ounces strained freshly squeezed lemon juice

6 ounces finely chopped candied ginger

2 ounces ginger liqueur

A few drops of pure vanilla extract

DAY 1

Combine the Apriums with the sugar and lemon juice in a large heatproof glass or hard plastic storage container. Press a sheet of plastic wrap directly onto the surface of the mixture, smoothing well to minimize air bubbles (this will help keep the fruit from browning as it sits). Cover the mixture tightly with a lid and let macerate in the refrigerator overnight.

DAY 2

Place a saucer with five metal spoons in a flat place in your freezer for testing the jam later.

Remove the Apriums from the refrigerator. Transfer the mixture to an 11- or 12-quart copper preserving pan or a wide nonreactive kettle. Add the ginger, ginger liqueur, and vanilla, stirring well to combine.

Bring the jam mixture to a boil over high heat, stirring frequently with a large heatproof rubber spatula. Boil, stirring frequently, for 4 minutes. Remove from the heat and, using a large stainless-steel spoon, skim the stiff foam from the top of the mixture and discard. Return the jam to a boil, then decrease the heat slightly. Continue to cook, monitoring the

heat closely, until the jam thickens, 30 to 45 minutes. Scrape the bottom of the pan often with your spatula, and decrease the heat gradually as more and more moisture cooks out of the jam. For the last 10 to 15 minutes of cooking, stir the jam slowly and steadily to keep it from scorching.

When the jam seems ready, test it for doneness. To test, carefully transfer a small representative half-spoonful of jam to one of your frozen spoons. Replace the spoon in the freezer for 3 to 4 minutes, then remove and carefully feel the underside of the spoon. It should be neither warm nor cold; if still warm, return it to the freezer for a moment. Tilt the spoon vertically to see how quickly the jam runs; if it is reluctant to run, and it seems thick and gloppy, it is done. If it runs very quickly, cook it for another few minutes, stirring, and test again as needed.

Turn off the heat but do not stir. Using a stainless-steel spoon, skim all the remaining foam from the surface of the jam. Pour the jam into sterilized jars and process according to the manufacturer's instructions or as directed on page 42.

Approximate Yield: **nine 8-ounce jars** *Shelf Life:* **6 to 8 months**

PEACH JAMS
AND MARMALADES

Peaches are one of the best summer fruits, and they make fantastic jam and marmalade. There are three peach recipes here for the beginning of summer and one in Chapter 6 for the end of summer. Each reflects a particular moment of the season, because from the start to the end of summer, peaches undergo a drastic change. The earliest varieties are small and tart; the later ones are large, dense, and rich. This lends an excitement to working with peaches: Because the season for each variety is so short, each one must be quickly treasured.

EARLY SUMMER PEACH MARMALADE

The earliest summer peaches, though sometimes overlooked, are excellent fruits for preserving; they are much smaller and subtler than later varieties, and cooking brings out their delicate almondy fragrance and deep peach essence. This gorgeous marmalade is unusual and strikingly beautiful: Peach pieces and thinly sliced lemon are suspended in a rosy jelly. For this marmalade, try to use a red-tinged variety, such as Super Rich; this will make your preserve even more exquisite.

1 pound seeded lemons (preferably Lisbon), halved crosswise,
each half cut into quarters lengthwise and sliced medium-thin

3½ pounds peeled small yellow clingstone peaches (see Note)

3½ pounds white cane sugar

2 to 3 extra lemons, to make 6 ounces strained freshly squeezed juice

½ teaspoon pure almond extract

DAY 1

Prepare the lemon slices: Place the slices in a wide stainless-steel kettle and cover amply with cold water. Bring to a boil over high heat, boil for 1 minute, and drain, discarding the liquid. Return the slices to the kettle and cover with 1 inch cold water. Bring to a boil over high heat, then decrease the heat to medium-low, and cook, covered, at a lively simmer for 30 to 40 minutes, or until the fruit is very tender.

While the lemons are cooking, slice the peaches: Place a cutting board on a rimmed baking sheet or sheet pan. Put the peaches on the board and cut enough flesh off the pits to make 3 pounds of prepared fruit. You should end up with pieces of all different shapes and sizes. When you are finished, discard the peach pits. Transfer the peach pieces, along with any juices that may have collected in the bottom of the baking sheet, to a hard plastic or glass storage container. Add the sugar, lemon juice, almond extract, and the cooked lemon slices and their liquid. Stir well. Press a sheet of plastic wrap directly onto the surface of the mixture, smoothing well to minimize air bubbles (this will help keep the fruit from

browning as it sits). Cover the mixture tightly with a lid and let macerate in the refrigerator overnight.

DAY 2

Place a saucer with five metal teaspoons in a flat place in your freezer for testing the jam later.

Remove the peach mixture from the refrigerator and transfer it to an 11- or 12-quart copper preserving pan or a wide nonreactive kettle, stirring well to incorporate any undissolved sugar.

Bring the mixture to a boil over high heat. Cook at a rapid boil until the setting point is reached; this will take a minimum of 30 minutes, but may take longer depending on your individual stove and pan. Initially, the mixture will bubble gently for several minutes; then, as more moisture cooks out of it and its sugar concentration increases, it will begin to foam. Do not stir it at all during the initial bubbling; then, once it starts to foam, stir it gently every few minutes with a heatproof rubber spatula. As it gets close to being done, stir it slowly every minute or two to prevent burning, decreasing the heat a tiny bit if necessary. The marmalade is ready for testing when its color darkens slightly and its bubbles become very small.

To test the marmalade for doneness, remove it from the heat and carefully transfer a small representative half-spoonful to one of your frozen spoons. It should look shiny, with tiny bubbles throughout. Replace the spoon in the freezer for 3 to 4 minutes, then remove and carefully feel the underside of the spoon. It should be neither warm nor cold; if still warm, return it to the freezer for a moment. Tilt the spoon vertically to see whether the marmalade runs; if it does not run, and if its top layer has thickened to a jelly consistency, it is done. If it runs, cook it for another few minutes, stirring, and test again as needed.

When the marmalade has finished cooking, turn off the heat but do not stir. Using a stainless-steel spoon, skim off any surface foam and discard. Pour the marmalade into sterilized jars and process according to the manufacturer's instructions or as directed on page 42.

Note: To peel peaches, drop them into boiling water for 1 to 2 minutes, then gently remove them with a slotted spoon and place them in a single layer on a baking sheet or sheet pan. Let the peaches rest until they are cool enough to handle, then carefully slip off the skins.

Approximate Yield: **eight 8-ounce jars** *Shelf Life:* **1 year**

EARLY SUMMER PEACH JAM
WITH GREEN ALMONDS

This delicate and supremely fresh-tasting peach jam heralds the arrival of summer. The jam is best made with small yellow clingstone peaches. It is also delicious without the green almonds if you prefer.

4½ to 5 pounds peeled ripe yellow clingstone peaches (see Note)

2 pounds white cane sugar

2 to 4 ounces strained freshly squeezed lemon juice

½ pound unshelled green almonds

1 teaspoon almond extract

DAY 1

Place a cutting board on a rimmed baking sheet or sheet pan. Put the peaches on the board and, using a paring knife, cut enough flesh off the pits to make 3 pounds 14 ounces of prepared fruit. You should end up with pieces of all different shapes and sizes.

When you are finished, discard the peach pits. Transfer the peach slices, along with any juices that may have collected in the bottom of the baking sheet, to a hard plastic or glass storage container. Add the sugar and 2 ounces of the lemon juice and stir well.

Press a sheet of plastic wrap directly onto the surface of the mixture, smoothing well to minimize air bubbles (this will help keep the fruit from browning as it sits). Cover the mixture tightly with a lid and let macerate in the refrigerator overnight.

DAY 2

Place a saucer with five metal teaspoons in a flat place in your freezer for testing the jam later.

Shell the green almonds: Using a paring knife, carefully cut a slit down one side of each almond shell, open the almond, and remove its inner nut. Discard the shells. Using your fingers or a small paring knife, carefully remove the thin outer skin of each almond.

(If your almonds are very soft and jelly-like, you may omit this step.) Set the almonds aside.

Remove the peaches from the refrigerator and stir well to incorporate any undissolved sugar. Taste the peach mixture and slowly add more lemon juice if necessary. You should be able to taste the lemon juice, but it should not be overpowering. Keep adding lemon juice only until you are just able to detect its tartness in the mixture. Add the almond extract and stir well to combine. Transfer the mixture to an 11- or 12-quart copper preserving pan or two smaller nonreactive kettles.

Place the jam mixture over high heat and bring it to a boil, stirring every couple of minutes or so. Continue to cook, monitoring the heat closely, until the jam thickens, 25 to 35 minutes. Scrape the bottom of the pan often with your spatula, and decrease the heat gradually as more and more moisture cooks out of the jam. For the last 10 to 15 minutes of cooking, stir the jam slowly and steadily to keep it from scorching. If necessary, mash up to half of the fruit with a potato masher as it cooks to encourage the fruit to break down. Skim any stiff foam from the surface of the jam as it cooks and discard. When the jam is nearly ready, stir in the green almonds.

When the jam has thickened, test it for doneness. To test, carefully transfer a small representative half-spoonful of jam to one of your frozen spoons. Replace the spoon in the freezer for 3 to 4 minutes, then remove and carefully feel the underside of the spoon. It should be neither warm nor cold; if still warm, return it to the freezer for a moment. Tilt the spoon vertically to see how quickly the jam runs; if it is reluctant to run, and if it has thickened to a gloppy consistency, it is done. If it runs very quickly or appears watery, cook it for another few minutes, stirring, and test again as needed. While you are waiting for the jam in the freezer to cool, skim off any white foam that appears on the surface of the jam in the pan.

When the jam is ready, pour it into sterilized jars and process according to the manufacturer's instructions or as directed on page 42.

Note: To peel peaches, drop them into boiling water for 1 to 2 minutes, and then gently remove them with a slotted spoon and place them in a single layer on a baking sheet or sheet pan. Let the peaches rest until they are cool enough to handle, and then carefully slip off the skins.

Approximate Yield: seven 8-ounce jars *Shelf Life:* 8 months

WHITE CHERRY & PEACH JAM

This jam's perfect balance of flavors makes it stand out. With its beautiful texture, warm color, and flecks of vanilla bean, this preserve is an unusual and delicious use for Rainier cherries.

2½ pounds peeled early-season yellow peaches (see Note page 154)

2½ pounds pitted Rainier or other white cherries

2 pounds 2 ounces white cane sugar

5 ounces strained freshly squeezed lemon juice

Several drops of pure almond extract

Several drops of maraschino liqueur

1 (1-inch) piece vanilla bean, split

Place a saucer with five metal teaspoons in a flat place in your freezer for testing the jam later.

Place a cutting board on a rimmed baking sheet or sheet pan. Put the peaches on the board and, using a paring knife, cut enough flesh off the pits to make 2 pounds of prepared fruit. You should end up with pieces of all different shapes and sizes. When you are finished, discard the peach pits.

Place the peach pieces and their collected juices from the baking sheet with the cherries, sugar, and lemon juice in a large mixing bowl, stirring well to combine. Add a few drops each of almond extract and maraschino. Taste, add a drop or two more of the flavorings if necessary, and add the vanilla bean. Transfer the mixture to an 11- or 12-quart copper preserving pan or a wide nonreactive kettle.

Place the jam mixture over high heat and bring it to a boil, stirring every couple of minutes or so. Continue to cook, monitoring the heat closely, until the jam thickens, 25 to 30 minutes. Scrape the bottom of the pan often with your spatula, and decrease the heat gradually as more and more moisture cooks out of the jam. For the last 10 to 15 minutes of cooking, stir the jam slowly and steadily to keep it from scorching. Skim any stiff foam from the surface of the jam as it cooks and discard.

When the jam has thickened and appears glossy, test it for doneness. To test, carefully transfer a small representative half-spoonful of jam to one of your frozen spoons. Replace the spoon in the freezer for 3 to 4 minutes, then remove and carefully feel the underside of the spoon. It should be neither warm nor cold; if still warm, return it to the freezer for a moment. Tilt the spoon vertically to see how quickly the jam runs; if it is reluctant to run, and if it has thickened to a gloppy consistency, it is done. If it runs very quickly or appears watery, cook it for another few minutes, stirring, and test again as needed. While you are waiting for the jam in the freezer to cool, skim off any white foam that appears on the surface of the jam in the pan.

When the jam is ready, pour it into sterilized jars and process according to the manufacturer's instructions or as directed on page 42.

Approximate Yield: six 8-ounce jars   *Shelf Life:* 8 months

BLACKBERRY JAMS

The words *blackberry jam* evoke days in the bramble patch, happily pop-
ping berries into one's mouth and a few into one's basket; and blackberry-
ing conjures up misty days in the countryside. Indeed, both blackberries
and dewberries, their wild bramble relatives, thrive most in cooler climes.
In England, they were for years considered peasant food.

In this book, there are many recipes for blackberry jams, each one tai-
lored to a specific variety or time of the season. Each blackberry variety
has its own distinct characteristics, and when you taste these jams side
by side, you may be amazed at the subtle differences between them.

Like all berry jams, blackberry jams should taste extremely fresh and
vibrant. To accomplish this, always cook these jams in extremely small
batches. They should be cooked as briefly as possible, just long enough to
set; be careful not to cook them even a minute past this point, as this can
cause their flavor to lose brightness. Blackberry jam is best eaten within
six months of being made; after that, its texture may start to change.

OLALLIEBERRY
JAM

Olallieberries make a particularly tart early-summer blackberry jam with a strikingly vivid flavor. In California, the olallieberry is among the most well-loved blackberry varieties.

3 pounds 5 ounces olallieberries

1 pound 10 ounces white cane sugar

3⅓ ounces strained freshly squeezed lemon juice

Place a saucer with five metal teaspoons in a flat place in your freezer for testing the jam later.

Combine the berries, sugar, and lemon juice in an 11- or 12-quart copper preserving pan or a wide nonreactive kettle. Heat slowly, stirring with a large heatproof rubber spatula, until the sugar is dissolving and the berries begin to release a lot of juice. Turn the heat up to high and cook, stirring frequently and skimming any stiff foam from the surface of the mixture. Test the jam for doneness 15 to 20 minutes from the time it reaches a rolling boil.

To test for doneness, carefully transfer a small representative half-spoonful of jam to one of your frozen spoons. Replace the spoon in the freezer for 3 to 4 minutes, then remove and carefully feel the underside of the spoon. It should be neither warm nor cold; if still warm, return it to the freezer for a moment. Tilt the spoon vertically to see whether the jam runs; if it just refuses to run, and if it has thickened to a near-jelly consistency, it is done. If it runs, cook it for another few minutes, stirring, and test again as needed.

Using a stainless-steel spoon, skim any remaining foam from the surface of the jam. Pour the jam into sterilized jars and process according to the manufacturer's instructions or as directed on page 42.

Approximate Yield: five to six 8-ounce jars *Shelf Life:* 6 months

APRICOT PRESERVES

Nothing quite matches the buttery flavor of a really perfect fresh apricot, and apricots make some of the most delectable preserves. Each summer, I spend a sunny day picking apricots high up in the branches of my friends Heather and Brock's tree, which is very old and at least twenty feet tall. When apricots ripen, they must be picked immediately, for they very quickly start to drop to the ground and bruise. There is something particularly luscious about apricots straight off the tree; their slight fragility and velvety skins make them extra-precious. For apricot jam, be sure to use perfectly ripe fruit and only the barest amount of sugar. Apricots combine well with numerous flavors; my favorites are those that combine seamlessly with the fruit but still allow its vaguely exotic flavor to shine.

APRICOT-ROSE JAM

This is a jam for late spring, when the first flavorful apricots begin to appear at the market. Apricots and rose are meant for each other, as this fruity and barely sweet jam attests.

5¼ pounds pitted and quartered apricots, pits reserved
2¼ pounds white cane sugar
3 ounces strained freshly squeezed lemon juice
2 to 3 small splashes of rose water

DAY 1

In a glass or hard plastic storage container, combine the apricots with the sugar and lemon juice. Press a sheet of plastic wrap directly onto the surface of the mixture, smoothing well to minimize air bubbles (this will help keep the fruit from browning as it sits). Cover the mixture tightly with a lid and let macerate in the refrigerator overnight.

DAY 2

Place a saucer with five metal teaspoons in a flat place in your freezer for testing the jam later.

Place several apricot pits on the floor between two old, clean cloths and, using a hammer, tap them through the top cloth until they crack. Carefully remove the almond-like kernel from each pit, discarding the shells, until you have enough to make 1 heaping tablespoon chopped. Place the chopped kernels into a fine-mesh stainless-steel tea infuser with a firm latch and set aside.

Remove the apricots from the refrigerator and transfer them to an 11- or 12-quart copper preserving pan or a wide nonreactive kettle. Place the tea infuser into the mixture, pressing down on it to submerge it.

Bring the apricot mixture to a boil over high heat, stirring frequently with a large heatproof rubber spatula.

Boil, stirring frequently, for 4 minutes. Remove from the heat and, using a large stainless-steel spoon, skim the stiff foam from the top of the mixture and discard. Return the jam to a boil, then decrease the heat slightly. Continue to cook, monitoring the heat closely, until the jam thickens, about 30 minutes. Scrape the bottom of the pan often with your spatula, and decrease the heat gradually as more and more moisture cooks out of the jam. For the last 10 to 15 minutes of cooking, stir the jam slowly and steadily to keep it from scorching.

When the jam has thickened, test it for doneness. To test, carefully transfer a small representative half-spoonful of jam to one of your frozen spoons. Replace the spoon in the freezer for 3 to 4 minutes, then remove and carefully feel the underside of the spoon. It should be neither warm nor cold; if still warm, return it to the freezer for a moment. Tilt the spoon vertically to see how quickly the jam runs; if it runs very slowly, and if it has thickened to a gloppy consistency, it is done. If it runs very quickly or appears watery, cook it for another few minutes, stirring, and test again as necessary.

Turn off the heat but do not stir. Remove the tea ball of kernels. Using a stainless-steel soup spoon, skim all the remaining foam and discard. Pour a small splash of rose water into the jam, stir well, and carefully taste. Add more rose water judiciously, tasting carefully as you go, until the rose flavor is present but not overpowering. Pour the jam into sterilized jars and process according to the manufacturer's instructions or as directed on page 42.

instructions or as directed on page 42.

Variation:
APRICOT-ROSE JAM WITH CARDAMOM
Add 1 tablespoon lightly crushed green cardamom pods to the apricot kernels in the mesh tea infuser, and proceed with the recipe as directed.

Approximate Yield: nine 8-ounce jars *Shelf Life:* 6 to 8 months

APRICOT-ORANGE MARMALADE

In this marmalade, apricot, orange, and saffron come together in an unusual and complex flavored preserve. Its gorgeous rust orange color, flecked with dark red saffron threads, is exquisite; its exotic flavor reminds me of an imagined Spain, with a dash of the Arabian nights.

1½ pounds seeded Valencia oranges, halved crosswise,
each half cut lengthwise into quarters and sliced crosswise medium-thin
3 pounds pitted and quartered apricots
4 pounds white cane sugar
4 ounces strained freshly squeezed lemon juice
A large pinch of saffron

DAY 1

In a nonreactive saucepan, place the sliced oranges with enough water to cover the tops by 1 inch. Cover tightly and let rest overnight at room temperature.

DAY 2

Prepare the apricot juice: Place the apricots in a medium stainless-steel kettle and cover with enough cold water for the fruit to bob freely. Bring to a boil over high heat, then decrease the heat to a lively simmer. Cover and cook the fruit for 2½ hours, or until the liquid has become syrupy. As the apricots cook, stir them every 20 to 30 minutes or so, adding more water if necessary. The level of water should stay consistently high enough for the fruit to remain submerged as it cooks.

Strain the apricot juice by pouring the hot fruit and liquid into a medium-fine-mesh strainer suspended over a heatproof storage container or nonreactive saucepan. Cover the entire setup well with plastic wrap and place in the refrigerator to drip overnight.

Meanwhile, cook the orange slices: Bring the pan with them to a boil over high heat, then decrease the heat to medium and cook, covered, at a lively simmer for 30 to 60 minutes, or until the fruit is very

tender. As the oranges cook, stir them gently every 15 minutes or so, adding a little more water if necessary. The water level should stay consistently high enough for the fruit to remain submerged as it cooks. Remove the pan from the heat, cover tightly, and let rest overnight at room temperature.

DAY 3

Place a saucer with five metal teaspoons in a flat place in your freezer for testing the marmalade later.

Remove the plastic wrap from the apricots and their juice and discard the apricots. Strain the juice well through a very fine-mesh strainer to remove any lingering solids.

In a large mixing bowl, combine the cooked apricot juice, sugar, lemon juice, saffron, and orange slices and their liquid. Stir well, then transfer the mixture to an 11- or 12-quart copper preserving pan or a wide stainless-steel kettle.

Bring the marmalade mixture to a boil over high heat. Cook at a rapid boil over high heat until the setting point is reached; this will take a minimum of 30 minutes, but may take longer depending upon your individual stove and pan. Initially, the mixture will bubble gently for several minutes; then, as more moisture cooks out of it and its sugar concentra-tion increases, it will begin foaming. Do not stir it at all during the initial bubbling; then, once it starts to foam, stir it gently every few minutes with a heatproof rubber spatula. As it gets close to being done, stir it slowly every minute or two to prevent burning. The marmalade is ready for testing when its color darkens slightly and its bubbles become very small.

To test the marmalade for doneness, remove it from the heat and carefully transfer a small representative half-spoonful to one of your frozen spoons. It should look shiny, with tiny bubbles throughout. Replace the spoon in the freezer for 3 to 4 minutes, then remove and carefully feel the underside of the spoon. It should be neither warm nor cold; if still warm, return it to the freezer for a moment. Tilt the spoon vertically to see whether the marmalade runs; if it does not run, and if its top layer has thickened to a jelly consistency, it is done. If it runs, cook it for another few minutes, stirring, and test again as needed.

When the marmalade has finished cooking, turn off the heat but do not stir. Let the marmalade rest for 10 minutes off the heat, then fill one jar. Wait a few moments to see if the rinds begin floating to the top; if so, let the marmalade rest for another 5 minutes. If not, quickly pour the marmalade into the remaining jars and process according to the manufacturer's instructions or as directed on page 42.

Approximate Yield: eight to nine 8-ounce jars *Shelf Life:* 2 years

ROYAL BLENHEIM
APRICOT JAM

Royal Blenheim apricots make a stellar jam. The key is to use as little sugar as possible so as best to showcase this apricot's extraordinarily sumptuous flavor. Among the many plain apricot jams I have tasted, this one is the best.

6 pounds pitted and halved Royal Blenheim apricots,
and 5 to 10 pits reserved
2½ pounds white cane sugar
2½ ounces strained freshly squeezed lemon juice

DAY 1

Have ready two glass or hard plastic storage containers with tight-fitting lids.

In each container, combine 3 pounds of the apricots with 1¼ pounds of the sugar and 1¼ ounces of the lemon juice, stirring well. Press a sheet of plastic wrap directly onto the surface of the mixture, smoothing well to minimize air bubbles (this will help keep the fruit from browning as it sits). Cover the mixture tightly with the lids and let macerate in the refrigerator overnight.

DAY 2

Place a saucer with five metal teaspoons in a flat place in your freezer for testing the jam later.

Place the apricot pits on the floor between two old, clean cloths and, using a hammer, tap them through the top cloth until they crack. Carefully remove the almond-like kernel from each pit, discarding the shells. Chop the kernels very coarsely, adding a few extra kernels if you like a really pronounced almond flavor. Place the chopped kernels into a fine-mesh stainless-steel tea infuser with a firm latch and set aside.

Remove the two containers of apricots from the refrigerator. Transfer the contents of one of them to an 11- or 12-quart copper preserving pan or a wide nonreactive kettle. Put the contents of the other through the fine holes of a food mill and then add them to the rest of the apricots in the preserving pan. Scrape any solids that will not go through the food mill back into the jam mixture, breaking up the chunks as you go. Place the tea infuser in the apricot mixture, pressing down on it to submerge it.

Bring the jam mixture to a boil over high heat, stirring frequently with a large heatproof rubber spatula. Boil, stirring frequently, for 4 minutes. Remove from the heat and, using a large stainless-steel spoon, skim the stiff foam from the top of the mixture and discard. Return the jam to a boil, then decrease the heat slightly. Continue to cook, monitoring the heat closely, until the jam thickens, 30 to 40 minutes. Scrape the bottom of the pan often with your spatula, and decrease the heat gradually as more and more moisture cooks out of the jam. For the last 10 to 15 minutes of cooking, stir the jam slowly and steadily to keep it from scorching.

When the jam seems ready, test it for doneness. To test, carefully transfer a small representative half-spoonful of jam to one of your frozen spoons. Replace the spoon in the freezer for 3 to 4 minutes, then remove and carefully feel the underside of the spoon. It should be neither warm nor cold; if still warm, return it to the freezer for a moment. Tilt the spoon vertically to see how quickly the jam runs; if it runs very slowly, and if it has thickened to a gloppy consistency, it is done. If it runs very quickly or appears watery, cook it for another few minutes, stirring, and test again as needed.

Turn off the heat but do not stir. Remove the tea ball of kernels. Using a stainless-steel soup spoon, skim all the remaining foam from the surface of the jam. Pour the jam into sterilized jars and process according to the manufacturer's instructions or as directed on page 42.

Variation:

ROYAL BLENHEIM APRICOT JAM WITH VANILLA
For this delicious version, add a split 1-inch piece of vanilla bean to the apricot kernels in the mesh tea infuser and proceed with the recipe as directed.

Approximate Yield: eight to nine 8-ounce jars *Shelf Life:* 6 to 8 months

WINTERTIME
RED CHERRY JAM

What Seville orange marmalade is to winter, this jam is to June: dark, rich, and complex. I've called this jam "wintertime" because of its special mix of flavors, which always reminds me of the holidays. This glorious jam perfectly captures the essence of Bing cherries at the height of their season.

2½ pounds pitted Bing cherries

1½ pounds plus 5 ounces white cane sugar

1½ thin strips sour orange rind, 1½ inches long by ⅜ inch wide

¼ of a star anise

1 pound unpitted Bing cherries

3 ounces strained freshly squeezed lemon juice

A scant 3 ounces strained freshly squeezed Seville or other sour orange juice

2 ounces brandy or Madeira

A few drops of kirsch

Place a saucer with five metal teaspoons in a flat place in your freezer for testing the jam later.

In a ceramic or stainless-steel bowl, combine the pitted cherries with 1½ pounds of the sugar and stir to combine. Place the orange rind and star anise into a fine-mesh stainless-steel tea infuser with a firm latch. Set the cherries and the infuser aside.

In an 11- or 12-quart copper preserving pan or a wide nonreactive kettle, combine the unpitted cherries with 6 ounces water and the remaining 5 ounces of the sugar. Place the pan over high heat and bring the cherries to a boil. Lower the heat slightly and cook, mashing occasionally with a potato masher, until the cherries have shriveled and the liquid has become syrupy, about 7 minutes. Add 1 to 2 ounces more water to the fruit during cooking if the liquid appears to be cooking down too rapidly. Immediately drain the cherries through a fine-mesh strainer, pressing

down on the fruit until every last drop goes through. Discard the drained cherries. Return the cherry syrup to the preserving pan, along with the lemon and orange juices, brandy, mesh tea infuser, and pitted cherries and their sugar. Stir well to combine.

Bring the jam mixture to a boil over high heat. Cook, stirring frequently with a heatproof rubber spatula, for 15 to 20 minutes, or until done. Monitor the heat closely as you stir; if the jam begins to stick, decrease the heat slightly. Between stirrings, skim the foam carefully off the top of the mixture and discard. After 15 minutes, remove from the heat and test the jam for doneness. It should by now look dark, glossy, and syrupy. Do not stir it.

To test for doneness, carefully transfer a small representative half-spoonful of jam to one of your frozen spoons. Replace the spoon in the freezer for 3 to 4 minutes, then remove and carefully feel the

underside of the spoon. It should be neither warm nor cold; if still warm, return it to the freezer for a moment. Tilt the spoon vertically to see whether the jam runs; if it is reluctant to run, and if it has thickened to a near-jelly consistency, it is done. If it runs very quickly, cook it for another few minutes, stirring, and test again as needed.

When the jam is ready, use a stainless-steel spoon to skim all the remaining foam from its surface.

Remove the tea ball. Stir in a few drops of kirsch. Pour the jam into sterilized jars and process according to the manufacturer's instructions or as directed on page 42.

Note: If sour oranges are unavailable, replace the sour orange juice with sweet orange juice mixed with a little lemon juice, and the sour orange rind with sweet orange rind.

Approximate Yield: six 8-ounce jars *Shelf Life:* 1 year

VANILLA-LACED WHITE CHERRY JAM

This romantic cherry jam seems forever old-fashioned to me, redolent of fine china and tea parties. However, it is also an unsurpassed dessert jam and a welcome companion to all manner of cakes and creams. Perhaps its nostalgic quality stems from its subtle flavors, which are somehow both simple and grown up, straightforward and complex. In its own special way, this recipe is the very essence of cherry jam.

2½ pounds pitted Rainier or other flavorful white cherries, pits reserved

1 pound 5 ounces plus 5 ounces white cane sugar

1 pound unpitted Rainier cherries

4 ounces strained freshly squeezed lemon juice

1 (¾-inch) piece vanilla bean, split

Splash of brandy

Place a saucer with five metal teaspoons in a flat place in your freezer for testing the jam later.

Spread several cherry pits on the floor between two old clean cloths and, using a hammer, tap them through the top cloth until they crack. Carefully remove the tiny almond-like kernel from each pit until you have enough kernels to make 1½ tablespoons coarsely chopped. Discard the shells and remaining pits. Place the chopped kernels into a fine-mesh stainless-steel tea infuser with a firm latch and set aside.

Combine the pitted cherries with 1 pound 5 ounces of the sugar in a ceramic or stainless-steel bowl, stir well, and set aside.

In an 11- or 12-quart copper preserving pan or a wide nonreactive kettle, combine the unpitted cherries with 8 ounces of water and the remaining 5 ounces of sugar. Bring the cherries to a boil over high heat. Lower the heat slightly and cook, mashing occasionally with a potato masher, until the cherries have shriveled and the liquid has become syrupy, about 20 minutes. Add 1 to 2 ounces more water to the fruit during cooking if the liquid appears to be cooking down too rapidly. Immediately drain the cherries through a fine-mesh strainer over a bowl, pressing down on the fruit until every last drop of juice goes through. Discard the drained cherries. Return the cherry syrup to the preserving pan, along with the lemon juice, vanilla bean, mesh tea infuser, and pitted cherries and their sugar. Pour in a little brandy and stir well to combine. Taste, adding more brandy if necessary; you should be able to just taste the brandy in the mixture.

Bring the jam mixture to a boil over high heat. Cook, stirring frequently with a heatproof rubber spatula, for 25 to 30 minutes. Monitor the heat closely as you stir; if the jam begins to stick, decrease the heat slightly. After 25 minutes, remove from the heat and test the jam for doneness. When ready, the jam will appear syrupy, with whole cherries throughout.

To test for doneness, carefully transfer a small representative half-spoonful of jam to one of your frozen spoons. Replace the spoon in the freezer for 3 to 4 minutes, then remove and carefully feel the underside of the spoon. It should be neither warm nor cold; if still warm, return it to the freezer for a moment. Tilt the spoon vertically to see how quickly the jam runs; if it runs very slowly and appears syrupy, it is done. If it runs very quickly, cook it for another few minutes, stirring, and test again as needed.

When the jam is ready, do not stir. Remove the vanilla bean and tea ball of kernels. Using a stainless-steel spoon, skim all the remaining foam from the surface of the jam. Pour the jam into sterilized jars and process according to the manufacturer's instructions or as directed on page 42.

Approximate Yield: five 8-ounce jars *Shelf Life:* 1 year

BOYSENBERRY JAM
WITH LEMON VERBENA

Boysenberries are among the most delicious of blackberry relatives, and this is an exceptionally vibrant berry jam. The lemon verbena offsets the boysenberries perfectly, though this jam is also excellent without it.

2 (10-inch) sprigs lemon verbena

1½ pounds plus 2 pounds boysenberries

2 pounds 2 ounces white cane sugar

4½ ounces strained freshly squeezed lemon juice

Place a saucer with five metal teaspoons in a flat place in your freezer for testing the jam later. Rinse the verbena well under cold water, pat it dry between two clean kitchen towels, and set aside.

Combine 1½ pounds berries with the sugar and lemon juice in an 11- or 12-quart copper preserving pan or a wide nonreactive kettle. Place the pan over medium-low heat and cook, stirring constantly, until the juice begins to run from the berries. Increase the heat to high and continue to cook, stirring very frequently, until the mixture boils.

Boil the mixture vigorously for 5 minutes, stirring frequently, and lowering the heat slightly if the jam begins to stick. After 5 minutes, add the remaining 2 pounds of boysenberries, stirring well to combine. Over high heat, bring the mixture back up to a boil, stirring every 30 seconds or so. Once it reaches a boil, cook it for 10 to 15 minutes more, stirring frequently. Begin testing for doneness after 10 minutes.

To test for doneness, carefully transfer a small representative half-spoonful of jam to one of your frozen spoons. Replace the spoon in the freezer for 3 to 4 minutes, then remove and carefully feel the underside of the spoon. It should be neither warm nor cold; if still warm, return it to the freezer for a moment. Tilt the spoon vertically to see whether the jam runs; if it just refuses to run, and if it has thickened to a near-jelly consistency, it is done. If it runs, cook it for another few minutes, stirring, and test again as needed.

Using a stainless-steel spoon, skim any remaining foam from the surface of the jam and discard. Place the verbena sprigs into the mixture and let steep for a few minutes off the heat. Carefully taste the jam and either remove the sprigs or leave them in for another minute or two, keeping in mind that their flavor will be slightly milder once the jam has cooled. Using tongs, discard the verbena. Pour the jam into sterilized jars and process according to the manufacturer's instructions or as directed on page 42.

Approximate Yield: **five to six 8-ounce jars** *Shelf Life:* **6 to 8 months**

CHILDREN'S
STRAWBERRY JAM

I call this jam "children's" because of its simple, unembellished strawberry flavor; with neither herbs, flowers, extracts, nor alcohol, this is the classic straight strawberry jam we all know and love, in an especially bright-tasting version. As with all strawberry jams, the key is to use an ample amount of lemon juice to balance and sharpen the natural sweetness of the berries.

4 pounds hulled large strawberries

2 pounds 10 ounces white cane sugar

3⅔ ounces plus 2⅔ ounces strained freshly squeezed lemon juice

Place a saucer with five metal teaspoons in a flat place in your freezer for testing the jam later.

In an 11- or 12-quart copper preserving pan or a wide nonreactive kettle, combine the berries with the sugar and 3⅔ ounces of the lemon juice. Place the pan over medium-low heat and cook, stirring constantly with a heatproof rubber spatula. After a few minutes, as the juice starts to run and the mixture begins foaming a little around the edges, gradually raise the heat to high, stirring often.

Boil the mixture vigorously for 20 to 30 minutes, gently scraping the bottom of the pan every minute or two with your spatula to be sure the jam is not sticking. If it begins to stick, decrease the heat slightly, being sure the jam continues to cook at a rapid boil. Continue to cook, stirring and scraping frequently, until the foam subsides, the mixture acquires a darker, shinier look, and the berries appear softened and saturated with liquid, about 25 minutes total.

At this point, stir in the remaining 2⅔ ounces of lemon juice, continuing to stir frequently. If necessary, lower the heat slightly to prevent scorching.

After 3 to 5 more minutes, your jam should look shiny and thickened. At this point, remove from the heat and test for doneness, using a stainless-steel spoon to carefully scrape all the white foam off the top of the mixture while you test. Do not stir. To test for doneness, carefully transfer a small representative half-spoonful of jam to one of your frozen spoons. Replace the spoon in the freezer for 3 to 4 minutes, then remove and carefully feel the underside of the spoon. It should be neither warm nor cold; if still warm, return it to the freezer for a moment. Tilt the spoon vertically to see how quickly the jam runs; if it runs slowly, and if it has thickened to a gloppy consistency, it is done. If it runs very quickly or appears watery, cook it for another couple of minutes, stirring, and test again as needed. This jam, while spreadable, has a relatively loose texture. Pour the jam into sterilized jars and process according to the manufacturer's instructions or as directed on page 42.

Approximate Yield: **seven 8-ounce jars** *Shelf Life:* **6 to 8 months**

GROWN-UP
STRAWBERRY JAM

This deliciously sophisticated cocktail of a strawberry jam takes the flavor of the berries a step beyond the simple flavors of childhood. The hard-to-place flavor of Drambuie liqueur lends the fruit an unexpectedly herby flavor. This sparkling jam reminds me of warm evenings spent on the back porch, slowly sipping a tall drink and listening to the evening crickets: summer in a jar.

3 pounds 14 ounces hulled strawberries

2½ pounds white cane sugar

4 ounces plus 2 ounces strained freshly squeezed lemon juice

2½ ounces Drambuie

Place a saucer with five metal teaspoons in a flat place in your freezer for testing the jam later.

In an 11- or 12-quart copper preserving pan or a wide nonreactive kettle, combine the berries with the sugar and 4 ounces of the lemon juice. Place the pan over medium-low heat and cook, stirring constantly with a heatproof rubber spatula. After a few minutes, as the juice starts to run and the mixture begins foaming a little around the edges, gradually raise the heat to high, stirring often.

Boil the mixture vigorously for 20 to 30 minutes, gently scraping the bottom of the pan every few minutes with your spatula to be sure the jam is not sticking. If it begins to stick, decrease the heat slightly, being sure the jam continues to cook at a rapid boil. Continue to cook, stirring and scraping the bottom frequently, until the foam subsides, the mixture acquires a darker, shinier look, and the berries appear softened and saturated with liquid, 20 to 25 minutes total.

Remove from the heat. Do not stir. Let the mixture rest for a moment, then use a metal soup spoon to carefully skim all the white foam from the top of the mixture. When you have removed every last bit of white, stir in the remaining 2 ounces of lemon juice and the Drambuie. Return the jam to medium or medium-low heat and continue to cook, stirring frequently. If necessary, gradually lower the heat to prevent scorching.

After 3 to 5 more minutes, your jam should again look glossy and dark. At this point, remove from the heat and test for doneness. Do not stir. To test for doneness, carefully transfer a small representative half-spoonful of jam to one of your frozen spoons. Replace the spoon in the freezer for 3 to 4 minutes, then remove and carefully feel the underside of the spoon. It should be neither warm nor cold; if still warm, return it to the freezer for a moment. Tilt the spoon vertically to see how quickly the jam runs; if it runs slowly, and if it has thickened to a gloppy consistency, it is done. If it runs very quickly or appears watery, cook it for another couple of minutes, stirring, and test again as needed. This jam, while spreadable, has a relatively loose texture.

When the jam is ready, skim all the remaining foam from its surface, then stir well to be sure the berries and liquid are evenly distributed. Pour the jam into sterilized jars and process according to the manufacturer's instructions or as directed on page 42.

Approximate Yield: five to six 8-ounce jars   *Shelf Life:* 6 months

TAYBERRY JAM

Tayberry jam is the king of berry jams; think of the most vivid raspberry and the darkest blackberry, brought together into a single and utterly dazzling berry flavor. With vanilla cake, cream, and a few fresh berries, it makes a luscious dessert.

1½ pounds plus 2 pounds tayberries

2 pounds 2 ounces sugar

4½ ounces strained freshly squeezed lemon juice

Place a saucer with five metal teaspoons in a flat place in your freezer for testing the jam later.

Combine 1½ pounds of the berries with the sugar and lemon juice in an 11- or 12-quart copper preserving pan or a wide nonreactive kettle. Place the pan over medium low heat and cook, stirring very frequently, until the juice begins to run from the berries. Increase the heat to high and continue to cook, stirring frequently, until the mixture boils.

Boil the mixture vigorously for 5 minutes, stirring frequently, and lowering the heat slightly if it begins to stick. After 5 minutes, add the remaining 2 pounds of tayberries, stirring well to combine. Over high heat, bring the mixture back up to a boil, stirring every 30 seconds or so. Once it reaches a boil, cook it for 10 to 15 minutes more, stirring frequently. Begin testing for doneness after 10 minutes.

To test for doneness, carefully transfer a small representative half-spoonful of jam to one of your frozen spoons. Replace the spoon in the freezer for 3 to 4 minutes, then remove and carefully feel the underside of the spoon. It should be neither warm nor cold; if still warm, return it to the freezer for a moment. Tilt the spoon vertically to see whether the jam runs; if it just refuses to run, and if it has thickened to a near-jelly consistency, it is done. If it runs, cook it for another few minutes, stirring, and test again as needed.

Using a stainless-steel spoon, skim any remaining foam from the surface of the jam. Pour the jam into sterilized jars and process according to the manufacturer's instructions or as directed on page 42.

Approximate Yield: five to six 8-ounce jars   *Shelf Life:* 6 to 8 months

EAST COAST
BLUEBERRY JAM

This excellent jam brings back memories of blueberry picking in the woods with my father, a ritual that was invariably followed by one of my mother's truly stellar blueberry pies. This recipe uses small, intensely flavored berries, such as the domestic Rancocas, or the wild ones found growing throughout the East. Blueberry jam makes an especially lively filling for linzer cookies.

2½ pounds small blueberries

1 pound 14 ounces white cane sugar

6 ounces strained freshly squeezed lemon juice

1 (1-inch) piece cinnamon stick

Several drops of pure vanilla extract

Place a saucer with five metal teaspoons in a flat place in your freezer for testing the jam later.

Combine all the ingredients in an 11- or 12-quart copper preserving pan or a wide nonreactive kettle. Place the pan over medium-high heat and cook, stirring constantly, until the juice begins to run from the berries. When the juice starts flowing freely, stop stirring and let the mixture cook for 1 to 2 minutes. Then, stir well and increase the heat to high. Continue to cook, stirring very frequently, until the mixture boils. Once it reaches a boil, cook it for 10 to 15 minutes more, stirring frequently, and decreasing the heat slightly if the jam starts to stick. Begin testing for doneness after 10 minutes.

To test for doneness, carefully transfer a small representative half-spoonful of jam to one of your frozen spoons. Replace the spoon in the freezer for 3 to 4 minutes, then remove and carefully feel the underside of the spoon. It should be neither warm nor cold; if still warm, return it to the freezer for a moment. Tilt the spoon vertically to see whether the jam runs; if it does not, it is ready. If it does, cook the jam for another few minutes, stirring, and test again as needed.

Turn off the heat but do not stir. Using a stainless-steel spoon, skim any foam from the surface of the jam. Pour the jam into sterilized jars and process according to the manufacturer's instructions or as directed on page 42.

Variation:
BLUEBERRY JAM WITH BALSAMIC
This is a subtle jam in the tradition of blueberry jams of the past, which often contained vinegar in place of lemon juice. Unlike these jams, which were often highly spiced, this version puts the fruit front and center. Substitute 1 ounce of aged balsamic vinegar for 1 ounce of the lemon juice, and follow the recipe as directed.

Approximate Yield: five to six 8-ounce jars *Shelf Life:* 1 year

BLUEBERRY JAM
WITH MINT

Blueberries and mint are a natural pair, and their flavors come together seamlessly in this jam, which is a fantastic accompaniment to yogurt. Of all summer jams, this one is particularly clean and refreshing: a welcome balm for a hot sunny day.

3 (8-inch) sprigs peppermint or chocolate mint

2 pounds 10 ounces blueberries

1 pound 10 ounces white cane sugar

6 ounces strained freshly squeezed lemon juice

Place a saucer with five metal teaspoons in a flat place in your freezer for testing the jam later. Rinse the mint well under cold water, pat it dry between two clean kitchen towels, and set aside.

Combine the blueberries, sugar, and lemon juice in an 11- or 12-quart copper preserving pan or a wide nonreactive kettle. Place the pan over medium-high heat and cook, stirring constantly, until the juice begins to run from the berries. When the juice starts flowing freely, increase the heat to high. Continue to cook, stirring very frequently, until the mixture boils. Once it reaches a boil, cook it for 10 to 15 minutes more, stirring frequently, and decreasing the heat slightly if the jam starts to stick. Begin testing for doneness after 10 minutes.

To test the jam for doneness, carefully transfer a small representative half-spoonful of jam to one of your frozen spoons. Replace the spoon in the freezer

for 3 to 4 minutes, then remove and carefully feel the underside of the spoon. It should be neither warm nor cold; if still warm, return it to the freezer for a moment. Tilt the spoon vertically to see whether the jam runs; if it does not, it is ready. If it does, cook the jam for another few minutes, stirring, and test again as needed.

Turn off the heat but do not stir. Using a stainless-steel spoon, skim any foam from the surface of the jam. Place the mint sprigs into the jam and let steep for a minute or two off the heat. Taste carefully and either remove the mint or leave it in for another minute or two, keeping in mind that its flavor will be slightly milder once the jam has cooled. When the flavor is strong enough for your liking, use tongs to discard the mint, and pour the jam into sterilized jars and process according to the manufacturer's instructions or as directed on page 42.

Approximate Yield: four to five 8-ounce jars *Shelf Life:* 1 year

BLACKBERRY JAM
WITH LEMON BASIL

This is one of the most summery jams and also one of the simplest to make. There is something about its dark flavor that always delights me. I love it just as much made with lemon balm in place of the lemon basil and, of course, if you prefer straight blackberry jam, that is delicious, too.

2 to 3 (10-inch) sprigs lemon basil or lemon balm

3½ pounds midsummer blackberries

1¾ pounds white cane sugar

3 ounces strained freshly squeezed lemon juice

Place a saucer with five metal teaspoons in a flat place in your freezer for testing the jam later. Rinse the herb sprigs under cold running water and pat them dry between two clean kitchen towels.

Combine the berries, sugar, and lemon juice in an 11- or 12-quart copper preserving pan or a wide stainless-steel kettle. Heat slowly, stirring with a large heatproof rubber spatula, until the sugar is dissolving and the berries begin releasing a lot of juice. Turn the heat up to high and cook, stirring frequently. Test the jam for doneness 15 to 20 minutes from the time it reaches a rolling boil.

To test for doneness, carefully transfer a small representative half-spoonful of jam to one of your frozen spoons. Replace the spoon in the freezer for 3 to 4 minutes, then remove and carefully feel the underside of the spoon. It should be neither warm nor cold; if still warm, return it to the freezer for a moment. Tilt the spoon vertically to see whether the jam runs; if it just refuses to run, and if it has thickened to a near-jelly consistency, it is done. If it runs, cook it for another few minutes, stirring, and test again as needed.

Using a stainless-steel spoon, skim any remaining foam from the surface of the jam. Place the herb sprigs into the jam, stir, and let steep for a couple of minutes off the heat. Carefully taste the jam and either remove the sprigs or leave them in for another minute or two, keeping in mind that their flavor will be milder once the jam has cooled. Using tongs, discard the sprigs. Pour the jam into sterilized jars and process according to the manufacturer's instructions or as directed on page 42.

Approximate Yield: five 8-ounce jars *Shelf Life:* 6 to 8 months

BLACK RASPBERRY
JAM

Black raspberries make a very flavorful, very dark berry jam. I prefer to leave the seeds in, but you may strain them out after the cooking is completed if you prefer. This jam always brings me back to special summer outings to the ice cream stand during my childhood, where black raspberry was my flavor of choice.

1 pound plus 2½ pounds black raspberries

2 pounds white cane sugar

5 ounces strained freshly squeezed lemon juice

Place a saucer with five metal teaspoons in a flat place in your freezer for testing the jam later.

Combine 1 pound of the berries with the sugar and lemon juice in an 11- or 12-quart copper preserving pan or a wide nonreactive kettle. Place the pan over medium-low heat and cook, stirring constantly, until the juice begins to run from the berries. Increase the heat to high and continue to cook, stirring very frequently, until the mixture boils.

Boil the mixture vigorously for 1 to 2 minutes, stirring every few seconds or so. Add the remaining 2½ pounds of berries, stirring well to combine. Over high heat, bring the mixture back up to a boil, stirring every 30 seconds or so. Once it reaches a boil, cook it for 10 to 12 minutes more, stirring frequently. Begin testing for doneness after 10 minutes.

To test the jam for doneness, carefully transfer a small representative half-spoonful of jam to one of your frozen spoons. Replace the spoon in the freezer for 3 to 4 minutes, then remove and carefully feel the underside of the spoon. It should be neither warm nor cold; if still warm, return it to the freezer for a moment. When ready, nudge the jam gently with your finger. If the surface crinkles slightly when you nudge it, it is either done or nearly done. Tilt the spoon vertically to see if the jam runs; if it just refuses to run, and if it crinkled when you nudged it, it is done. If the jam is not quite ready, cook it for another 2 to 3 minutes, stirring, and test again as needed.

Turn off the heat but do not stir. Using a stainless-steel spoon, skim any foam from the surface of the jam. Pour the jam into sterilized jars and process according to the manufacturer's instructions or as directed on page 42.

Approximate Yield: six 8-ounce jars *Shelf Life:* 1 year

WHITE NECTARINE JAM
WITH ELDERFLOWER & GREEN ALMONDS

High-acid nectarines work best for this pretty jam, which one of our clients once described as "fanciful." For a simpler version, it may be made without the elderflower liqueur or green almonds, in which case you may wish to add a few drops of kirsch to it as it cooks. Either way, it's a gem.

6 pounds pitted and halved high-acid white nectarines (see Note)

4 pounds white cane sugar

4 ounces strained freshly squeezed lemon juice

1¼ pounds unshelled green almonds

A few drops of pure almond extract

1 to 2 ounces elderflower liqueur

DAY 1

Cut each nectarine half into 4 equal wedges. Combine the nectarines with the sugar and lemon juice in a hard plastic or glass storage container. Stir well, cover, and let macerate in the refrigerator for 24 to 48 hours.

DAY 2 OR 3

Place a saucer with five metal teaspoons in a flat place in your freezer for testing the jam later.

Shell the green almonds: Using a paring knife, carefully cut a slit down one side of each almond shell, open the almond, and remove its inner kernel. Discard the shells. Using your fingers or a small paring knife, carefully remove the thin outer skin of each almond. (If your almonds are very soft and jelly-like, you may omit this step.) Set the almonds aside.

Remove the nectarines from the refrigerator. By this time, they should have released a large quantity of juice, and most of the sugar should be dissolved. Stir well to incorporate any undissolved sugar. Add the almond extract and stir well to combine. Taste

and add a drop or two more extract if necessary; it should be very subtle, just enough to bring out the flavor of the nectarines. Transfer the mixture to an 11- or 12-quart copper preserving pan or a wide nonreactive kettle.

Bring the jam mixture to a boil over high heat, stirring frequently with a large heatproof rubber spatula. Boil, stirring frequently, for 5 minutes. Remove from the heat and, using a large stainless-steel spoon, skim the foam from the top of the mixture and discard. Mash half of the fruit with a potato masher to encourage it to break down. Return the jam to high heat. Cook until the jam has thickened and become cohesive, 25 to 40 minutes, decreasing the heat slightly if the mixture starts sticking.

When the jam has thickened, stir in the green almonds. Continue to cook for another minute or two, then test the jam for doneness. To test, carefully transfer a small representative half-spoonful of jam to one of your frozen spoons. Replace the spoon in the freezer for 3 to 4 minutes, then remove and

carefully feel the underside of the spoon. It should be neither warm nor cold; if still warm, return it to the freezer for a moment. Nudge the jam gently with your finger; if it seems thickened and gloppy when you nudge it, it is either done or nearly done. Tilt the spoon vertically to see how quickly the jam runs; if it is reluctant to run, and if it has thickened to a gloppy consistency, it is done. If it runs very quickly or appears watery, cook it for another few minutes, stirring, and test again as needed. While you are waiting for the jam in the freezer to cool, skim off any white foam that appears on the surface of the jam in the pan.

When the jam is ready, stir in 1 ounce elderflower liqueur. Taste carefully and add a little more liqueur if necessary; the flavor should be present, but subtle. Pour the jam into sterilized jars and process according to the manufacturer's instructions or as directed on page 42.

Note: Although this jam ideally should be made with early-season high-acid nectarines, other nectarines may be used. If using less acidic nectarines, be sure to taste the mixture before cooking, since you will probably need to increase the quantity of lemon juice and flavorings slightly.

Approximate Yield: twelve to thirteen 8-ounce jars *Shelf Life:* 8 to 10 months

STRAWBERRY-MEYER LEMON MARMALADE WITH ROSE GERANIUM

This delicately perfumed marmalade is a perfect marriage of summer berry and tart citrus. Its rosy jelly, punctuated by slices of Meyer lemon rind, has a heady fragrance. This recipe is a most unusual use for strawberries. In many recipes they dominate, but here they meld seamlessly with the lemon and geranium, subtly enfolded into the overall flavor of the marmalade.

2¼ pounds hulled strawberries

1½ pounds seeded Meyer lemons, halved crosswise,
each half cut into quarters lengthwise and sliced crosswise medium-thin

3 (8- to 10-inch) sprigs rose geranium

2 pounds 10 ounces white cane sugar

3 ounces strained freshly squeezed Eureka or Lisbon lemon juice

DAY 1

Prepare the strawberry juice: Place the strawberries in a medium stainless-steel kettle and add enough cold water to just cover the fruit. Bring to a boil over high heat, then decrease the heat to a simmer. Cover and cook the fruit for 1 to 2 hours, or until the berries are brown and shapeless and the liquid has become syrupy.

Strain the strawberry juice by pouring the hot fruit and liquid into a medium-fine-mesh strainer suspended over a heatproof storage container or nonreactive saucepan. Cover the entire setup well with plastic wrap and place in the refrigerator to drip overnight.

While the strawberries are cooking, place the lemon slices in a separate nonreactive saucepan with enough water to cover the fruit by 1 inch. Cover tightly and let rest overnight at room temperature.

DAY 2

Place a saucer with five metal teaspoons in a flat place in your freezer for testing the marmalade later. Rinse the rose geranium sprigs under cold running water and pat them dry between two clean kitchen towels.

Bring the pan with the lemon slices to a boil over high heat, decrease the heat to medium, and cook, uncovered, at a lively simmer for 20 to 30 minutes, or until the fruit is tender.

While the lemon slices are cooking, remove the plastic wrap from the strawberries and their juice and discard the berries. Strain the juice through a very fine-mesh strainer to remove any lingering solids.

When the lemon slices have finished cooking, place them with their liquid into a large mixing bowl with the sugar, cooked strawberry juice, and fresh lemon juice. Stir well to combine, taste, and slowly add a little more lemon juice if necessary. You should be able to taste the lemon juice, but it should not be overpowering. Keep adding lemon juice only until you are just able to detect its tartness. Transfer the mixture to an 11- or 12-quart copper preserving pan or a wide nonreactive kettle.

Bring the mixture to a boil over high heat. Cook at a rapid boil until the setting point is reached; this will take a minimum of 35 minutes, but may take longer depending on your individual stove and pan. Initially, the mixture will bubble gently for several minutes; then, as more moisture cooks out of it and its sugar concentration increases, it will begin foaming. Do not stir it at all during the initial bubbling; then, once it starts to foam, stir it gently every few minutes with a heatproof rubber spatula. As it gets close to being done, stir it slowly every minute or two to prevent burning, decreasing the heat a tiny bit if necessary. The marmalade is ready for testing when its color darkens slightly and its bubbles become very small.

To test the marmalade for doneness, remove it from the heat and carefully transfer a small representative half-spoonful to one of your frozen spoons. It should look shiny, with tiny bubbles throughout. Replace the spoon in the freezer for 3 to 4 minutes, then remove and carefully feel the underside of the spoon. It should be neither warm nor cold; if still warm, return it to the freezer for a moment. Tilt the spoon vertically to see whether the marmalade runs; if it does not run, and if its top layer has thickened to a jelly consistency, it is done. If it runs, cook it for another few minutes, stirring, and test again as needed.

When the marmalade is ready, turn off the heat but do not stir. Using a stainless-steel spoon, skim off any surface foam. Rub the rose geranium sprigs briefly between your fingers to release their oils, place them into the marmalade, and let them steep for a minute or two off the heat. Taste carefully and either remove the sprigs or leave them in for another minute or two, keeping in mind that the rose geranium flavor will be slightly milder once the marmalade has cooled. When the flavor is to your liking, use tongs to discard the sprigs. Pour the marmalade into sterilized jars and process according to the manufacturer's instructions or as directed on page 42.

Approximate Yield: six to seven 8-ounce jars   *Shelf Life:* 1 year

AMARELLE JAM

Amarelle cherries are sour cherries with bright red skin and clear juice. This elegant, dessert-like jam is best eaten soon after opening.

2½ pounds pitted Montmorency cherries, pits reserved
2½ pounds white cane sugar
1½ pounds unpitted Montmorency cherries
6 ounces strained freshly squeezed lemon juice
Several drops of maraschino liqueur (optional)

Place a saucer with five metal spoons in a flat place in your freezer for testing the jam later.

Spread several cherry pits on the floor between two old, clean cloths and, using a hammer, tap them through the top cloth until they crack. Carefully remove the tiny almond-like kernel from each pit, discarding the shells, until you have enough kernels to make 1 tablespoon chopped. Place the chopped kernels into a fine-mesh stainless-steel tea infuser with a firm latch and set aside while you proceed with the rest of the recipe.

In a ceramic or stainless-steel bowl, combine the pitted cherries with the sugar and stir well. Set the cherries aside.

Place the unpitted cherries in a medium stainless-steel kettle and add enough cold water to reach 1 inch above the tops of the fruit. Place the pan over high heat and bring to a boil. Lower the heat slightly and cook, mashing occasionally, until the cherries shrivel and the liquid thickens and turns slightly syrupy, 45 to 60 minutes. Immediately drain the cherries through a fine-mesh strainer, pressing down on the fruit to get as much juice as possible. Discard the drained cherries and add their juice to the pitted cherries and sugar. Transfer the cherry mixture to an 11- or 12-quart copper preserving pan or a wide nonreactive kettle. Add the lemon juice, mesh tea infuser, and maraschino, if using. Stir well to combine.

Bring the cherry mixture to a boil over high heat. Cook, stirring frequently with a heatproof rubber spatula, for 25 to 30 minutes, or until done. Monitor the heat closely; if the jam begins to stick, decrease the flame slightly. After 25 minutes, remove from the heat and test the jam for doneness. When ready, the jam will appear syrupy, with whole cherries throughout.

To test for doneness, carefully transfer a small representative half-spoonful of jam to one of your frozen spoons. Replace the spoon in the freezer for 3 to 4 minutes, then remove and carefully feel the underside of the spoon. It should be neither warm nor cold; if still warm, return it to the freezer for a moment. Tilt the spoon vertically to see how quickly the jam runs; if it runs very slowly or is reluctant to run, and if it has thickened to a viscous syrupy consistency, it is done. If it runs quickly, cook it for another few minutes, stirring, and test again as needed.

When the jam is ready, do not stir. Remove the tea ball of kernels. Using a stainless-steel spoon, skim all the remaining foam from the surface of the jam.

Pour the jam into sterilized jars and process according to the manufacturer's instructions or as directed on page 42.

Approximate Yield: **five 8-ounce jars** *Shelf Life:* **10 months**

PLUM JAM

This is my favorite plain plum jam: very tart, and studded with plum skins and whole pieces of fruit. For this jam, use any extra-flavorful red or black variety. For reds, consider Showtime, Santa Rosa, or Elephant Heart; and for blacks, Black Splendor or Laroda.

2 pounds 3 ounces pitted and halved ripe plums
1¼ pounds plus ¾ pound white cane sugar
2 to 6 ounces strained freshly squeezed lemon juice
2 pounds 5 ounces pitted ripe plums,
halved or quartered depending on softness and size

DAY 1

Combine the 2 pounds 3 ounces plum halves with 1¼ pounds of the sugar and 1 ounce of the lemon juice in a medium nonreactive kettle. Combine the 2 pounds 5 ounces plum pieces with the remaining ¾ pound of sugar and 1 ounce of the lemon juice in a large heatproof glass or hard plastic storage container. Cover both plum mixtures tightly and let macerate in the refrigerator for 24 hours.

DAY 2

Place a saucer with five metal teaspoons in a flat place in your freezer for testing the jam later.

Remove both sets of plums from the refrigerator. Heat the 2 pounds 3 ounces plum halves over medium-high heat, stirring often, until they soften, 5 to 10 minutes. Remove them from the heat, put them through the fine holes of a food mill, and add them to the rest of the uncooked plums. Scrape any solids that will not go through the food mill back into the plum mixture, breaking up the chunks as you go.

Taste the plum mixture. Gradually add a little more lemon juice, tasting as you go. You should be able to taste the lemon juice, but it should not be overpowering. Keep adding lemon juice until you are just able to detect its tartness in the mixture. Transfer the mixture to an 11- or 12-quart copper preserving pan or a wide nonreactive kettle.

Bring the jam mixture to a boil over high heat, stirring frequently with a large heatproof rubber spatula. Boil, stirring frequently, until the jam thickens, 30 to 45 minutes. As the jam cooks, use a stainless-steel spoon to skim the stiff foam from its surface and discard. Scrape the bottom of the pan often with your

spatula, and decrease the heat gradually as more and more moisture cooks out of the jam. For the last 10 to 15 minutes of cooking, you will need to stir the jam slowly and steadily to keep it from scorching.

When the jam has thickened, test it for doneness. To test, carefully transfer a small representative half-spoonful of jam to one of your frozen spoons. Replace the spoon in the freezer for 3 to 4 minutes, then remove and carefully feel the underside of the spoon. It should be neither warm nor cold; if still warm, return it to the freezer for a moment. Tilt the spoon vertically to see how quickly the jam runs; if it is reluctant to run, and it seems thick and gloppy, it is done. If it runs very quickly, cook it for another few minutes, stirring, and test again as needed.

Turn off the heat but do not stir. Using a stainless-steel spoon, skim all the remaining foam from the surface of the jam. Pour the jam into sterilized jars and process according to the manufacturer's instructions or as directed on page 42.

Approximate Yield: seven to eight 8-ounce jars *Shelf Life:* 1 year

RANGPUR LIME MARMALADE

Certain fruits just seem to beg to be made into marmalade, and Rangpur limes are one of them. Rangpurs can produce a large midsummer crop, providing a welcome change from berries and stone fruits. Not only is the flavor of Rangpur limes perfectly tart and clear, but they also contain exactly the right amount of pectin to make an exquisite and finely textured jelly. For best results, keep a very close eye on your lime slices when making this recipe; the skin of Rangpurs is quite porous and can easily turn to mush. This marmalade is a delight for citrus lovers.

2 pounds Rangpur limes, quartered

2 pounds Rangpur limes, halved lengthwise and sliced crosswise into thin half-moons

3 pounds 9 ounces white cane sugar

¾ ounce strained freshly squeezed lemon juice

A large pinch of saffron (optional)

DAY 1

Place the lime quarters in a nonreactive saucepan where they will fit snugly in a single layer. Add enough cold water for the fruit to bob freely. Cover tightly and let rest overnight at room temperature.

DAY 2

Prepare the cooked lime juice: Bring the pan with the lime quarters to a boil over high heat, then decrease the heat to medium. Cook the fruit at a lively simmer, covered, for 2 hours, or until the limes are very soft and the liquid has become slightly syrupy. As the limes cook, press down on them gently with a spoon every 30 minutes or so, adding a little more water if necessary. The water level should stay consistently high enough for the fruit to remain submerged as it cooks.

When the lime quarters have finished cooking, strain their juice by pouring the hot fruit and liquid into a medium strainer or colander suspended over a heat-proof storage container or nonreactive saucepan. Cover the entire setup well with plastic wrap and let drip overnight at room temperature.

Meanwhile, place the sliced limes in a nonreactive saucepan. Add cold water to reach ½ to ¾ inch above the tops of the slices, pressing down on the fruit to be sure the water level is correct. Cover tightly and let rest overnight at room temperature.

DAY 3

Place a saucer with five metal teaspoons in a flat place in your freezer for testing the marmalade later.

Remove the plastic wrap from the lime quarters and their juice and discard the limes. Strain the juice well through a very fine-mesh strainer to remove any lingering solids.

Bring the pan with the lime slices to a boil over high heat, decrease the heat to medium, and cook at a lively simmer, uncovered, for 13 to 15 minutes, or until tender.

In a large mixing bowl, combine the sugar, cooked lime juice, fresh lemon juice, saffron, and lime slices and their liquid, stirring well. Transfer the mixture to

an 11- or 12-quart copper preserving pan or a wide nonreactive kettle.

Bring the mixture to a boil over high heat. Cook at a rapid boil until the setting point is reached; this will take a minimum of 30 minutes, but may take longer depending on your individual stove and pan. Initially, the mixture will bubble gently for several minutes; then, as more moisture cooks out of it and its sugar concentration increases, it will begin foaming. Do not stir it at all during the initial bubbling; then, once it starts to foam, stir it gently every few minutes with a heatproof rubber spatula. As it gets close to being done, stir it slowly every minute or two to prevent burning, decreasing the heat a tiny bit if necessary. The marmalade is ready for testing when its color darkens slightly and its bubbles become very small.

To test the marmalade for doneness, remove it from the heat and carefully transfer a small representative half-spoonful to one of your frozen spoons. It should look shiny, with tiny bubbles throughout. Replace the spoon in the freezer for 3 to 4 minutes, then remove and carefully feel the underside of the spoon. It should be neither warm nor cold; if still warm, return it to the freezer for a moment. Tilt the spoon vertically to see whether the marmalade runs; if it does not run, and if its top layer has thickened to a jelly consistency, it is done. If it runs, cook it for another few minutes, stirring, and test again as needed.

Turn off the heat but do not stir. Skim any foam from the surface of the marmalade. Pour immediately into sterilized jars and process according to the manufacturer's instructions or as directed on page 42.

Approximate Yield: five to six 8-ounce jars *Shelf Life:* 2 years

RED CURRANT JAM

Red currants have a bright flavor and natural tartness that make them extremely versatile; in Europe, red currant jelly is traditionally used both as a dessert glaze and as an accompaniment to meats. The spiced variation makes a stellar addition to braised red cabbage at the holidays. Because it foams up so high in the pan, this jam is cooked in two small batches instead of one larger one.

2½ pounds plus ¾ pound stemmed red currants

2½ pounds white cane sugar

2 ounces strained freshly squeezed lemon juice

DAY 1

Place 2½ pounds of currants in a medium nonreactive kettle and fill with enough water to cover the tops by 1 inch. Bring to a boil over high heat, then decrease the heat to a lively simmer. Simmer the fruit for 1 hour, or until the liquid has thickened to a slightly syrupy consistency. Strain the juice by suspending a medium-fine-mesh strainer over a heatproof storage container or nonreactive saucepan. Cover the entire setup well with plastic wrap and let drip overnight at room temperature.

DAY 2

Place a saucer with five metal teaspoons in a flat place in your freezer for testing the jam later.

Remove the plastic wrap from the currants and discard the fruit. Strain the juice through a very fine mesh strainer to remove any lingering solids.

Combine the cooked currant juice, sugar, lemon juice, and the remaining ¾ pound of currants in a large ceramic or glass mixing bowl, stirring to dissolve the sugar. Divide the mixture into two equal portions; you may cook the portions simultaneously or one after the other. Place each portion into an 11-

or 12-quart copper preserving pan or a wide nonreactive kettle. Bring the mixture to a boil over high heat and boil vigorously for several minutes. Do not stir. The jam will foam up very high in the pan. It is done when the bubbles have darkened slightly in color and become smaller and glossier. When you think it may be ready, test it for doneness.

To test, carefully transfer a small representative half-spoonful of jam to one of your frozen spoons. Replace the spoon in the freezer for 3 to 4 minutes, then remove and carefully feel the underside of the spoon. It should be neither warm nor cold; if still warm, return it to the freezer for a moment. Tilt the spoon vertically to see how quickly the jam runs; if it does not run, and if it has thickened to a jelly consistency, it is done. If it runs, cook it for another few minutes, stirring, and test again as needed.

Turn off the heat but do not stir. Using a stainless-steel spoon, skim any remaining foam from the surface of the jam. Pour the jam into sterilized jars and process according to the manufacturer's instructions or as directed on page 42.

Variation:

SPICED RED CURRANT JAM

For a more savory preserve than the original, have a fine-mesh stainless-steel tea infuser with a firm latch for each jam kettle. Into each infuser, place a ½-inch piece of cinnamon stick, 5 pink peppercorns, 1 clove, half a petal of star anise, and a ¼-inch square piece of orange zest. Place one tea infuser in each pot at the start of the final cooking, removing promptly when the cooking is completed. Follow the rest of the recipe as directed.

Approximate Yield: five to six 8-ounce jars *Shelf Life:* 2 years

RASPBERRY-RED CURRANT JAM
WITH ROSE GERANIUM

This ravishingly delicious jam is positively jewel-like: barely cooked red raspberries suspended in a garnet jelly. Though the rose geranium makes it extra-special, this jam is also excellent without it. It is the ultimate partner for toast and butter.

2½ pounds stemmed red currants

2 (10-inch) sprigs rose geranium

2½ pounds white cane sugar

2½ ounces strained freshly squeezed lemon juice

1 pound red raspberries

DAY 1

Place the currants in a medium nonreactive kettle and fill with water to approximately 1 inch above the tops of the currants. Bring to a boil over high heat, then decrease the heat to a lively simmer. Simmer the fruit for 1 hour, or until the liquid has thickened to a slightly syrupy consistency. Strain the juice by suspending a medium-fine-mesh strainer over a heat-proof storage container or nonreactive saucepan. Cover the entire setup with plastic wrap and let drip overnight at room temperature.

DAY 2

Place a saucer with five metal teaspoons in a flat place in your freezer for testing the jam later. Rinse the rose geranium sprigs under cold running water and pat them dry between two clean kitchen towels.

Remove the plastic wrap from the currants and discard the fruit. Strain the juice well through a very fine mesh strainer to remove any lingering solids.

Combine the cooked currant juice, sugar, and lemon juice in an 11- or 12-quart copper preserving pan or a wide nonreactive kettle. Bring the mixture to a boil over high heat and boil vigorously for 5 minutes without stirring. Stir in the raspberries and continue to cook over high heat. The jam will foam up very high in the pan; if it appears at risk of boiling over, decrease the heat to medium and stir the jam briefly to calm it down. Continue to boil, stirring occasionally, until the bubbles become smaller, it has acquired a glossier look, and the color has darkened slightly. Depending upon how viscous your initial juice was, this may take 10 minutes or longer. At this point, test the jam for doneness.

To test, carefully transfer a small representative half-spoonful of jam to one of your frozen spoons. Replace the spoon in the freezer for 3 to 4 minutes, then remove and carefully feel the underside of the spoon. It should be neither warm nor cold; if still warm, return it to the freezer for a moment. Tilt the spoon vertically to see how quickly the jam runs; if it does not run, and if it has thickened to a soft jelly consistency, it is done. If it runs, cook it for another few minutes, stirring, and test again as needed.

Turn off the heat but do not stir. Using a stainless-steel spoon, skim off any surface foam. Rub the rose geranium sprigs briefly between your fingers to release their oils, place them into the jam, and let steep for a minute or two off the heat. Taste carefully and either remove the sprigs or leave them in for another minute or two, keeping in mind that the rose geranium flavor will be slightly milder once the jam has cooled. When the flavor is to your liking, use tongs to discard the sprigs. Let the jam rest for 10 minutes off the heat, then fill 1 jar. Wait a few moments to see if the raspberries seem to be floating to the top; if so, let the jam rest for another 5 minutes. If not, quickly pour the jam into the remaining jars and process according to the manufacturer's instructions or as directed on page 42.

Approximate Yield: five to six 8-ounce jars *Shelf Life:* 1 year

FLAVORELLA PLUMCOT JAM

This jam is a special gift for lovers of sour tastes. Plumcots have a very tart golden plum flavor, with a hint of apricot. A touch of brandy provides a subtle counterpart to their acidity.

3 pounds plus 3 pounds pitted and quartered Flavorella plumcots

1 pound 14 ounces plus 1 pound white cane sugar

4 ounces strained freshly squeezed lemon juice

1 ounce brandy

DAY 1

Combine 3 pounds of the plumcots with 1 pound 14 ounces of the sugar and 2 ounces of the lemon juice in a medium glass or hard plastic storage container. Combine the remaining 3 pounds of plumcots, 1 pound of sugar, and 2 ounces of lemon juice in a medium nonreactive kettle. Press a sheet of plastic wrap directly onto the surface of each plumcot mixture, smoothing well to minimize air bubbles (this will help keep the fruit from browning as it sits). Cover the mixtures tightly with lids and let macerate in the refrigerator overnight.

DAY 2

Place a saucer with five metal spoons in a flat place in your freezer for testing the jam later.

Remove the plumcots from the refrigerator. Heat the plumcots in the kettle over medium-high heat, stirring often, until they soften, 5 to 10 minutes. Remove them from the heat, put them through the fine holes of a food mill, and add the resulting puree to the remaining uncooked plumcots. Scrape any solids that will not go through the food mill back into the plumcot mixture, breaking up the chunks as you go. Stir in the brandy. Transfer the mixture to an 11- or 12-quart copper preserving pan or a wide nonreactive kettle.

Bring the jam mixture to a boil over high heat, stirring occasionally with a large heatproof rubber spatula. Boil, stirring frequently, for 4 minutes. Remove from the heat and, using a large stainless-steel spoon, skim the stiff foam from the top of the mixture and discard. Return the jam to high heat and bring it back up to a boil. Continue to cook, stirring often, and gradually decreasing the heat if the jam starts to sputter, until thickened, 20 to 30 minutes total. For the last 5 to 10 minutes of cooking, stir the jam slowly and steadily to keep it from scorching.

When the jam has thickened, test it for doneness. To test, carefully transfer a small representative half-spoonful of jam to one of your frozen spoons. Replace the spoon in the freezer for 3 to 4 minutes, then remove and carefully feel the underside of the spoon. It should be neither warm nor cold; if still warm, return it to the freezer for a moment. Tilt the spoon vertically to see how quickly the jam runs; if it runs very slowly, and if it has thickened to a gloppy consistency, it is done. If it runs very quickly or appears watery, cook it for another few minutes, stirring, and test again as needed.

Turn off the heat but do not stir. Using a stainless-steel spoon, skim all the remaining foam from the surface of the jam. Pour the jam into sterilized jars and process according to the manufacturer's instructions or as directed on page 42.

Approximate Yield: eight 8-ounce jars *Shelf Life:* 8 months

MIXED-FRUIT PLUM JAMS

Plums are among the most versatile summer fruits, and they combine well with a wide array of flavors. Their ability to simultaneously thicken and add tartness to jams makes them especially well suited to being mixed with other fruits. Since there are numerous excellent varieties of plum, the potential for such combinations is truly endless. The next two recipes, though closely related, produce quite different results. In the first, rich Santa Rosa plums are combined with strawberries and rosemary to make a wholesome jam with a deep flavor. In the second, bright Showtime plums are combined with rhubarb and sour cherries to produce a whimsical and much lighter jam.

SANTA ROSA PLUM
& STRAWBERRY JAM WITH ROSEMARY

1¼ pounds pitted and halved Santa Rosa plums

1¼ pounds pitted Santa Rosa plums, thickly sliced

¾ pound plus ¾ pound hulled strawberries, thickly sliced

14 ounces plus 14 ounces white cane sugar

2 to 5 ounces strained freshly squeezed lemon juice

2 to 3 (10-inch) sprigs rosemary

DAY 1

Have ready 2 medium glass or hard plastic storage containers with tight-fitting lids.

In the first container, combine the halved plums with ¾ pound of the strawberries and 14 ounces of the sugar. Cover and let macerate in the refrigerator for 24 to 48 hours.

In the second container, combine the sliced plums with the remaining ¾ pound of berries and 14 ounces of sugar. Cover and let macerate in the refrigerator for 24 to 48 hours.

DAY 2 OR 3

Place a saucer with five metal teaspoons in a flat place in your freezer for testing the jam later.

Remove the fruit from the refrigerator. Put the halved plums and their sugar through the fine holes of a food mill and add them to the second container with the sliced plums. Scrape any solids that will not go through the food mill back into the jam mixture, breaking up the chunks as you go. Transfer the mixture to an 11- or 12-quart copper preserving pan or a wide nonreactive kettle.

Stir in 2 ounces of the lemon juice. Taste and slowly add more lemon juice if necessary. You should be able to taste the lemon juice, but it should not be overpowering. Keep adding lemon juice only just until you are able to detect its presence in the mixture.

Bring the jam mixture to a boil over high heat. Boil, stirring frequently, for 4 minutes. Remove from the heat and, using a large stainless-steel spoon, skim the foam from the top of the mixture and discard. Return the jam to high heat and continue to cook, monitoring the heat closely, until the jam thickens, about 30 minutes. Scrape the bottom of the pan often with your spatula, and decrease the heat gradually as more and more moisture cooks out of the jam. For the final 10 minutes of cooking, stir it very frequently to prevent scorching.

To test the jam for doneness, carefully transfer a small representative half-spoonful of jam to one of your frozen spoons. Replace the spoon in the freezer for 3 to 4 minutes, then remove and carefully feel the underside of the spoon. It should be neither warm nor cold; if still warm, return it to the freezer for a moment. Tilt the spoon vertically to see how quickly the jam runs; if it runs very slowly, and if it has thickened to a gloppy consistency, it is done. If it runs very quickly or appears watery, cook it for another few minutes, stirring, and test again as needed.

Turn off the heat but do not stir. Using a stainless-steel spoon, skim all the remaining foam from the

surface of the jam. Place the rosemary into the mixture and let steep for a few minutes off the heat. Stir and carefully taste the jam and either remove the sprigs or leave them in for another minute or two, keeping in mind that their flavor will be slightly milder once the jam has cooled. Using tongs, discard the rosemary. Pour the jam into sterilized jars and process according to the manufacturer's instructions or as directed on page 42.

Approximate Yield: six 8-ounce jars   *Shelf Life:* 1 year

SHOWTIME PLUM JAM
WITH RHUBARB & SOUR CHERRIES

This lighthearted jam may be varied either by using another midsummer red plum variety or by replacing the sour cherries with sweet. The important thing is that the fruits be bright and lively so that they can shine and play off each other.

3 pounds pitted and halved Showtime plums

3 pounds white cane sugar

1 pound trimmed rhubarb stalks, cut into 1- to 2-inch lengths

11 ounces pitted Montmorency cherries

A scant 3 ounces strained freshly squeezed lemon juice

A few drops of kirsch

Place a saucer with five metal teaspoons in a flat place in your freezer for testing the jam later.

In a stainless-steel saucepan or kettle, combine the halved plums with the sugar and stir well. Place over medium-high heat and cook, stirring often, until the plums soften, 5 to 10 minutes. Remove the plums from the heat. Put them through the fine holes of a food mill, scraping any solids that will not go through the food mill back into the resulting puree. Add the rhubarb, cherries, and lemon juice and stir well to combine. Transfer the mixture to an 11- or 12-quart copper preserving pan or a wide nonreactive kettle.

Bring the jam mixture to a boil over high heat, stirring frequently with a large heatproof rubber spatula. Boil, stirring frequently, for 4 minutes. Remove from the heat and, using a large stainless-steel spoon, skim the foam from the top of the mixture and discard. Return the jam to high heat and continue to cook, monitoring the heat closely, until the jam thickens, about 30 minutes. Scrape the bottom of the pan often with your spatula, and decrease the heat grad-

ually as more and more moisture cooks out of the jam. For the final 10 minutes, stir it very frequently to prevent scorching.

When the jam has thickened, test it for doneness. To test, carefully transfer a small representative half-spoonful of jam to one of your frozen spoons. Replace the spoon in the freezer for 3 to 4 minutes, then remove and carefully feel the underside of the spoon. It should be neither warm nor cold; if still warm, return it to the freezer for a moment. Tilt the spoon vertically to see how quickly the jam runs; if it runs very slowly, and if it has thickened to a cohesive gloppy consistency, it is done. If it runs very quickly or appears watery, cook it for another few minutes, stirring, and test again as needed.

Turn off the heat but do not stir. Using a stainless-steel spoon, skim all the remaining foam from the surface of the jam. Stir in a few drops of kirsch. Pour the jam into sterilized jars and process according to the manufacturer's instructions or as directed on page 42.

Approximate Yield: six to seven 8-ounce jars *Shelf Life:* 8 to 10 months

BLACK MULBERRY JAM

Few things could be easier to make or more satisfying to eat than black mulberry jam. Its distinctively woodsy flavor, ultra-dark color, and pie-like texture place it among the best breakfast or dessert jams. It is especially good with creamy desserts, which are the perfect foil for its large berries and midnight color.

1 pound white cane sugar

⅓ ounce powdered apple pectin

3 pounds black mulberries

2 ounces strained freshly squeezed lemon juice

Place a saucer with five metal teaspoons in a flat place in your freezer for testing the jam later.

In a bowl, combine the sugar and pectin and whisk well to evenly distribute the pectin granules throughout the sugar. Place the mulberries and lemon juice in an 11- or 12-quart copper preserving pan or a wide nonreactive kettle and immediately pour the sugar-pectin mixture over the fruit, stirring as you pour to prevent the pectin from clumping.

Place the pan over medium-low heat and cook, stirring constantly, until the juice begins to run from the berries. Increase the heat to high and continue to cook, stirring very frequently, until the mixture boils. At this point, lower the heat slightly, maintaining a boil.

Mash half to three-quarters of the fruit with a potato masher. Boil the mixture for 10 to 15 minutes, stirring frequently. Begin testing for doneness after 10 minutes.

To test for doneness, carefully transfer a small representative half-spoonful of jam to one of your frozen spoons. Replace the spoon in the freezer for 3 to 4 minutes, then remove and carefully feel the underside of the spoon. It should be neither warm nor cold; if still warm, return it to the freezer for a moment. Tilt the spoon vertically to see whether the jam runs; if it is reluctant to run, and if it has thickened to a near-jelly consistency, it is done. If it runs very quickly, cook it for another few minutes, stirring, and test again as needed.

Pour the jam into sterilized jars and process according to the manufacturer's instructions or as directed on page 42.

Approximate Yield: **three to four 8-ounce jars** *Shelf Life:* **1 year**

chapter 6

LATE SUMMER
THROUGH FALL

In the waning days of summer, the bounty of fruit seems to multiply, and each day brings something different. Autumn ushers an eclectic and exciting mix of fruits into the kitchen. It always feels to me at this time as if nature is trying to fit in every last possible fruit before the onset of winter. Fruits of this season include apples, Concord grapes, melons, tomatoes, elderberries, figs, cranberries, quinces, pears, and also the last of summer's berries and stone fruits.

It has taken me years to come to a true understanding of the fruits of this time of year, to see clearly what ties them together. The late-season summer and fall fruits have a warmth and fullness that midsummer fruits typically lack. And since so many of these fruits seem uniquely suited to spice, the preserves made from them just clamor to be served with cheeses or meats. These jams and marmalades say *holiday*; they are the mulled ciders and wines of the jam world and point toward cold winter. Fall fruit always inspires me to reach into my spice chest and liquor cabinet, where a whole world of playful possibilities lies before me. Growing up in New York State, I used to love the sudden coolness in October's air and the fall leaves crunching underfoot. And now, in California, it is not only the cooler air but also the changing fruit that tells me winter is coming.

I have included December in this chapter for two reasons: first, because the fruits of November and December are essentially the same, December being a slow month for fruit; and second, because of the Christmassy nature of many late summer and fall preserves, which differ so much from those of any other time of year. It is a comfort indeed, in summer, to think that the warm spice of the holidays lies just around the corner.

august

FIG JAMS

Fig jam is one of early fall's greatest treats. Each of the fig recipes included here is intended for a different variety of fig. Fig jam may be flavored with a wide range of ingredients, but it is best to keep your flavorings subtle; the goal should always be to support the naturally warm and gentle flavor of the figs. Like quinces and citrons, figs are among the most ancient of cultivated fruits; working with them always gives me a special sense of connection to the past. This, combined with their extraordinary visual beauty and unique flavor, makes these jams especially satisfying both to make and to eat.

ADRIATIC FIG JAM

Adriatic figs are particularly flavorful, and they make an exceptional plain fig jam. Like all figs, they are best slowly savored, and are most at home with a hard, sharp cheese. I also love this jam on sandwiches or oat scones. The key to serving it is in choosing an accompaniment that will allow its warm flavor to shine.

2½ pounds plus 3 pounds stemmed Adriatic figs (see Note)

3 pounds white cane sugar

6 ounces strained freshly squeezed lemon juice

2 ounces yellow Chartreuse

A few drops of Benedictine

Place a saucer with five metal spoons in a flat place in your freezer for testing the jam later.

Slice 2½ pounds of the figs into sixths or, if the figs are very large, into eighths. Combine the slivered figs with the sugar in a large heatproof mixing bowl and let macerate while you proceed with the rest of the recipe.

Place the remaining 3 pounds of figs in a stainless-steel kettle wide enough to hold them in a single layer. Add enough cold water to make a ¼-inch layer in the bottom of the pan. Cover the pan and bring the fruit to a simmer over medium-high heat. Stir, decrease the heat to medium-low, cover again, and cook for 5 minutes. Then, use a potato masher to crush the figs well and release their juices. Stir, cover once more, and cook for 20 to 30 minutes, stirring every 5 minutes or so, until the figs are mushy and translucent.

When the figs are ready, put them through the finest disk of a food mill and add them to the slivered figs and sugar. Scrape any fruit that does not go through the mill back into the rest of the fruit, breaking up the chunks as you go. Stir well to dissolve the sugar,

then add the lemon juice, Chartreuse, and Benedictine. Transfer the mixture to an 11- or 12-quart copper preserving pan or a wide nonreactive kettle.

Bring the jam to a boil over high heat, stirring a few times with a heatproof rubber spatula. When the jam boils, decrease the heat to a lively simmer. After 7 minutes of simmering, mash the fruit a little with a potato masher. Continue cooking, stirring very frequently and lowering the heat slightly if the jam begins to stick.

After 25 minutes of simmering, or when the jam has thickened, test the jam for doneness. To test, remove the jam from the heat and carefully transfer a small representative half-spoonful to one of your frozen spoons. Replace the cold spoon in the freezer for 3 to 4 minutes, then remove and carefully feel the underside of the spoon. It should be neither warm nor cold; if still warm, return it to the freezer for a moment. Nudge the jam gently with your finger, then tilt the spoon vertically to see how quickly the jam runs; if it runs slowly, and if it has thickened to a gloppy consistency, it is done. If it runs very quickly or appears watery, cook it for another few minutes, stirring, and test again as needed.

When the jam is ready, pour it into sterilized jars and process according to the manufacturer's instructions or as directed on page 42.

Note: Although Adriatic figs are best, other green figs, such as Kadota or Greek Royal, may be used for this jam. However, these other figs tend to have thicker skins than the Adriatics, so to use such figs, you will need to precook the slivers while the whole figs are simmering. To precook, simmer the slivers with a thin film of water in a covered nonreactive saucepan. Check the fig slivers every couple of minutes; simmer them until just tender, then proceed with the recipe as directed.

or as directed on page 42.

Variation:

ADRIATIC FIG & CANDIED GINGER JAM

Figs are famously good with ginger, and this not-too-sweet jam always wins raves. Omit the Chartreuse and Benedictine. Instead, add 5 ounces finely chopped candied ginger, 2 ounces ginger liqueur, and a scant few drops vanilla extract to the fig mixture at the start of the final cooking. When cooking this jam, be sure to monitor the heat carefully, since the candied ginger tends to adhere to the bottom of the pan. Follow the rest of the recipe as directed.

Approximate Yield: eleven 8-ounce jars   *Shelf Life:* 1 year

BROWN TURKEY FIG JAM WITH SHERRY & FENNEL

In this unusual jam, the subtle buttery flavor of Brown Turkey figs is accentuated by the addition of sherry and fennel seeds. This gentle jam is particularly good on turkey sandwiches or with soft cheese and a sprinkling of toasted hazelnuts for dessert. If you are lucky enough to live where figs are grown, honor them by making this jam.

1¾ pounds plus 2½ pounds stemmed Brown Turkey figs

2 pounds 2 ounces white cane sugar

3 scant teaspoons fennel seeds

2 ounces cream sherry or Marsala

2 ounces strained freshly squeezed lemon juice

Place a saucer with five metal teaspoons in a flat place in your freezer for testing the jam later.

Slice 1¾ pounds of the figs into sixths or, if the figs are very large, into eighths. Combine the slivered figs with the sugar in a large heatproof mixing bowl and let macerate while you proceed with the recipe.

Place the remaining 2½ pounds of figs in a stainless-steel kettle wide enough to hold them in a single

225

layer. Add enough cold water to make a ¼-inch layer in the bottom of the pan. Cover the pan and bring the fruit to a simmer over medium-high heat. Stir, decrease the heat to medium-low, cover again, and cook for 5 minutes. Then, using a potato masher, crush the figs well to release their juices. Stir, cover once more, and cook for 20 to 30 minutes, or until the figs are mushy and translucent, stirring every 5 minutes or so to prevent sticking.

While the figs are cooking, crush the fennel seeds in a mortar or grind them coarsely in a spice grinder. Place the sherry and fennel seeds in a small saucepan and heat them slowly until the sherry just starts to steam. Remove the mixture from the heat, cover, and set aside to steep.

When the whole figs are finished cooking, put them through the finest disk of a food mill and add them to the slivered figs and sugar. Scrape any fruit that does not go through the mill back into the rest of the fruit, breaking up the chunks as you go. Stir well to dissolve the sugar, then add the lemon juice. Transfer the mixture to an 11- or 12-quart copper preserving pan or a wide nonreactive kettle.

Bring the jam to a boil over high heat, stirring a few times with a heatproof rubber spatula. When the jam boils, decrease the heat to a lively simmer, stirring frequently. After 7 minutes of simmering, mash the fruit a little with a potato masher. Continue cooking, stirring very frequently, and lowering the heat slightly if the jam begins to stick.

After 20 minutes of simmering, or when the jam has thickened, strain the sherry and add it to the jam. Cook a minute or two more, then test the jam for doneness. To test, remove the jam from the heat and carefully transfer a small representative half-spoonful to one of your frozen spoons. Replace the cold spoon in the freezer for 3 to 4 minutes, then remove and carefully feel the underside of the spoon. It should be neither warm nor cold; if still warm, return it to the freezer for a moment. Nudge the jam gently with your finger, then tilt the spoon vertically to see how quickly the jam runs; if it runs slowly, and if it has thickened to a gloppy consistency, it is done. If it runs very quickly or appears watery, cook it for another few minutes, stirring, and test again as needed.

When the jam is ready, pour it into sterilized jars and process according to the manufacturer's instructions or as directed on page 42.

Approximate Yield: eight to nine 8-ounce jars *Shelf Life:* 1 to 2 years

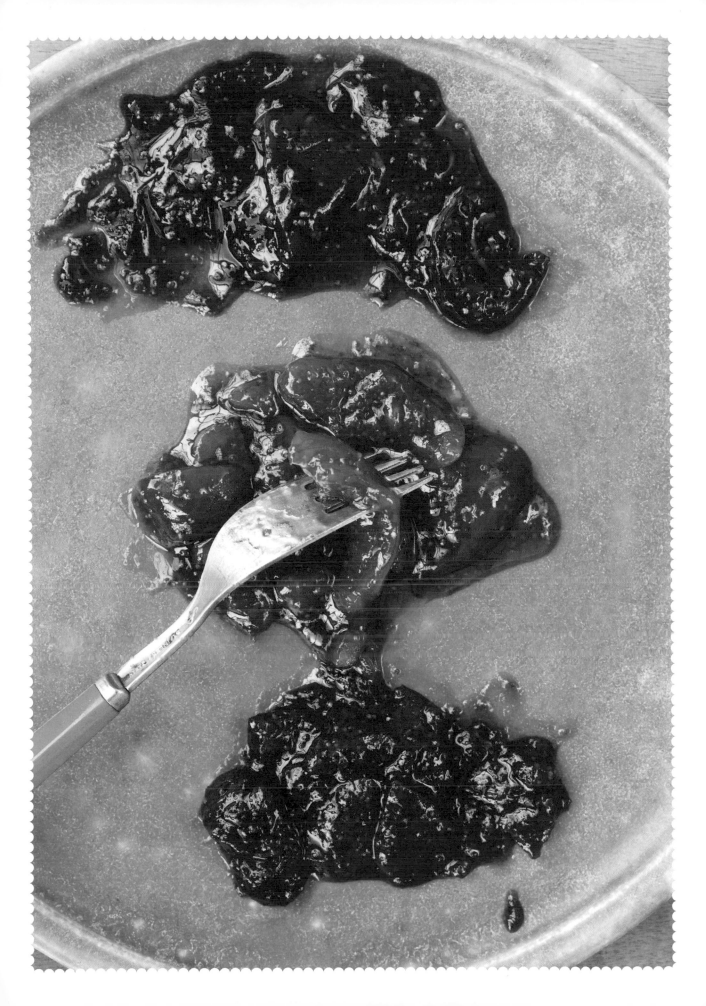

BLACK FIG
& CANDIED CITRUS JAM

Black Mission figs can sometimes vary in flavor, so I often like to spice them up a bit. In this lively jam, citrus peel brings out a different side of the figs; unlike more savory fig jams, this one is just as at home on the breakfast table as after dinner. My favorite citrus peels to use here are Meyer or plain lemon, orange, and citron, but whatever you have on hand is sure to be delicious.

3½ pounds plus 2 pounds stemmed Black Mission figs

2½ pounds white cane sugar

10 ounces chopped mixed candied citrus peel (see page 314)

6 ounces strained freshly squeezed lemon juice

Several drops of Benedictine

A few drops of triple sec

DAY 1

Chop 3½ pounds of the figs into medium-small pieces. Place the pieces in a stainless-steel kettle wide enough to hold them in a double layer. Add enough cold water to make a ½-inch layer in the bottom of the pan. Cover the pan and bring the fruit to a simmer over medium-high heat. Stir, decrease the heat to medium-low, cover again, and cook for 5 minutes. Stir, cover once more, and cook for 10 to 20 minutes, or until the figs are tender, stirring every 5 minutes or so to prevent sticking. Combine the chopped figs and their liquid with the sugar, citrus peel, and lemon juice and set aside.

Place the remaining 2 pounds of figs in a stainless-steel kettle wide enough to hold them in a single layer. Add enough cold water to make a ¼-inch layer in the bottom of the pan. Cover the pan and bring the fruit to a simmer over medium-high heat. Stir, decrease the heat to medium-low, cover again, and cook for 5 minutes. Then, using a potato masher, crush the figs well to release their juices. Stir, cover once more, and cook for 20 to 30 minutes, or until

the figs are mushy and translucent, stirring every 5 minutes or so to prevent sticking.

When the whole figs have finished cooking, put them through the finest disk of a food mill and add them to the chopped figs and sugar. Scrape any fruit that will not go through the mill back into the rest of the fruit, breaking up the chunks as you go. Stir well to dissolve the sugar, cover tightly, and let macerate in the refrigerator overnight.

DAY 2

Place a saucer with five metal teaspoons in a flat place in your freezer for testing the jam later.

Remove the figs from the refrigerator. Stir in the Benedictine and triple sec to taste; the flavor should be subtle. Transfer the mixture to an 11- or 12-quart copper preserving pan or a wide nonreactive kettle.

Bring the mixture to a boil over high heat, stirring a few times with a heatproof rubber spatula. When

the jam boils, decrease the heat to a lively simmer. After 7 minutes of simmering, mash the fruit a little with a potato masher. Continue cooking, stirring frequently and lowering the heat slightly if the jam begins to stick.

After 25 minutes of simmering, or when the jam has thickened, test the jam for doneness. To test, remove the jam from the heat and carefully transfer a small representative half-spoonful to one of your frozen spoons. Replace the cold spoon in the freezer for 3 to 4 minutes, then remove and carefully feel the underside of the spoon. It should be neither warm nor cold; if still warm, return it to the freezer for a moment. Nudge the jam gently with your finger, then tilt the spoon vertically to see how quickly the jam runs; if it runs slowly, and if it has thickened to a gloppy consistency, it is done. If it runs very quickly or appears watery, cook it for another few minutes, stirring, and test again as needed.

When the jam is ready, pour it into sterilized jars and process according to the manufacturer's instructions or as directed on page 42.

Approximate Yield: twelve 8-ounce jars *Shelf Life:* 1 year

MEM'S
RED RASPBERRY JAM

One spring day when I was a little girl, my father took me over to a local farm to help him pick up some manure for his vegetable garden. Always quick to observe the details of his surroundings, he immediately noticed the white plastic bucket, containing six or seven bare twigs, that languished in a corner of the farmyard. Upon inquiry, he learned that these twigs were the seemingly dead remnants of a raspberry patch somewhere on the property and were ours for the taking. We brought them home, stuck them in the ground, and for the next ten or fifteen years enjoyed an ever-growing bounty of the most perfectly delicious red raspberries I have ever tasted. As my parents didn't like the seeds, my mother always made seedless jam throughout the summer, which we would then enjoy the rest of the year. It is the simplest jam and also one of the best.

2¼ pounds red raspberries

3 pounds white cane sugar

Place a saucer with five metal teaspoons in a flat place in your freezer for testing the jam later. Have ready a medium-mesh strainer or chinois suspended over a heatproof mixing bowl.

Combine the berries and sugar in an 11- or 12-quart copper preserving pan or a wide nonreactive kettle. Place the pan over medium-low heat and cook, stirring and mashing constantly with a heatproof rubber spatula, until the juice begins to run from the berries. As soon as the sugar dissolves, increase the heat to high. Continue to cook, stirring very frequently, until the mixture boils. Boil the mixture vigorously for 10 to 15 minutes, stirring frequently. Begin testing for doneness after 10 minutes.

To test, carefully transfer a small representative half-spoonful of jam to one of your frozen spoons. Replace the spoon in the freezer for 3 to 4 minutes, then remove and carefully feel the underside of the spoon. It should be neither warm nor cold; if still warm, return it to the freezer for a moment. Tilt the spoon vertically to see whether the jam runs; if it does not run, and if it has thickened to a near-jelly consistency, it is done. If it runs, cook it for another few minutes, stirring, and test again as needed.

Using a stainless-steel spoon, skim any remaining foam from the surface of the jam. Transfer the jam immediately to the mesh strainer and force as much of the jam as possible through it. Discard the seeds. Skim any foam from the surface of the strained jam. Pour the jam into sterilized jars and process according to the manufacturer's instructions or as directed on page 42.

Approximate Yield: five 8-ounce jars *Shelf Life:* 2 years

MY RASPBERRY JAM

Though nothing could compare to my mother's raspberry jam, I do love whole berries in my jams. This recipe is equally delicious made with either golden or red raspberries; their flavors resemble each other very closely. It is beautiful to look at either way, with the little berries suspended in it, but it is particularly lovely with goldens.

2 pounds plus 1 pound red or golden raspberries

3 pounds white cane sugar

Place a saucer with five metal teaspoons in a flat place in your freezer for testing the jam later.

Combine 2 pounds of the berries with the sugar in an 11- or 12-quart copper preserving pan or a wide nonreactive kettle. Place the pan over medium-low heat and cook, stirring and mashing constantly with a heatproof rubber spatula, until the juice begins to run from the berries. As soon as the sugar dissolves, increase the heat to high. Continue to cook, stirring very frequently, until the mixture boils. Boil the mixture vigorously for exactly 12 minutes, stirring frequently. At 12 minutes, quickly stir in the remaining 1 pound of raspberries; cook, stirring frequently and carefully so as not to break the berries, until they just turn translucent but still hold their shape, 1 to 3 more minutes. At this point, test the jam for doneness.

To test, carefully transfer a small representative half-spoonful of jam to one of your frozen spoons. Replace the spoon in the freezer for 3 to 4 minutes, then remove and carefully feel the underside of the spoon. It should be neither warm nor cold; if still warm, return it to the freezer for a moment. Tilt the spoon vertically to see whether the jam runs; if it does not run, and if it has thickened to a near-jelly consistency, it is done. If it runs, cook it for another minute or two, stirring, and test again as needed.

Using a stainless-steel spoon, skim any remaining foam from the surface of the jam. Pour the jam into sterilized jars and process according to the manufacturer's instructions or as directed on page 42.

Variations:

RED RASPBERRY JAM WITH ROSE GERANIUM

For this classic variation, rinse 2 (10-inch) sprigs of rose geranium leaves well under cold water, pat them dry between two clean kitchen towels, and set them aside while you cook the jam as directed. When the cooking is completed, rub the rose geranium sprigs briefly between your fingers to release their oils, place them into the jam, and let them steep for a minute or two off the heat. Taste carefully and either remove the sprigs or leave them in for another minute or two, keeping in mind that the rose geranium flavor will be slightly milder once the jam has cooled. When the flavor is strong enough for your liking, use tongs to discard the sprigs and pour the jam into jars as directed.

GOLDEN RASPBERRY JAM WITH LEMON VERBENA

This variation creates a subtle marriage of flavors. Follow the recipe for the rose geranium variation, but use 3 sprigs lemon verbena in place of the rose geranium. Complete the recipe as directed.

Approximate Yield: six to seven 8-ounce jars *Shelf Life:* 1 year

CRABAPPLE MARMALADE

This marmalade, a soft jelly flecked with floating threads of fruit, is simultaneously very tart and very sweet. Crabapples are extraordinarily high in pectin, so it is important to stay well organized when using them. Transfer the marmalade immediately into jars when it finishes cooking, since it quickly thickens and becomes difficult to pour. This marmalade makes an excellent glaze for sweet or savory foods, and is also an excellent partner for toast.

2 pounds crabapples, halved
1 pound 13 ounce white cane sugar
2½ ounces strained freshly squeezed lemon juice
2⅔ ounces peeled and cored crabapples,
cut into matchsticks about 1 inch long by ⅛ inch wide

DAY 1

Place the halved crabapples in a nonreactive sauce-pan where they will fit snugly in a single layer. Add enough cold water for the fruit to bob freely. Bring the crabapples to a boil over high heat, then decrease the heat to medium. Cook the fruit at a lively simmer, covered, for 1 to 2 hours, or until the liquid has become slightly syrupy. As the crabapples cook, check them every 20 minutes or so, adding a little more water if the mixture appears to be cooking down so much that it is likely to stick or scorch.

Strain the crabapple juice by suspending a medium-fine-mesh strainer over a heatproof storage container or nonreactive saucepan. Cover the entire setup well with plastic wrap and let drip overnight at room temperature.

DAY 2

Place a saucer with five metal teaspoons in a flat place in your freezer for testing the jam later.

Remove the plastic wrap from the crabapples and discard the fruit. Strain the juice well through a very fine-mesh strainer to remove any lingering solids.

Combine the cooked crabapple juice, sugar, and lemon juice in a large mixing bowl, stirring well. Transfer the mixture to an 11- or 12-quart copper preserving pan or a wide nonreactive kettle. Bring the mixture to a boil over high heat and boil vigorously for 3 minutes, skimming off any stiff surface foam with a stainless-steel spoon. Add the crabapple matchsticks and stir briefly. Continue to boil, without stirring further, for 10 minutes, or until the bubbles become smaller, the marmalade has acquired a glossier look, and the color has darkened. At this point, test the marmalade for doneness.

To test, carefully transfer a small representative half-spoonful of marmalade to one of your frozen spoons. Replace the spoon in the freezer for 3 to 4 minutes, then remove and carefully feel the underside of the spoon. It should be neither warm nor cold; if still warm, return it to the freezer for a moment. Nudge the marmalade gently with your finger; if it has formed a solid jelly, it is either done or nearly done. Tilt the spoon vertically to see whether the marmalade runs; if it does not run, and if it has thickened to a jelly consistency, it is done. If it runs, cook it for another minute or two, stirring, and test again as needed.

Using a stainless-steel spoon, skim any remaining foam from the surface of the marmalade. Be sure to work quickly, as this marmalade tends to set right away. Pour the marmalade into sterilized jars and process according to the manufacturer's instructions or as directed on page 42.

Approximate Yield: four to five 8-ounce jars   *Shelf Life:* 1 year

GREENGAGE JAM

I always describe this as a marmalade lover's jam because it is so tart, but it is in fact above all a very British flavor, like gooseberry or black currant. Greengage jam is one of the best summer jams, but it can be hard to get right. The high amount of pectin in these plums causes the jam to thicken dramatically as it cools, much more so than most other plum jams. To assess doneness, it is therefore very helpful to turn the heat off, wait a minute or two, and examine the surface of the jam; if it has formed a skin across the top and seems leathery and slightly thickened when you drag a spoon through it, it is ready.

2½ pounds plus 2½ pounds pitted and halved greengage plums
1 pound 2½ ounces plus 1 pound 2½ ounces white cane sugar
1¼ ounces plus 1¼ ounces strained freshly squeezed lemon juice

DAY 1

Have ready two glass or hard plastic storage containers with tight-fitting lids.

In each container, combine 2½ pounds of the plums with 1 pound 2½ ounces of the sugar and 1¼ ounces of the lemon juice, stirring well to combine. Cover both plum mixtures tightly and let macerate in the refrigerator for 24 hours.

DAY 2

Place a saucer with five metal teaspoons in a flat place in your freezer for testing the jam later.

Remove both sets of plums from the refrigerator. Force the contents of one container through the fine holes of a food mill and add this puree to the remaining plums in the second container. Scrape any solids that will not go through the food mill back into the plum mixture, breaking up the chunks as you go. Transfer the mixture to an 11- or 12-quart copper preserving pan or a wide nonreactive kettle.

Bring the jam mixture to a boil over high heat, stirring frequently with a large heatproof rubber spatula.

Boil, stirring frequently, until the jam thickens, 30 to 45 minutes. As the jam cooks, use a stainless-steel spoon to skim any stiff foam from its surface and discard. Scrape the bottom of the pan often with your spatula, and decrease the heat gradually as more and more moisture cooks out of the jam. For the last 10 to 15 minutes of cooking, stir the jam slowly and steadily to keep it from scorching.

When the jam has thickened, test it for doneness. To test, carefully transfer a small representative half-spoonful of jam to one of your frozen spoons. Replace the spoon in the freezer for 3 to 4 minutes, then remove and carefully feel the underside of the spoon. It should be neither warm nor cold; if still warm, return it to the freezer for a moment. Tilt the spoon vertically to see how quickly the jam runs; if it runs very slowly, it is done. If it runs very quickly, cook it for another few minutes, stirring, and test again as needed. While the jam sample in the freezer is cooling, examine the surface of the jam in the pan as described in the recipe headnote.

When the jam is ready, use a stainless-steel spoon to skim all the remaining foam from the surface of the jam. Pour the jam into sterilized jars and process according to the manufacturer's instructions or as directed on page 42.

Approximate Yield: six to seven 8-ounce jars *Shelf Life:* 1 year

PLUM & PINK PEARL
APPLE JAM

This tart-sweet jam is a fantastic way to use apples, especially those with pink flesh. Each August, I raid my friend Yvette's plum tree for its lovely gagelike plums, which I use to make this excellent jam. Their warm color and flavor combine perfectly with apples, and the fact of having picked the plums myself makes the whole experience extra-special. Tart-skinned green or yellow plum varieties are best for this jam, which pairs beautifully with hard sharp cheese.

4 pounds 11 ounces pitted and halved greengage or other similar plums

2 pounds 13 ounces white cane sugar

3 ounces strained freshly squeezed lemon juice

1 pound 5 ounces peeled and cored tart apples, such as Pink Pearl

Place a saucer with five metal teaspoons in a flat place in your freezer for testing the jam later.

In a large mixing bowl, combine the plums, sugar, and lemon juice. Cover loosely and let macerate at room temperature for 3 hours.

Meanwhile, cut the apples into a mixture of small and medium pieces about ⅓ to ½ inch thick.

When the plums have finished macerating, add the apples to them, stirring well to combine. Transfer the mixture to an 11- or 12-quart copper preserving pan or a wide nonreactive kettle.

Bring the jam mixture to a boil over high heat, stirring frequently with a large heatproof rubber spatula. Skim off any stiff surface foam with a large stainless-steel spoon and discard. Continue to cook, monitoring the heat closely, until the jam thickens, 35 to 45 minutes. Scrape the bottom of the pan often with your spatula, and decrease the heat gradually as more and more moisture cooks out of the jam. As the jam continues to cook, stir it frequently to prevent scorching. For the final 10 to 15 minutes of cooking, stir the jam every 30 to 60 seconds to prevent burning.

To test the jam for doneness, carefully transfer a small representative half-spoonful of jam to one of your frozen spoons. Replace the spoon in the freezer for 3 to 4 minutes, then remove and carefully feel the underside of the spoon. It should be neither warm nor cold; if still warm, return it to the freezer for a moment. Nudge the jam gently with your finger; if it seems thickened and gloppy when you nudge it, it is either done or nearly done. Tilt the spoon vertically to see how quickly the jam runs; if it runs very slowly or not at all, and if it has thickened to a gloppy consistency, it is done. If it runs very quickly or appears watery, cook it for another few minutes, stirring, and test again as needed.

When the jam is ready, use a stainless-steel spoon to skim any remaining foam from the surface of the jam. Pour the jam into sterilized jars and process according to the manufacturer's instructions or as directed on page 42.

Approximate Yield: ten to eleven 8-ounce jars *Shelf Life:* 1 year

PINK PEARL APPLE
& WHITE CURRANT JELLY

This very pretty and versatile late-summer jelly, studded with currants, is a particularly fun use for early-season apples. The currants add a touch of tartness, and the natural pectin in both fruits makes for a gorgeous velvety texture. The unexpected little bites of currant give the jelly a whimsical quality, which to me perfectly captures the spirit of summer's end.

4 pounds tart apples, such as Pink Pearl, quartered

½ pound plus ½ pound stemmed white currants

3 pounds 5 ounces white cane sugar

4½ to 5 ounces strained freshly squeezed lemon juice

A few drops of Calvados or brandy

DAY 1

Place the apple quarters and ½ pound of the currants in a medium-large stainless-steel kettle and fill with water to about 1 inch above the tops of the fruit. Bring to a boil over high heat, then decrease the heat to a lively simmer. Simmer the fruit, covered, for 2 hours, or until the liquid has thickened to a slightly syrupy consistency. Strain the juice by suspending a medium-mesh strainer over a tall heatproof storage container or nonreactive saucepan. Cover the entire setup well with plastic wrap and let drip overnight at room temperature.

DAY 2

Place a saucer with five metal teaspoons in a flat place in your freezer for testing the jam later.

Remove the plastic wrap from the apples and currants and discard the fruit. Strain the juice well through a very fine-mesh strainer to remove any lingering solids.

In a large mixing bowl, combine the apple-currant juice, sugar, lemon juice, the remaining ½ pound of currants, and the Calvados, stirring well. Transfer the mixture to an 11- or 12-quart copper preserving pan or a wide nonreactive kettle. Bring the mixture to a boil over high heat and boil vigorously for about 35 minutes, or until the jelly has become shiny and darkened slightly and the bubbles have become very small.

To test the jelly for doneness, carefully transfer a small representative half-spoonful to one of your frozen spoons. Replace the spoon in the freezer for 3 to 4 minutes, then remove and carefully feel the underside of the spoon. It should be neither warm nor cold; if still warm, return it to the freezer for a moment. Nudge the jelly gently with your finger, then tilt the spoon vertically to see whether the jelly runs; if it does not run, and if it has thickened to a semisolid consistency, it is done. If it runs, cook it for another few minutes, stirring, and test again as needed.

When the jelly has finished cooking, turn off the heat but do not stir. Skim off any surface foam and

discard. Let the jelly rest for 10 minutes off the heat, then fill 1 jar. Wait a few moments to see if the currents begin floating to the top; if so, let the jelly rest for another 5 minutes. If not, quickly pour the jelly into the remaining jars and process according to the manufacturer's instructions or as directed on page 42.

Approximate Yield: eight to nine 8-ounce jars *Shelf Life:* 2 years

MELON JAM

Melon jams, though commonly found in France, are rare in this country. A good melon jam is a truly surprising and delectable treat. The important thing is the melon itself: It must be highly flavorful, aromatic, and perfectly buttery and ripe. A tender peachy-fleshed variety of muskmelon is best for this jam.

1 pound plus 1 pound white cane sugar

⅓ ounce plus ⅓ ounce powdered apple pectin

2 pounds 15 ounces seeded and skinned Crenshaw or other flavorful peach-fleshed muskmelon,
sliced into pieces about ¼ inch thick by ⅝ inch wide by 1 inch long

3 pounds 5 ounces seeded and skinned Crenshaw melon, cut into 2-inch chunks

A scant 6 ounces strained freshly squeezed lemon juice

DAY 1

Have ready two large glass or hard plastic storage containers with tight-fitting lids.

In a bowl, combine 1 pound of the sugar with ⅓ ounce pectin and whisk well to evenly distribute the pectin granules throughout the sugar. Place the sliced melon in one of the storage containers and pour the sugar-pectin mixture over the fruit, stirring the fruit as you pour to prevent the pectin from clumping.

In the same bowl, combine the remaining 1 pound of sugar with the remaining ⅓ ounce pectin, whisking well. Place the melon chunks in the second storage container and pour the sugar-pectin mixture over the fruit, stirring as you pour. Cover both containers and let macerate in the refrigerator for 48 hours.

DAY 2

Place a saucer with five metal teaspoons in a flat place in your freezer for testing the jam later.

Remove the melon from the refrigerator. Put the melon chunks through the fine holes of a food mill and add them to the sliced melon. Scrape any solids that will not go through the food mill back into the jam mixture, breaking up the chunks as you go. Add the lemon juice and stir well to combine. Transfer the mixture to an 11- or 12-quart copper preserving pan or a wide nonreactive kettle.

Bring the jam mixture to a boil over high heat, stirring occasionally with a large heatproof rubber spatula. Cook, stirring frequently and decreasing the heat slightly if you detect any sticking, for 60 to

70 minutes, or until the jam has thickened and any hint of wateriness has gone. As the jam cooks, use a stainless-steel spoon to skim off any stiff surface foam and discard. If you are using a firmer variety, such as Charentais, you may wish to mash the fruit partway through the cooking process with a potato masher to help it along; if you are using Crenshaw or another softer variety, this should not be necessary.

To test the jam for doneness, carefully transfer a small representative half-spoonful to one of your frozen spoons. Replace the spoon in the freezer for 3 to 4 minutes, then remove and carefully feel the underside of the spoon. It should be neither warm nor cold; if still warm, return it to the freezer for a moment. Tilt the spoon vertically to see how quickly the jam runs; if it runs very slowly, and if it has thickened to a gloppy consistency, it is done. If it runs very quickly or appears watery, cook it for another few minutes, stirring, and test again as needed.

Turn off the heat but do not stir. Using a stainless-steel spoon, skim any remaining foam from the surface of the jam. Pour the jam into sterilized jars and process according to the manufacturer's instructions or as directed on page 42.

Approximate Yield: six 8-ounce jars *Shelf Life:* 10 months

END-OF-SUMMER YELLOW PEACH JAM

Rich late-season peaches plus peach kernels and leaves: the last word in peach jam. The final peaches of summer are large, dense, and bursting with flavor. Peach kernels bring out the fruit's almondy side, and the leaves impart an immediately recognizable flavor that is at once peachy, almondy, and green. Because this jam uses all parts of the fruit, its flavor is both extra-peachy and unexpectedly complex.

6½ pounds large ripe yellow freestone peaches (approximately),

peeled (see Note)

3 pounds white cane sugar

3½ ounces strained freshly squeezed lemon juice

3 to 4 (12-inch) branches yellow peach leaves

DAY 1

Prepare the peaches: Place a cutting board on a rimmed baking sheet to catch any juice that may run from the fruit. Place the peeled peaches on the board, halve them lengthwise, and pit them, reserving the pits. Cut enough of the peaches into slices about ⅓ inch thick to make 5½ pounds of prepared fruit and juices. Transfer the sliced peaches to a hard plastic or glass storage container. Add the sugar and lemon juice and stir well. Press a sheet of plastic wrap directly onto the surface of the mixture, smoothing well to minimize air bubbles (this will help keep the fruit from browning as it sits). Cover the mixture tightly and let macerate in the refrigerator overnight. Place the peach pits in a separate container, cover, and refrigerate overnight.

DAY 2

Place a saucer with five metal teaspoons in a flat place in your freezer for testing the jam later. Rinse the peach branches well under cold water, pat them dry between two clean kitchen towels, and set aside.

Remove the peach pits from the refrigerator. Place several pits on the floor between two old, clean cloths. Using a hammer, hit each pit through the top cloth a few times to crack it. Carefully remove the almond-like kernel from inside each pit until you have enough kernels to make 1 tablespoon coarsely chopped. Discard the shells and remaining pits. Place the chopped kernels into a fine-mesh stainless-steel tea infuser with a firm latch and set aside.

Remove the peaches from the refrigerator and transfer them to an 11- or 12-quart copper preserving pan or a wide stainless-steel kettle. Stir well to incorporate any undissolved sugar. Taste and slowly add a drop or two more lemon juice if necessary. You should be able to taste the lemon juice, but it should not be overpowering. Add the mesh tea infuser and press down on it to submerge it.

Bring the peaches to a boil over high heat, stirring frequently with a large heatproof rubber spatula. Boil, stirring frequently, for 5 minutes. Remove from the heat and, using a large stainless-steel spoon, skim the stiff foam from the top of the mixture and discard. Mash half of the fruit with a potato masher to encourage it to break down. Return the jam to the stove over medium-high heat. Cook until the jam has thickened and become cohesive, 25 to 40 minutes, decreasing the heat slightly if the mixture starts sticking.

When the jam seems ready, test it for doneness. To test, carefully transfer a small representative half-spoonful of jam to one of your frozen spoons. Replace the spoon in the freezer for 3 to 4 minutes, then remove and carefully feel the underside of the spoon. It should be neither warm nor cold; if still warm, return it to the freezer for a moment. Tilt the spoon vertically to see how quickly the jam runs; if it runs very slowly, and if it has thickened to a gloppy consistency, it is done. If it runs very quickly or appears watery, cook it for another few minutes, stirring, and test again as needed. While you are waiting for the jam in the freezer to cool, skim off any white foam that appears on the surface of the jam in the pan.

When the cooking is completed, remove the mesh tea infuser. Place the peach leaf sprigs into the mixture and let steep for a few minutes off the heat. Carefully taste the jam and either remove the sprigs or leave them in for another minute or two, keeping in mind that their flavor will be slightly weaker once the jam has cooled. Using tongs, discard the peach leaf sprigs. Pour the jam into sterilized jars and process according to the manufacturer's instructions or as directed on page 42.

Note: To peel peaches, drop them into lightly simmering water for 1 to 2 minutes, and then drain them and let them rest until they are cool enough to handle. Carefully slip off the skins and proceed with the recipe.

Variation:
END-OF-SUMMER WHITE PEACH JAM
For this lighter variation, follow the recipe as directed, substituting white peaches for yellow. Add 1 extra ounce of lemon juice and substitute white peach leaf branches for the yellow.

Approximate Yield: **twelve 8-ounce jars** *Shelf Life:* **8 months**

AUGUST
RED NECTARINE JAM

This sumptuous jam is best made with red-tinged nectarines, since these fruits have a fantastic flavor and gorgeous rusty color when cooked. Of the late-summer varieties, August Reds are particularly flavorful, with high acidity and dense flesh. Their flavor has more bite to it than that of peaches, and they also have more natural pectin. Pulling this jam out of the cupboard in winter brings me immediately back to the warmer days of early fall. I have put this jam in the September section because this fruit is usually at its peak in the first week of September.

6 pounds 5 ounces pitted and halved August Red or other late-season yellow nectarines

3½ pounds white cane sugar

8 to 11 ounces strained freshly squeezed lemon juice

DAY 1

Cut each nectarine half into 6 equal wedges. Place the wedges in a hard plastic or glass storage container. Pour the sugar evenly over the fruit, jiggle to help the sugar settle, and drizzle 8 ounces of lemon juice over the mixture. Do not stir. Press a sheet of plastic wrap directly onto the surface of the mixture, smoothing well to minimize air bubbles (this will help keep the fruit from browning as it sits). Cover the nectarines and let macerate in the refrigerator for 3 to 6 days.

3 TO 6 DAYS LATER

Place a saucer with five metal spoons in a flat place in your freezer for testing the jam later.

Remove the nectarines from the refrigerator and transfer them to an 11- or 12-quart copper preserving pan or a wide nonreactive kettle. By this time, they should have released a large quantity of juice, and most of the sugar should be dissolved. Stir the fruit well to incorporate any undissolved sugar. Taste the mixture and slowly add more lemon juice if necessary. You should be able to taste the lemon juice, but it should not be overpowering. Keep adding lemon juice until you are just able to detect its presence in the mixture.

Bring the jam mixture to a boil over high heat, stirring frequently with a large heatproof rubber spatula. Boil, stirring frequently, for 5 minutes. Remove from the heat and, using a large stainless-steel spoon, skim the stiff foam from the top of the mixture and discard. Mash two-thirds or more of the fruit with a potato masher to encourage it to break down. Return the jam to the stove over medium-high heat. Cook until the jam has thickened and become cohesive, 25 to 40 minutes, decreasing the heat slightly if the mixture starts sticking.

When the jam has thickened, test it for doneness. To test, carefully transfer a small representative half-spoonful of jam to one of your frozen spoons.

Replace the spoon in the freezer for 3 to 4 minutes, then remove and carefully feel the underside of the spoon. It should be neither warm nor cold; if still warm, return it to the freezer for a moment. Nudge the jam gently with your finger; if it seems thickened and gloppy when you nudge it, it is either done or nearly done. Tilt the spoon vertically to see how quickly the jam runs; if it is reluctant to run, and if it has thickened to a gloppy consistency, it is done. If it runs very quickly or appears watery, cook it for another few minutes, stirring, and test again as needed. While you are waiting for the jam in the freezer to cool, skim off any white foam that appears on the surface of the jam in the pan.

When the jam is ready, pour it into sterilized jars and process according to the manufacturer's instructions or as directed on page 42.

Variation:
AUGUST RED NECTARINE & CANDIED GINGER JAM
For this fabulous jam, follow the recipe as directed, but stir in 2½ ounces finely chopped candied ginger and 1½ ounces ginger liqueur just before cooking.

Approximate Yield: twelve to thirteen 8-ounce jars *Shelf Life:* 8 months

PLUOT JAM WITH SLOE GIN & ORANGE FLOWERS

Pluots and orange flower water are natural partners and make a lovely jam. The sloe gin adds a subtle touch of plumminess, and lemon sharpens the flavors.

3 pounds plus 3 pounds pitted and halved Flavor King Pluots

1 pound 4 ounces plus 1 pound 4 ounces white cane sugar

4 ounces strained freshly squeezed lemon juice

A large splash of sloe gin

Several drops of orange flower water

DAY 1

Combine 3 pounds of the Pluots with 1 pound 4 ounces of the sugar and half the lemon juice in a large heatproof glass or hard plastic storage container. Combine the remaining 3 pounds Pluots with the remaining 1 pound 4 ounces sugar and the remaining lemon juice in a medium stainless-steel kettle. Cover both mixtures tightly with lids and let macerate in the refrigerator for 24 hours.

DAY 2

Place a saucer with five metal teaspoons in a flat place in your freezer for testing the jam later.

Remove both sets of Pluots from the refrigerator. Heat the Pluots in the stainless-steel kettle over medium-high heat, stirring often until they soften, 5 to 10 minutes. Remove them from the heat, put them through the fine holes of a food mill, and add them to the remaining Pluot halves. Scrape any solids that will not go through the food mill back into the rest of the fruit, breaking up the chunks as you go. Transfer the mixture to an 11- or 12-quart copper preserving pan or a wide nonreactive kettle.

Bring the jam mixture to a boil over high heat, stirring frequently with a large heatproof rubber spatula.

Boil, stirring frequently, for 4 minutes. Remove from the heat and, using a large stainless-steel spoon, skim the stiff foam from the top of the mixture and discard. Return the jam to a boil, then decrease the heat slightly. Continue to cook, monitoring the heat closely, until the jam thickens, 25 to 40 minutes. Scrape the bottom of the pan often with your spatula, and decrease the heat gradually as more and more moisture cooks out of the jam. For the last 10 to 15 minutes of cooking, stir the jam every 15 seconds or so to keep it from scorching.

To test the jam for doneness, carefully transfer a small representative half-spoonful of jam to one of your frozen spoons. Replace the spoon in the freezer for 3 to 4 minutes, then remove and carefully feel the underside of the spoon. It should be neither warm nor cold; if still warm, return it to the freezer for a moment. Tilt the spoon vertically to see how quickly the jam runs; if it runs very slowly, and if it has thickened to a gloppy consistency, it is done. If it runs very quickly or appears watery, cook it for another few minutes, stirring, and test again as needed.

Turn off the heat and skim all the remaining foam from the surface of the jam. Stir in the sloe gin and

orange flower water. Carefully taste the jam and add a few more drops of each if necessary, keeping in mind that the flavors should be subtle and will be slightly milder once the jam has cooled. Pour the jam into sterilized jars and process according to the manufacturer's instructions or as directed on page 42.

Approximate Yield: seven to eight 8-ounce jars *Shelf Life:* 1 year

STRAWBERRY-PLUOT JAM

This recipe is one of my favorite ways to make the most of late-season plums and Pluots. Its melt-in-your-mouth texture and bright strawberry flavor make it universally popular, and the hidden dash of rose is key to bringing out the luscious summeriness of the fruit. This jam benefits from having a mix of different Pluot and plum varieties serving as a backdrop for the strawberries.

2½ pounds pitted and halved late-season Pluots,
such as Flavor Grenade or Flavor Rosa
1 pound 3 ounces pitted and halved late-season plums,
such as Elephant Heart, or a mixture of Pluots and plums
2 pounds 9 ounces hulled strawberries
2 pounds 9 ounces white cane sugar
6 to 10 ounces strained freshly squeezed lemon juice
Several drops of rose water

DAY 1

Place the Pluots, plums, strawberries, and sugar in alternating layers in a large glass or hard plastic storage container. Drizzle 3 ounces lemon juice over the fruit, cover tightly, and refrigerate for 24 to 48 hours, until the fruit has released its juices.

DAY 2 OR 3

Place a saucer with five metal teaspoons in a flat place in your freezer for testing the jam later.

Remove the fruit from the refrigerator, stir well to dissolve the sugar, and add 3 ounces of lemon juice. Taste the liquid part of the mixture and slowly add more lemon juice if necessary. You should be able to taste the lemon juice, but it should not be overpowering. Keep adding lemon juice until you are just able to detect its tartness in the mixture. Transfer the mixture to an 11- or 12-quart copper preserving pan or a wide nonreactive kettle.

Bring the fruit to a boil over high heat, stirring occasionally with a large heatproof rubber spatula. Boil, stirring frequently, for 4 minutes. Remove from the heat and, using a large stainless-steel spoon, skim the stiff foam from the top of the mixture and discard. Return the jam to high heat and bring it back up to the boil. Continue to cook, decreasing the heat slightly if the jam starts to sputter violently or stick, until thickened, 20 to 30 minutes total. For the last 5 to 10 minutes of cooking, you will need to stir the jam slowly and steadily to keep it from scorching.

When the jam has thickened, test it for doneness. To test, carefully transfer a small representative half-spoonful of jam to one of your frozen spoons. Replace the spoon in the freezer for 3 to 4 minutes, then remove and carefully feel the underside of the spoon. It should be neither warm nor cold; if still warm, return it to the freezer for a moment. Tilt the spoon vertically to see how quickly the jam runs; if it runs very slowly, and if it has thickened to a gloppy consistency, it is done. If it runs very quickly or appears watery, cook it for another few minutes, stirring, and test again as needed.

Turn off the heat but do not stir. Using a stainless-steel spoon, skim all the remaining foam from the surface of the jam. Sprinkle several drops of rose water over the jam and stir to combine. Taste carefully, and add a little more rose water if necessary; the rose should be a subtle accent to the other flavors. Pour the jam into sterilized jars and process according to the manufacturer's instructions or as directed on page 42.

Approximate Yield: six to seven 8-ounce jars   *Shelf Life:* 6 to 8 months

STRAWBERRY JAM
WITH AGED BALSAMIC & BLACK PEPPER

This jam's inspiration comes from Italy, where the combination of strawberries and balsamic vinegar is common. The balsamic enriches the flavor of the berries, and the black pepper lends subtle warmth to the overall flavor. My favorite berries to use for this jam are late-summer Aromas or Albions; their richness is perfect with the vinegar and pepper.

A scant 5 ounces strained freshly squeezed lemon juice

1 to 1½ ounces aged balsamic vinegar

4 pounds hulled strawberries

2 pounds 10 ounces white cane sugar

Freshly ground black pepper

Place a saucer with five metal teaspoons in a flat place in your freezer for testing the jam later.

Measure out the lemon juice in a glass measuring cup, then add enough balsamic vinegar to it to bring it up to just over 6 ounces.

In an 11- or 12-quart copper preserving pan or a wide nonreactive kettle, combine the berries with the sugar and half the lemon juice mixture. Place the pan over medium-low heat and cook, stirring constantly with a heatproof rubber spatula. After a few minutes, when the juice starts to run and the mixture begins foaming a little around the edges, gradually raise the heat to high, stirring often. Add several twists of finely ground black pepper to taste.

Boil vigorously for 20 to 30 minutes, gently scraping the bottom of the pan every few minutes with your spatula to prevent the jam from sticking. If it begins to stick, decrease the heat slightly, being sure the jam continues to cook at a rapid boil. After 15 minutes, carefully taste the jam and add more black pepper if necessary. Continue to cook, stirring and scraping the bottom of the pan frequently, until the foam subsides, the jam acquires a darker, shinier look, and the berries appear softened and saturated with liquid, about 25 minutes total.

Remove from the heat. Do not stir. Let the mixture rest for a moment, then stir in the remaining half of the lemon juice mixture. Return the jam to the stove over medium heat and continue to cook, stirring frequently. If necessary, lower the heat slightly to prevent scorching.

After 3 to 5 more minutes, the jam should again look glassy and dark. At this point, remove from the heat and test for doneness, using a metal spoon to carefully scrape all the white foam from the top of the mixture while you test. Do not stir. To test, carefully transfer a small representative half-spoonful of jam to one of your frozen spoons. Replace the spoon in the freezer for 3 to 4 minutes, then remove and carefully feel the underside of the spoon. It should be neither warm nor cold; if still warm, return it to the freezer for a moment. Tilt the spoon vertically to see how quickly the jam runs; if it runs slowly, and if it has thickened to a gloppy consistency, it is done. If it runs very quickly or appears watery, cook it for another couple of minutes, stirring, and test again as needed.

When the jam is ready, skim all the remaining foam from its surface, then stir well to be sure the berries and liquid are evenly distributed. Pour the jam into sterilized jars and process according to the manufacturer's instructions or as directed on page 42.

Approximate Yield: six 8-ounce jars *Shelf Life:* 6 to 8 months

STRAWBERRY-MARSALA JAM
WITH ROSEMARY

In this sophisticated jam, Marsala deepens the naturally bright flavor of strawberries, and rosemary adds a savory edge. The result is a stunningly rich jam with a dramatic and intense berry flavor. This jam is very versatile and is one of our most popular jams. Try it with breakfast, tea, or dessert. Like the Strawberry Jam with Aged Balsamic and Black Pepper (page 258), it makes a stellar partner for fresh cheese.

3 pounds 14 ounces hulled strawberries

2 pounds 6 ounces white cane sugar

A scant 6 ounces strained freshly squeezed lemon juice

3 to 4 (6-inch) sprigs rosemary

1 to 2 ounces sweet or medium-sweet Marsala

DAY 1

Place the strawberries in a glass or hard plastic storage container and add the sugar and lemon juice. Shake the container slightly to evenly distribute the sugar, cover tightly, and let macerate in the refrigerator for 24 to 48 hours, or until the berries release their juice.

DAY 2 OR 3

Place a saucer with five metal teaspoons in a flat place in your freezer for testing the jam later. Rinse the rosemary well under cold water, pat it dry between two clean kitchen towels, and set aside.

Remove the strawberry mixture from the refrigerator and transfer it to an 11- or 12-quart copper preserving pan or a wide nonreactive kettle. Place the pan over medium-low heat and cook, stirring constantly with a heatproof rubber spatula. After a few minutes, as the juice starts to run and the mixture begins foaming a little around the edges, gradually raise the heat to high, stirring often.

Boil the mixture hard for 20 to 30 minutes, gently scraping the bottom of the pan every few minutes with your spatula to be sure the jam is not sticking.

If it does begin to stick, decrease the heat slightly, being sure the jam continues to cook at a rapid boil. Continue to cook, stirring and scraping the bottom frequently, until the foam subsides, the mixture acquires a darker, shinier look, and the berries appear softened and saturated with liquid, about 25 minutes total. At this point, stir in the Marsala.

Continue to cook the jam. After 3 to 5 more minutes, it should again look glossy and dark. At this point, remove the jam from the heat and test for doneness, using a stainless-steel spoon to carefully scrape all the white foam from the top of the mixture while you test. Do not stir. To test for doneness, carefully transfer a small representative half-spoonful of jam to one of your frozen spoons. Replace the spoon in the freezer for 3 to 4 minutes, then remove and carefully feel the underside of the spoon. It should be neither warm nor cold; if still warm, return it to the freezer for a moment. Tilt the spoon vertically to see how quickly the jam runs; if it runs slowly, and if it has thickened to a gloppy consistency, it is done. If it runs very quickly or appears watery, cook it for another couple of minutes, stirring, and test again as needed.

When the jam is ready, skim all the foam from its surface, then stir well to be sure the berries and liquid are evenly distributed. Place the rosemary into the mixture and let steep for a few minutes off the heat. Carefully taste the jam and either remove the sprigs or leave them in for another minute or two, keeping in mind that their flavor will be slightly milder once the jam has cooled. Using tongs, discard the rosemary. Pour the jam into jars and process according to the manufacturer's instructions or as directed on page 42.

Approximate Yield: six 8-ounce jars *Shelf Life:* 6 to 8 months

BLACK FIG
& TEMPRANILLO GRAPE JAM

The effect of the wine grapes in this jam is to darken and enhance the flavor of the figs. This rich preserve makes a perfect partner for strong aged cheeses.

2 pounds 9 ounces stemmed Black Mission figs, quartered lengthwise

2 pounds 14 ounces stemmed Tempranillo grapes or other good red wine grapes

2 pounds white cane sugar

2½ ounces strained freshly squeezed lemon juice

2 (4- by 1-inch) strips mandarin rind or orange rind

½ ounce yellow Chartreuse

DAY 1

Place the figs in a nonreactive kettle wide enough to hold them in a single layer. Add cold water to come ¼ inch up the sides of the pan. Cover the pan and bring the fruit to a simmer over medium-high heat. Stir, decrease the heat to medium-low, cover again, and cook for 5 minutes. Then, using a potato masher, crush the figs well to release their juices. Stir, cover once more, and cook for 20 to 30 minutes, or until the figs are tender and translucent, stirring every 5 minutes or so to prevent sticking.

Meanwhile, place the grapes in a separate medium stainless-steel kettle. Add cold water to come ½ inch up the sides of the pan. Cover the pan and bring the fruit to a simmer over medium-high heat. Stir, decrease the heat to medium-low, cover again, and cook for 10 to 15 minutes, or until the grapes have popped and released their juices, stirring every 5 minutes or so to prevent sticking.

When the grapes have finished cooking, force them through a fine-mesh sieve and discard the seeds. Combine the grape puree, sugar, and cooked figs and their liquid in a glass or hard plastic storage con-

tainer. Stir well to dissolve the sugar, cover tightly, and let macerate in the refrigerator overnight.

DAY 2

Place a saucer with five metal teaspoons in a flat place in your freezer for testing the jam later.

Remove the fig mixture from the refrigerator and add the lemon juice, mandarin rind, and Chartreuse, stirring well to combine. Transfer the mixture to an 11- or 12-quart copper preserving pan or a wide non-reactive kettle.

Bring the jam mixture to a boil over high heat, stirring a few times with a heatproof rubber spatula. When the jam boils, decrease the heat to a lively simmer. After 7 minutes of simmering, mash the figs a little with a potato masher. Continue cooking, stirring frequently and lowering the heat slightly if the jam begins to stick.

After 30 minutes of simmering, or when the jam has thickened, test the jam for doneness. To test, remove the jam from the heat and carefully transfer a small representative half-spoonful to one of your frozen spoons. Replace the cold spoon in the freezer for 3 to 4 minutes, then remove and carefully feel the underside of the spoon. It should be neither warm nor cold; if still warm, return it to the freezer for a moment. Nudge the jam gently with your finger, then tilt the spoon vertically to see how quickly the jam runs; if it runs slowly, and if it has thickened to a gloppy consistency, it is done. If it runs very quickly or appears watery, cook it for another few minutes, stirring, and test again as needed.

When the jam is ready, use a stainless-steel spoon to skim any white foam from its surface. Discard the mandarin rind. Pour the jam into sterilized jars and process according to the manufacturer's instructions or as directed on page 42.

Approximate Yield: ten 8-ounce jars *Shelf Life:* 1 year

CONCORD GRAPE JAM

Concord grape skins paired with the subtlest hint of orange and lemon make a wow of a jam. Its flavor is intensely grapy, and its bright purple color is entrancing. Unlike familiar store-bought grape jelly, this jam is bursting with fruit, and it has just enough sugar to balance its flavor.

4 pounds stemmed Concord grapes

2½ pounds white cane sugar

3 ounces strained freshly squeezed lemon juice

Very finely grated zest of ½ an orange (orange part only)

½ ounce strained freshly squeezed orange juice

Place a saucer with five metal teaspoons in a flat place in your freezer for testing the jam later.

Working directly over a small nonreactive saucepan, use your fingers to gently squeeze the flesh from each grape, being careful to catch all the grape juices in the pan. Set the skins aside in a large mixing bowl.

Over medium heat, bring the grape innards and juices to a simmer, cover, and cook until soft, 3 to 5 minutes. Immediately force as much of the pulp as possible through a fine-mesh strainer or chinois. Discard the seeds.

Add the sieved grape pulp, sugar, lemon juice, orange zest, and orange juice to the grape skins, stirring well. Transfer the mixture to an 11- or 12-quart copper preserving pan or a wide nonreactive kettle. Bring to a boil over high heat. Continue to cook until done, 20 to 30 minutes. Stir very frequently during the cooking with a heatproof rubber spatula; if the jam starts sticking, lower the heat slightly. To avoid overcooking the jam, test it for doneness after 20 minutes of cooking. When the jam is done, it will acquire a glossier sheen and will have a thicker, more luxurious look than it did initially.

To test, remove the jam from the heat and carefully transfer a small representative half-spoonful to one of your frozen spoons. Replace the cold spoon in the freezer for 3 to 4 minutes, then remove and carefully feel the underside of the spoon. It should be neither warm nor cold; if still warm, return it to the freezer for a moment. Tilt the spoon vertically to see how quickly the jam runs; if it is reluctant to run, and if it has thickened to a spreadable consistency, it is done. If it runs quickly, cook it for another minute or two, stirring, and test again as needed.

When the jam is ready, skim any white foam from its surface with a stainless-steel spoon. Pour the jam into sterilized jars and process according to the manufacturer's instructions or as directed on page 42.

Approximate Yield: **five to six 8-ounce jars** *Shelf Life:* **1 year**

WILD BLACKBERRY JAM

The flavor of wild blackberries, like that of damsons and huckleberries, is deeper and richer than that of their domestic counterparts. While cultivated blackberries tend to be sparklingly bright in flavor, wild blackberries have a mysteriously dark quality that sets them apart. Because their flavor is so distinct and unexpected, I love them unadorned, as in this delicious late-summer jam.

1 pound 6 ounces plus 2 pounds 2 ounces wild blackberries
1¾ pounds white cane sugar
2½ to 3 ounces strained freshly squeezed lemon juice

Place a saucer with five metal teaspoons in a flat place in your freezer for testing the jam later.

Combine 1 pound 6 ounces of the blackberries with the sugar and lemon juice in an 11- or 12-quart copper preserving pan or a wide nonreactive kettle. Place the pan over medium-low heat and cook, stirring very frequently, until the juice begins to run from the berries. Increase the heat to high and continue to cook, stirring often, until the mixture boils.

Boil the mixture vigorously for 3 to 4 minutes, stirring frequently. After 3 to 4 minutes, add the remaining 2 pounds 2 ounces blackberries, stirring well to combine. Bring the mixture back up to a boil, stirring every 30 seconds or so. Once it reaches a boil, cook it for 10 to 15 minutes more, stirring frequently. Begin testing for doneness after 10 minutes.

To test for doneness, carefully transfer a small representative half-spoonful of jam to one of your frozen spoons. Replace the spoon in the freezer for 3 to 4 minutes, then remove and carefully feel the underside of the spoon. It should be neither warm nor cold; if still warm, return it to the freezer for a moment. Tilt the spoon vertically to see how quickly the jam runs; if it just refuses to run, and if it has thickened to a spreadable consistency, it is done. If it runs, cook it for another few minutes, stirring, and test again as needed.

Using a stainless-steel spoon, skim any remaining foam from the surface of the jam. Pour the jam into sterilized jars and process according to the manufacturer's instructions or as directed on page 42.

Approximate Yield: five 8-ounce jars *Shelf Life:* 6 to 8 months

DAMSON JAM

Damson plums make a famously dark, flavorful, and prune-like jam. Every year, I anxiously await the arrival of this very special autumn plum, which, like the fall prune plum varieties, is best enjoyed cooked rather than raw. This classic English preserve is reminiscent of dried fruit, with a very concentrated and luxurious flavor.

4½ pounds pitted and halved damsons
1½ pounds white cane sugar
3½ ounces strained freshly squeezed lemon juice
A scant few drops of almond extract or several drops of amaretto

DAY 1

Combine the damsons with the sugar and lemon juice in a medium glass or hard plastic storage container. Cover tightly and let macerate in the refrigerator for 24 to 48 hours, or until the damsons have released their juice.

DAY 2 OR 3

Place a saucer with five metal teaspoons in a flat place in your freezer for testing the jam later.

Remove the damsons from the refrigerator and stir them to dissolve the sugar. Transfer the damson mixture to an 11- or 12-quart copper preserving pan or a wide nonreactive kettle. Cautiously add some almond extract to taste; the flavor should be very subtle, just enough to bring out the flavor of the fruit.

Bring the jam mixture to a boil over high heat, stirring frequently with a large heatproof rubber spatula. Boil, stirring frequently, until the jam thickens, 30 to 45 minutes. Scrape the bottom of the pan often with your spatula, and decrease the heat gradually as more and more moisture cooks out of the jam. For the last 10 to 15 minutes of cooking, stir the jam slowly and steadily to keep it from scorching.

When the jam has thickened, test it for doneness. To test, carefully transfer a small representative half-spoonful of jam to one of your frozen spoons. Replace the spoon in the freezer for 3 to 4 minutes, then remove and carefully feel the underside of the spoon. It should be neither warm nor cold; if still warm, return it to the freezer for a moment. Tilt the spoon vertically to see how quickly the jam runs; if it is reluctant to run, and if it seems thick and gloppy, it is done. If it runs very quickly, cook it for another few minutes, stirring, and test again as needed.

Turn off the heat but do not stir. Using a stainless-steel spoon, skim all the remaining foam from the surface of the jam. Pour the jam into sterilized jars and process according to the manufacturer's instructions or as directed on page 42.

Approximate Yield: six 8-ounce jars *Shelf Life:* 1 year

october

TOMATO PRESERVES

Although tomato preserves may be made at any point in the summer, my favorite time to do so is the fall, for by that time summer's berries and stone fruits have slowly started to slip away. Tomato preserves have largely been forgotten in this country, but they are extremely delicious; people are always surprised upon tasting them, since the fruit's flavor becomes quite intensified through cooking and sweetening. The possibilities for tomato preserves are endless, though tomatoes have a particular affinity for spice. I offer three tomato recipes here; the first two are my take on classic tomato jam and tomato marmalade; the third is a fabulous spiced tomato jam with plums and brandy.

EARLY GIRL TOMATO JAM

This most simple of tomato jams reminds us that tomatoes are a fruit, and one of the very best. Early Girl tomatoes, especially when dry farmed, are spectacularly sweet and thick skinned. Mace and salt bring out their flavor perfectly.

9 pounds medium sweet tomatoes, such as Early Girl

3 pounds 15 ounces white cane sugar

2¼ ounces strained freshly squeezed lemon juice

1 small blade of mace

2 small pinches of salt

Place a saucer with five metal teaspoons in a flat place in your freezer for testing the jam later.

Bring a medium kettle of water to a boil, then carefully drop the tomatoes into the water to loosen their skins. Leave the tomatoes immersed for 1 minute, then drain them in a large colander. When they are cool enough to handle, peel them over a large heatproof mixing bowl, discarding the skins. Place a cutting board on a rimmed baking sheet and chop the tomatoes into medium pieces. Transfer the tomatoes and their juices back into the mixing bowl. Add the sugar and lemon juice, stirring well to combine. Transfer the mixture to an 11- or 12-quart copper preserving pan or a wide nonreactive kettle. Place the mace into a fine-mesh stainless-steel tea infuser with a firm latch and add it to the mixture.

Bring the jam mixture to a boil over high heat. Add the salt and decrease the heat slightly. Skim off any surface foam with a large stainless-steel spoon. Continue to cook, monitoring the heat closely, until the jam thickens and no longer seems watery, 30 to 45 minutes. Scrape the bottom of the pan often with a heatproof rubber spatula, and decrease the heat

gradually as more and more moisture cooks out of the jam. For the final 15 to 20 minutes of cooking, or when the jam starts to visibly thicken, stir the jam gently and constantly to prevent burning.

To test the jam for doneness, carefully transfer a small representative half-spoonful to one of your frozen spoons. Replace the spoon in the freezer for 3 to 4 minutes, then remove and carefully feel the underside of the spoon. It should be neither warm nor cold; if still warm, return it to the freezer for a moment. Nudge the jam gently with your finger; if it seems thickened and gloppy when you nudge it, it is either done or nearly done. Tilt the spoon vertically to see how quickly the jam runs; if it runs very slowly, and if it has thickened to a cohesive consistency, it is done. If it runs very quickly or appears watery, cook it for another few minutes, stirring, and test again as needed.

When the jam is ready, remove the mesh tea infuser. Skim any remaining foam from the surface of the jam. Pour the jam into sterilized jars and process according to the manufacturer's instructions or as directed on page 42.

Approximate Yield: eleven to twelve 8-ounce jars *Shelf Life:* 1 year

EARLY GIRL TOMATO MARMALADE

Tomato marmalades are the perfect partners for crackers, cornbread, or sourdough. They have a long history in the United States, where they were traditionally seen as a way to use up extra fruit during summer's long tomato season. Like tomato jam, they tended to be heavily spiced with cinnamon and cloves. For this lighter version, I have introduced saffron into the mix. The result is magic.

1 pound seeded lemons, halved crosswise,
each half cut lengthwise into quarters and sliced crosswise medium-thin
1 pound navel or seeded Valencia oranges, halved crosswise,
each half cut lengthwise into quarters and sliced crosswise medium-thin
3½ pounds Early Girl or other sweet red tomatoes
4 pounds 14 ounces white cane sugar
4 ounces strained freshly squeezed lemon juice
A large pinch of saffron
1 (1½-inch) piece cinnamon stick

DAY 1

First, prepare the lemon and orange slices: Place the slices in a wide stainless-steel kettle and cover amply with cold water. Bring to a boil over high heat, boil for 1 minute, and then drain, discarding the liquid. Return the slices to the kettle and cover with 1 inch cold water. Bring to a boil over high heat, then decrease the heat to medium and cook, covered, at a lively simmer for 30 to 40 minutes, or until the fruit is very tender.

While the citrus is cooking, prepare the tomatoes: Bring a medium kettle of water to a boil, then carefully drop the tomatoes into the water to loosen their skins. Leave the tomatoes immersed for 1 minute, then drain them in a large colander. When they are cool enough to handle, peel them over a large bowl, discarding the skins. Using your hands, gently tear the tomatoes into medium pieces.

When both the citrus slices and tomatoes are ready, put them together into a nonreactive heatproof storage container with the sugar, lemon juice, and saffron, stirring well to combine. Cover tightly and refrigerate overnight.

DAY 2

Place a saucer with five metal teaspoons in a flat place in your freezer for testing the marmalade later.

Remove the tomato mixture from the refrigerator and transfer it to an 11- or 12-quart copper preserving pan or a wide nonreactive kettle. Add the cinnamon stick and stir well to incorporate any undissolved sugar.

Bring the mixture to a boil over high heat. Cook at a rapid boil until the setting point is reached; this will

take a minimum of 30 minutes, but may take longer depending on your individual stove and pan. Initially, the mixture will bubble gently for several minutes; then, as more moisture cooks out of it and its sugar concentration increases, it will begin to foam. Do not stir it at all during the initial bubbling; then, once it starts to foam, stir it gently every few minutes with a heatproof rubber spatula. As it gets close to being done, stir it slowly every minute or two to prevent burning, decreasing the heat a tiny bit if necessary. The marmalade is ready for testing when it turns slightly shiny and its bubbles become very small.

To test the marmalade for doneness, remove it from the heat and carefully transfer a small representative half-spoonful to one of your frozen spoons. It should look glossy, with tiny bubbles throughout. Replace the spoon in the freezer for 3 to 4 minutes, then remove and carefully feel the underside of the spoon. It should be neither warm nor cold; if still warm, return it to the freezer for a moment. Tilt the spoon vertically to see whether the marmalade runs; if it does not run, and if its top layer has thickened to a jelly consistency, it is done. If it runs, cook it for another few minutes, stirring, and test again as needed

When the marmalade has finished cooking, turn off the heat but do not stir. Using a stainless-steel spoon, skim off any surface foam and discard. Remove the cinnamon stick. Pour the marmalade into sterilized jars and process according to the manufacturer's instructions or as directed on page 42.

Approximate Yield: eleven to twelve 8-ounce jars   *Shelf Life:* 2 years

TWO SPICED JAMS

Fall and winter are the undisputed times for spice, and these next two jams are autumn standouts. Spiced jams of the past were often heavy in flavor due to the inclusion of large quantities of powdered spices, but here the spices are more restrained, serving primarily to enhance the original flavors of the fruit. I always think of these jams as siblings representing two sides of the same idea, and they are indeed perfect alongside each other. In the first, the spectacular holiday combination of prune-like damsons, super-sweet red tomatoes, and cloves makes for a vivid and bright-tasting jam; in the second, Italian prune plums and white cardamom come together in a lovely and genteel marriage of flavors.

EARLY GIRL TOMATO & DAMSON JAM

This is a drop-dead delicious jam that is one of my personal all-time favorites. People are always delighted and surprised upon tasting it, for it is at once spicier than most plum jams, sweeter than tomato sauce, and unique in its brilliant rust red color. It pairs perfectly with sharp aged cheese, and it also adds a vivid burst of flavor to meats and curries.

2¼ pounds pitted and halved damsons

2¼ pounds white cane sugar

2 ounces strained freshly squeezed lemon juice

3½ pounds Early Girl or other sweet red tomatoes

1 ounce brandy

1 (1-inch) piece cinnamon stick

3 cloves

DAY 1

Place the damsons, sugar, and lemon juice in a hard plastic or glass storage container and set aside.

Have ready a large mesh strainer suspended over a heatproof glass or ceramic mixing bowl. Bring a medium kettle of water to a boil, then carefully drop the tomatoes into the water to loosen their skins. Leave the tomatoes immersed for 1 minute, then drain them in a large colander. When they are cool enough to handle, peel them over the large mesh strainer, discarding the skins. Using your hands, gently squeeze the juice and seeds of the tomatoes into the strainer, leaving a few seeds still on the tomatoes. Tear the tomatoes into medium pieces and add them to the damsons and sugar. When you are finished peeling and tearing, force as much juice through the strainer as possible, then add the resulting juice to the damsons, discarding the extra tomato seeds. Stir well to combine, cover, and refrigerate overnight.

DAY 2

Place a saucer with five metal teaspoons in a flat place in your freezer for testing the jam later.

Remove the tomato-damson mixture from the refrigerator and transfer it to an 11- or 12-quart copper preserving pan or a wide stainless-steel kettle. Stir in the brandy. Place the cinnamon and cloves into a fine-mesh stainless-steel tea infuser with a firm latch and add it to the mixture, pressing down on it to be sure it is submerged.

Bring the jam mixture to a boil over high heat, stirring frequently with a large heatproof rubber spatula. Skim off any stiff surface foam with a large stainless-steel spoon. Continue to cook, monitoring the heat closely, until the jam thickens, 25 to 30 minutes. Scrape the bottom of the pan often with your spatula, and decrease the heat very gradually as more and more moisture cooks out of the jam. For the final 10 to 15 minutes of cooking, stir the jam gently every 10 to 20 seconds to prevent burning.

To test the jam for doneness, carefully transfer a small representative half-spoonful to one of your frozen spoons. Replace the spoon in the freezer for 3 to 4 minutes, then remove and carefully feel the underside of the spoon. It should be neither warm nor cold; if still warm, return it to the freezer for a moment. Nudge the jam gently with your finger; if it seems thickened and gloppy when you nudge it, it is either done or nearly done. Tilt the spoon vertically to see how quickly the jam runs; if it runs very slowly, and if it has thickened to a gloppy consistency, it is done. If it runs very quickly or appears watery, cook it for another few minutes, stirring, and test again as needed.

When the jam is ready, remove the mesh tea infuser. Use a stainless-steel spoon to skim any remaining foam from the surface of the jam. Pour the jam into sterilized jars and process according to the manufacturer's instructions or as directed on page 42.

Approximate Yield: seven to eight 8-ounce jars *Shelf Life:* 1 year

ITALIAN PRUNE
& CARDAMOM CONSERVE

The term *conserve* typically refers to a jam involving both fresh and dried fruit, often with the addition of liquor, spices, and nuts. These preserves are traditionally served alongside savory dishes or with cheeses, as well as for breakfast. In this delicious fall conserve, Italian prune plums are accentuated by dried currants and a generous splash of plum brandy.

4 pounds pitted and halved Italian prune plums

1½ pounds white cane sugar

3 ounces strained freshly squeezed lemon juice

2 ounces slivovitz or other dry plum brandy

2 ounces dried currants

½ teaspoon white cardamom seeds

DAY 1

Place the prune plums, sugar, lemon juice, slivovitz, and currants into a glass or hard plastic storage container. Stir well to combine, cover tightly, and refrigerate for 48 to 72 hours, stirring once each day.

2 TO 3 DAYS LATER

Place a saucer with five metal teaspoons in a flat place in your freezer for testing the jam later.

Transfer the plum mixture to an 11- or 12-quart copper preserving pan or a wide nonreactive kettle. Place the cardamom seeds into a fine-mesh stainless-steel tea infuser with a firm latch and add it to the mixture.

Bring the mixture to a boil over high heat, stirring frequently with a large heatproof rubber spatula. Continue to cook, monitoring the heat closely, until the conserve thickens, 35 to 45 minutes. Skim off any surface foam with a large stainless-steel spoon. Scrape the bottom of the pan often with a heatproof rubber spatula, and decrease the heat gradually as more and more moisture cooks out of the conserve.

For the final 10 to 15 minutes of cooking, stir the conserve nearly constantly to prevent burning.

To test the conserve for doneness, carefully transfer a small representative half-spoonful of conserve to one of your frozen spoons. Replace the spoon in the freezer for 3 to 4 minutes, then remove and carefully feel the underside of the spoon. It should be neither warm nor cold, if still warm, return it to the freezer for a moment. Nudge the conserve gently with your finger; if it seems thickened and gloppy when you nudge it, it is either done or nearly done. Tilt the spoon vertically to see how quickly the conserve runs; if it runs very slowly, and if it has thickened to a gloppy consistency, it is done. If it runs very quickly or appears watery, cook it for another few minutes, stirring, and test again as needed.

When the conserve is ready, remove the tea infuser, then skim any remaining foam and discard. Pour the conserve into sterilized jars and process according to the manufacturer's instructions or as directed on page 42.

Approximate Yield: **five to six 8-ounce jars** *Shelf Life:* **18 months**

ELDERBERRY-APPLE JELLY

Elderberries have a distinctively musty aroma and are a classic sweet-savory accompaniment to meat and game. They grow wild all over the United States and Europe. Elderberries historically were often combined with apples, which both soften their strong flavor and provide a boost of pectin. In this recipe, the two fruits meld together into a versatile and luscious dark jelly that is equally at home with dinner or on the breakfast table.

2 pounds tart apples, such as Pippin or Sierra Beauty, quartered

1 pound elderberries

2 pounds 10 ounces white cane sugar

3½ ounces strained freshly squeezed lemon juice

1 ounce elderflower liqueur (optional)

DAY 1

Place the apples and elderberries in a nonreactive saucepan where they will fit snugly in a single layer. Add enough cold water for the fruit to bob freely. Bring the fruit to a boil over high heat, then decrease the heat to medium. Cook the fruit at a lively simmer, covered, for 2 hours, or until the liquid has become slightly syrupy. As the fruit cooks, check it every 20 minutes or so, adding a little more water if necessary. The water level should stay consistently high enough for the fruit to remain submerged as it cooks.

When the apples and elderberries have finished cooking, strain their juice by pouring the hot fruit and liquid into a medium strainer or colander suspended over a heatproof storage container or nonreactive saucepan. Cover the entire setup well with plastic wrap and let drip overnight at room temperature.

DAY 2

Place a saucer with five metal teaspoons in a flat place in your freezer for testing the jelly later.

Remove the fruit and juice from the refrigerator and discard the fruit. Strain the juice well through a triple layer of cheesecloth to remove any linger-ing sediments.

Combine the cooked apple-elderberry juice, sugar, lemon juice, and elderflower liqueur, if using, in a large mixing bowl, then transfer the mixture to an 11- or 12-quart copper preserving pan or a wide nonreactive kettle. Bring the mixture to a boil over high heat and cook vigorously, skimming off any surface scum with a stainless-steel spoon. Continue to boil, stirring occasionally, until the bubbles become smaller, the jelly has acquired a glossier look, and the color has darkened slightly. Depending upon how viscous your initial juice was, this could take anywhere from 25 to 45 minutes. At this point, test the jelly for doneness.

To test, carefully transfer a small representative half-spoonful of jelly to one of your frozen spoons. Replace the spoon in the freezer for 3 to 4 minutes, then remove and carefully feel the underside of the spoon. It should be neither warm nor cold; if still warm, return it to the freezer for a moment. Nudge the jelly gently with your finger; if it is cohesive, it is either done or nearly done. Tilt the spoon vertically to

see whether the jelly runs; if it does not run, and if it has thickened to a semisolid consistency, it is done. If it runs, cook it for another minute or two, stirring, and test again as needed.

Using a stainless-steel spoon, skim any remaining foam from the surface of the jelly. Pour the jelly into sterilized jars and process according to the manufacturer's instructions or as directed on page 42.

Approximate Yield: five 8-ounce jars *Shelf Life:* 1 year

ELDERBERRY-ORANGE MARMALADE

This unusual and beautiful marmalade bridges the gap between fall and winter with its dark color and winy orange flavor. It has just a hint of elderberry to accentuate the vibrant sweetness of the oranges. This marmalade is one of my favorites for breakfast; I particularly love it on some really good rye bread.

2 pounds seeded Valencia oranges, halved crosswise,
each half cut lengthwise into quarters and sliced crosswise medium-thin
1 pound elderberries
2 pounds 2 ounces tart apples, such as Pippin or Sierra Beauty, quartered
4 pounds 14 ounces white cane sugar
3½ ounces strained freshly squeezed lemon juice

DAY 1

In a nonreactive saucepan, place the sliced oranges with water to reach 1 inch above the tops. Cover tightly and let rest overnight at room temperature.

DAY 2

Prepare the elderberry-apple juice: Place the elderberries and apples in a medium nonreactive saucepan and add enough cold water for the fruit to bob freely. Bring the fruit to a boil over high heat, then decrease the heat to medium. Cook the fruit at a lively simmer, covered, for 2 hours, or until the liquid has become slightly syrupy. As the fruit cooks, check it every 20 minutes or so, adding a little more water if necessary. The water level should stay consistently high enough for the fruit to remain submerged as it cooks.

When the apples and elderberries have finished cooking, strain their juice by pouring the hot fruit and liquid into a medium strainer or colander suspended over a heatproof storage container or nonreactive saucepan. Cover the entire setup well with plastic wrap and let drip overnight at room temperature.

Meanwhile, cook the orange slices: Bring the pan with them to a boil over high heat, then decrease the heat to medium and cook, covered, at a lively simmer for 30 to 60 minutes, or until the fruit is very tender. As the oranges cook, stir them gently every 15 minutes or so, adding a little more water if necessary. The water level should stay consistently high enough for the fruit to remain submerged as it cooks. Remove the pan from the heat, cover tightly, and let rest overnight at room temperature.

DAY 3

Place a saucer with five metal teaspoons in a flat place in your freezer for testing the marmalade later.

Remove the plastic wrap from the berries and apples and discard the solids. Strain the juice well through a triple layer of cheesecloth to remove any lingering solids.

In a large mixing bowl, combine the sugar, cooked elderberry-apple juice, lemon juice, and orange slices and their liquid, stirring well. Transfer the mixture to an 11- or 12-quart copper preserving pan or a wide nonreactive kettle.

Bring the mixture to a boil over high heat. Cook at a rapid boil until the setting point is reached; this will take a minimum of 20 minutes, but may take longer depending upon your individual stove and pan. Initially, the mixture will bubble gently for several minutes; then, as more moisture cooks out of it and its sugar concentration increases, it will begin foaming. Do not stir it at all during the initial bubbling; then, once it starts to foam, stir it gently every few minutes with a heatproof rubber spatula. As it gets close to being done, stir it slowly every minute or two to prevent burning, decreasing the heat a tiny bit if necessary. The marmalade is ready for testing when its color darkens slightly and its bubbles become very small.

To test the marmalade for doneness, remove it from the heat and carefully transfer a small representative half-spoonful of marmalade to one of your frozen spoons. It should look shiny, with tiny bubbles throughout. Replace the spoon in the freezer for 3 to 4 minutes, then remove and carefully feel the underside of the spoon. It should be neither warm nor cold; if still warm, return it to the freezer for a moment. Tilt the spoon vertically to see whether the marmalade runs; if it does not run, and if its top layer has thickened to a jelly consistency, it is done. If it runs, cook it for another few minutes, stirring, and test again as needed.

When the marmalade has finished cooking, turn off the heat but do not stir. Using a stainless-steel spoon, skim off any surface foam and discard. Fill 1 jar. Wait a few moments to see if the rinds seem to be floating to the top; if so, let the marmalade rest for 10 to 15 minutes before filling the remaining jars. If not, pour the marmalade into jars and process according to the manufacturer's instructions or as directed on page 42.

Approximate Yield: seven to eight 8-ounce jars   *Shelf Life:* 18 months

PEAR PRESERVES

Though not as acidic or bright as berries or plums, pears are surprisingly intense, and they rank among the best jam and marmalade fruits. They are famously good for dessert; pear jam with crepes and a light drizzle of chocolate makes a uniquely satisfying autumn treat. The three recipes that follow each represent a different aspect of this fruit's complex flavor. Whether combined with herbs, vanilla, or spices, one thing is important above all: use the ripest, most flavorful pears you can find.

PEAR JAM
WITH ROSEMARY & PINE

Pear goes naturally with herbs, and the combination of pear and rosemary is particularly delicious. Pinecone bud syrup has a dark chestnut color and wintry pine flavor. Here, it combines seamlessly with the rosemary and pears to create a warm and very autumnal jam.

8 pounds 2 ounces peeled and cored very ripe pears, such as Warren or Bartlett

3 pounds 14 ounces white cane sugar

14 ounces strained freshly squeezed lemon juice

2 to 3 (6-inch) sprigs rosemary

A generous drizzle of pinecone bud syrup

DAY 1

Chop the pears into pieces ¼ inch to ½ inch in diameter. Combine the pears, sugar, and lemon juice in a hard plastic or glass storage container, stirring well to combine. Press a sheet of plastic wrap directly onto the surface of the mixture, smoothing well to minimize air bubbles (this will help keep the fruit from browning as it sits). Cover the mixture tightly with a lid and let macerate in the refrigerator overnight.

DAY 2

Place a saucer with five metal teaspoons in a flat place in your freezer for testing the jam later. Rinse the rosemary well under cold water, pat it dry between two clean kitchen towels, and set aside.

Remove the pears from the refrigerator and transfer them to an 11- or 12-quart copper preserving pan or a wide nonreactive kettle, stirring well. Position a food mill over the storage container that held the pears and set aside.

Bring the pears to a boil over high heat, stirring every 2 minutes or so. Cook, stirring frequently with a heatproof rubber spatula, until the mixture starts to thicken and the pear pieces are semitranslucent,

15 to 20 minutes. Remove from the heat and transfer one-third of the mixture to the food mill. Put as much fruit as possible through the mill, then scrape any solids that will not go through back into the jam mixture. Return the pureed fruit to the jam kettle, breaking up the chunks as you go. Place the jam over medium-high heat and continue to cook, stirring gently and constantly, until the jam has thickened and no longer appears watery, about 15 minutes more.

When the jam seems ready, test it for doneness. To test, carefully transfer a small representative half-spoonful of jam to one of your frozen spoons. Replace the spoon in the freezer for 3 to 4 minutes, then remove and carefully feel the underside of the spoon. It should be neither warm nor cold; if still warm, return it to the freezer for a moment. Tilt the spoon vertically to see how quickly the jam runs; if it runs slowly, and if it has thickened to a gloppy consistency, it is done. If it runs very quickly or appears watery, cook it for another few minutes, stirring, and test again as needed. While you are waiting for the jam in the freezer to cool, skim off any white foam that appears on the surface of the jam in the pan.

When the cooking is completed, place the rosemary into the mixture and let steep for a few minutes off the heat. Stir and carefully taste the jam and either remove the sprigs or leave them for another minute or two, keeping in mind that their flavor will be slightly weaker once the jam has cooled. Using tongs, discard the rosemary. Add a generous drizzle of pinecone bud syrup and stir well. Pour the jam into sterilized jars and process according to the manufacturer's instructions or as directed on page 42.

Variation:
PEAR JAM WITH VANILLA & ELDERFLOWER
To make this delicately flavored jam, follow the recipe as directed, omitting the rosemary and pinecone bud syrup and instead substituting a 2- to 3-inch piece of split vanilla bean to the mixture at the start of cooking. Just moments before the jam is finished cooking, stir in a generous splash of elderflower liqueur. Cook for a minute or two more to allow some of the alcohol to evaporate, then remove the vanilla bean, pour into jars, and process as directed.

Approximate Yield: ten to eleven 8-ounce jars   *Shelf Life:* 8 to 10 months

PEAR JAM
WITH CHESTNUT HONEY & SAGE

The unmistakable fragrance of sage is front and center in this autumn jam, whose flavor keeps opening up before you; it begins with pear and ends with honey. This preserve was partly inspired by an unforgettable chestnut honey and sage ice cream I once had. It was one of the most delectable things I have ever tasted.

8 pounds peeled and cored very ripe pears, such as Warren or Bartlett

3 pounds 7 ounces white cane sugar

9 ounces strained freshly squeezed lemon juice

1 small bunch of fresh sage

1 to 2 ounces chestnut honey

Several drops of chestnut honey vinegar or cider vinegar

DAY 1

Chop the pears into pieces ¼ inch to ½ inch in diameter. Combine the pears, sugar, and lemon juice in a hard plastic or glass storage container, stirring well to combine. Press a sheet of plastic wrap directly onto the surface of the mixture, smoothing well to minimize air bubbles (this will help keep the fruit from browning as it sits). Cover the mixture tightly with a lid and let macerate in the refrigerator overnight.

Place a saucer with five metal teaspoons in a flat place in your freezer for testing the jam later. Rinse the sage well under cold water, pat it dry between two clean kitchen towels, and set aside.

Remove the pears from the refrigerator and transfer them to an 11- or 12-quart copper preserving pan or a wide nonreactive kettle, stirring well. Position a food mill over the storage container that held the pears and set aside.

Bring the pears to a boil over high heat, stirring every couple of minutes or so. Cook, stirring frequently with a heatproof rubber spatula, until the mixture starts to thicken and the pear pieces appear semi-translucent, 15 to 20 minutes. Remove from the heat and transfer one-third of the mixture to the food mill. Put as much fruit as possible through the mill, then scrape any solids that will not go through back into the jam mixture. Return the pureed fruit to the jam kettle, breaking up the chunks as you go. Place the jam over medium-high heat and continue to cook, stirring gently and constantly, until the jam has thickened and no longer appears watery, about 15 minutes more.

When the jam seems ready, test it for doneness. To test, carefully transfer a small representative half-spoonful of jam to one of your frozen spoons.

Replace the spoon in the freezer for 3 to 4 minutes, then remove and carefully feel the underside of the spoon. It should be neither warm nor cold; if still warm, return it to the freezer for a moment. Tilt the spoon vertically to see how quickly the jam runs; if it runs slowly, and if it has thickened to a gloppy consistency, it is done. If it runs very quickly or appears watery, cook it for another few minutes, stirring, and test again as needed. While you are waiting for the jam in the freezer to cool, skim off any white foam that appears on the surface of the jam in the pan.

When the cooking is completed, stir in the chestnut honey and several drops of vinegar to taste; its flavor should be mild. Place the sage into the mixture and let steep for 1 to 2 minutes off the heat. Stir and carefully taste the jam and either remove the sage or leave it in for another minute or two; its flavor should be subtle, but keep in mind that it will mellow slightly as the jam cools. Using tongs, discard the sage. Pour the jam into sterilized jars and process according to the manufacturer's instructions or as directed on page 42.

Approximate Yield: **ten to eleven 8-ounce jars** *Shelf Life:* **8 to 10 months**

PEAR-LEMON MARMALADE

The word for this marmalade is *lovely*: the warm flavor of pear enlivened by tart lemon, with just the faintest hint of spice. It makes a particularly delectable morning or teatime treat, especially with oatmeal or oat scones.

2 pounds 5 ounces very ripe pears, such as Warren or Bartlett

1¾ pounds seeded lemons (preferably Lisbon), halved crosswise,
each half quartered lengthwise and sliced medium-thin

3 pounds 10 ounces white cane sugar

1 to 2 extra lemons, to make 4 ounces strained freshly squeezed juice

1 (1½-inch) piece cinnamon stick (preferably Ceylon)

4 cloves

6 green cardamom pods, crushed lightly in a mortar to release their seeds

DAY 1

First, prepare the pear juice: Cut the pears into quarters or eighths, depending on their size. Place the pear pieces in a medium stainless-steel kettle and cover with enough cold water for the fruit to bob freely. Bring to a boil over high heat, then decrease the heat to a lively simmer. Cover and cook the fruit for 2 to 3 hours, or until the pears are very soft and the liquid has become syrupy. As the pears cook, stir them every 20 to 30 minutes or so, adding more water if necessary. The level of water should stay consistently high enough for the fruit to remain submerged as it cooks.

Strain the pear juice by pouring the hot fruit and liquid into a medium-fine-mesh strainer suspended over a heatproof storage container or nonreactive saucepan. Cover the entire setup well with plastic wrap and place in the refrigerator to drip overnight.

Meanwhile, prepare the sliced lemons: Place the slices in a wide stainless-steel kettle and cover amply with cold water. Bring to a boil over high heat,

then decrease the heat and simmer for 5 minutes. Drain, discarding the liquid. Return the lemon slices to the kettle and cover with 1 inch cold water. Bring to a boil over high heat, then decrease the heat to medium and cook, covered, at a lively simmer for 30 to 40 minutes, or until the fruit is very tender and the liquid has reduced significantly. Remove the pan from the heat, cover tightly, and let rest overnight at room temperature.

DAY 2

Place a saucer with five metal teaspoons in a flat place in your freezer for testing the marmalade later.

Remove the plastic wrap from the pears and their juice and discard the pears. Strain the juice well through a very fine mesh strainer to remove any lingering solids.

Place the sugar in an 11- or 12-quart copper preserving pan or a wide stainless-steel kettle. Gradually stir in the pear juice, fresh lemon juice, and cooked lemon slices and their liquid. Put the spices into a fine-mesh stainless-steel tea infuser with a firm latch and add it to the mixture, pressing down on it to be sure it is submerged.

Bring the mixture to a boil over high heat. Cook at a rapid boil over high heat until the setting point is reached; this will take a minimum of 30 minutes, but may take longer depending upon your individual stove and pan. Initially, the mixture will bubble gently for several minutes; then, as more moisture cooks out of it and its sugar concentration increases, it will begin foaming. Do not stir it at all during the initial bubbling; then, once it starts to foam, stir it gently every few minutes with a heatproof rubber spatula. As it gets close to being done, stir it slowly every minute or two to prevent burning. The marmalade is ready for testing when its color darkens slightly and its bubbles become very small.

To test the marmalade for doneness, remove it from the heat and carefully transfer a small representa-tive half-spoonful of marmalade to one of your fro-zen spoons. It should look shiny, with tiny bubbles throughout. Replace the spoon in the freezer for 3 to 4 minutes, then remove and carefully feel the underside of the spoon. It should be neither warm nor cold; if still warm, return it to the freezer for a moment. Tilt the spoon vertically to see whether the marmalade runs; if it does not run, and if its top layer has thickened to a jelly consistency, it is done. If it runs, cook it for another few minutes, stirring, and test again as needed.

When the marmalade has finished cooking, turn off the heat but do not stir. Remove the tea infuser and use a stainless-steel spoon to skim off any surface foam. Let the marmalade rest for 10 minutes off the heat, then fill 1 jar. Wait a few moments to see if the rinds begin floating to the top; if so, let the marma-lade rest for another 5 minutes. If not, quickly pour the marmalade into the remaining jars and process according to the manufacturer's instructions or as directed on page 42.

Approximate Yield: eight to nine 8-ounce jars   *Shelf Life:* 2 years

QUINCE MARMALADE

This beautiful marmalade, a velvety dark red jelly flecked with tiny shreds of quince, is an exceptionally elegant use for this ancient fruit. The technique for cooking the quince shreds comes from Deborah Madison's inspiring book *The Savory Way*. Butter and sheep's cheese are this marmalade's natural partners.

½ pound peeled and cored quinces

1 pound plus 2¼ pounds white cane sugar

5 pounds quinces, cut into eighths

3½ ounces strained freshly squeezed lemon juice

1 star anise (optional)

1 (½-inch) piece vanilla bean, split (optional)

1 to 2 ounces quince brandy or brandy

DAY 1

First, prepare the quince shreds: Using a sharp knife, slice the peeled quince very thinly, then cut it into small matchsticks. Combine the matchsticks with 1 pound of the sugar in a wide stainless-steel kettle. Add 2 inches of water. Bring the mixture to a boil over high heat, then partially cover and decrease the heat to a simmer. Cook, without stirring, until the liquid has turned a rosy-tawny color and the quince shreds are translucent, 2½ to 3 hours. While the mixture cooks, check it every 20 minutes or so; if it starts bubbling a lot or looking too syrupy, add a little water to thin it out. When the quince has finished cooking, cover it and let rest overnight at room temperature.

Meanwhile, prepare the quince juice: Place the quince eighths in a large stainless-steel kettle and fill with cold water to about 1 inch above the tops of the fruit. Bring to a boil over high heat, then decrease the heat to a simmer. Cover and cook the fruit for 2 to 2½ hours, or until the liquid has turned rosy and thickened to a slightly syrupy consistency. As the quinces cook, press down on them gently with a spoon every 30 minutes or so, adding a little more water if necessary. The water level should stay consistently high enough for the fruit to remain submerged as it cooks.

Strain the juice from the quince eighths by pouring the fruit into a medium-fine-mesh strainer suspended over a heatproof storage container or nonreactive saucepan. Cover the entire setup well with plastic wrap and place in the refrigerator to drip overnight.

DAY 2

Place a saucer with five metal teaspoons in a flat place in your freezer for testing the jam later.

Remove the quince eighths and their juice from the refrigerator and discard the fruit. Strain the juice well through a very fine-mesh strainer to remove any lingering solids.

In a large mixing bowl, combine the quince shreds and their liquid, cooked quince juice, remaining 2¼ pounds of sugar, lemon juice, star anise, and vanilla bean, if using, stirring well. Transfer the mixture to an 11- or 12-quart copper preserving pan or a wide nonreactive kettle.

Bring the mixture to a boil over high heat. Cook at a rapid boil until the setting point is reached; this will take a minimum of 25 minutes, but may take longer depending on your individual stove and pan. Initially, the mixture will bubble gently for several minutes; then, as more moisture cooks out of it and its sugar concentration increases, it will begin foaming. Do not stir it at all during the initial bubbling; then, once it starts to foam, stir it gently every few minutes with a heatproof rubber spatula. After several minutes of foaming, stir in the brandy. As the marmalade gets close to being done, stir it slowly every minute or two to prevent burning, decreasing the heat a tiny bit if necessary. The marmalade is ready for testing when its color darkens slightly and its bubbles become very small.

To test, carefully transfer a small representative half-spoonful of marmalade to one of your frozen spoons. Replace the spoon in the freezer for 3 to 4 minutes, then remove and carefully feel the underside of the spoon. It should be neither warm nor cold; if still warm, return it to the freezer for a moment. Nudge the marmalade gently with your finger; if it has formed a cohesive jelly, it is either done or nearly done. Tilt the spoon vertically to see whether the marmalade runs; if it does not run, and if it has thickened to a semisolid consistency, it is done. If it runs, cook it for another minute or two, stirring, and test again as needed.

Using a stainless-steel spoon, skim any remaining foam from the surface of the marmalade. Remove the vanilla bean and star anise. Pour immediately into sterilized jars and process according to the manufacturer's instructions or as directed on page 42.

Variations:

QUINCE MARMALADE WITH ROSE GERANIUM
The exceptional combination of peppery rose and perfumy quince makes an especially heady marmalade, delicious with butter and toast. Follow the recipe as directed. While the marmalade is coming to a boil, rinse 2 (8-inch) sprigs rose geranium under cold running water and pat them dry between two clean kitchen towels. When the marmalade has finished cooking, rub the rose geranium sprigs briefly between your fingers to release their oils, place them into the marmalade, and let them steep for a minute or two off the heat. Taste carefully and either remove the stalks or leave them in for another minute or two, keeping in mind that the rose geranium flavor will be slightly weaker once the marmalade has cooled. When the flavor is to your liking, discard the sprigs and process as directed

QUINCE MARMALADE WITH GINGER
Follow the previous recipe as directed, using only 1 ounce of brandy. Place 5 tablespoons chopped peeled fresh young ginger in a fine-mesh stainless-steel tea infuser with a firm latch and add it to the marmalade mixture for the final cooking. Just before you check the marmalade for doneness, stir in 1 ounce of ginger liqueur. The flavor of this version is quite subtle; if you prefer more bite, you may increase the quantity of fresh ginger. Remove the tea infuser and process as directed.

Approximate Yield: eleven to twelve 8-ounce jars *Shelf Life:* 1 year

QUINCE
& CANDIED GINGER JAM

In this method of preparation, perhaps more common in Europe and the Middle East than here, the quinces are chopped and cooked with sugar all on the same day, resulting in a deliciously rustic jam with an earthy and satisfying flavor. Candied ginger adds an extra-special spice to this scrumptious jam which, like all quince preserves, is particularly good with cheese.

1 pound 13 ounces plus 2 pounds peeled and cored quinces

2 pounds 5 ounces white cane sugar

3¾ ounces strained freshly squeezed lemon juice

5 ounces finely chopped candied ginger

2 ounces ginger liqueur

Place a saucer with five metal teaspoons in a flat place in your freezer for testing the jam later.

Chop 1 pound 13 ounces of the quince into pieces ¼ inch to ½ inch in diameter. Cut the remaining 2 pounds of quince into eighths. Place the small pieces and eighths into two separate nonreactive saucepans and add enough cold water to each pan to cover the fruit by 1 inch. Bring both pans to a boil, then decrease the heat to low, cover, and simmer for 2½ to 3 hours, or until the fruit has turned orangey-pink. Check the fruit every 20 minutes or so, adding a tiny bit more water if necessary; nearly all the liquid should evaporate by the end of cooking.

When the quinces have finished cooking, combine the cooked small pieces and their liquid in a large mixing bowl with the sugar, lemon juice, candied ginger, and ginger liqueur. Put the cooked quince eighths through a food mill or chinois, then add them to the rest of the fruit in the bowl. Transfer the mixture to an 11- or 12-quart copper preserving pan or a wide nonreactive kettle.

Bring the quince mixture to a boil over high heat, then decrease the heat slightly and cook, stirring frequently with a heatproof rubber spatula, until the jam has thickened and no longer appears watery, 30 to 40 minutes. Scrape the bottom of the pan often with your spatula, and decrease the heat gradually as more and more moisture cooks out of the jam. For the last 10 to 15 minutes of cooking, you will need to stir the jam slowly and steadily to keep it from scorching.

When the jam seems ready, test it for doneness. To test, carefully transfer a small representative half-spoonful of jam to one of your frozen spoons. Replace the spoon in the freezer for 3 to 4 minutes, then remove and carefully feel the underside of the spoon. It should be neither warm nor cold; if still warm, return it to the freezer for a moment. Tilt the spoon vertically to see how quickly the jam runs; if it runs slowly or not at all, and if it has thickened to a gloppy consistency, it is done. If it runs very quickly or appears watery, cook it for another few minutes, stirring, and test again as needed. While you are waiting for the jam in the freezer to cool, skim off any white foam that appears on the surface of the jam in the pan. Pour the jam into sterilized jars and process according to the manufacturer's instructions or as directed on page 42.

or as directed on page 42.

Variation:

QUINCE-CRANBERRY JAM

This jam is tarter in flavor and rosier in color. For this version, follow the recipe as directed. Omit the candied ginger and ginger liqueur and add 5 ounces fresh cranberries in their place.

Approximate Yield: five to six 8-ounce jars *Shelf Life:* 8 months

PARADISE MARMALADE

The term *paradise* refers to the classic combination of quince, apple, and cranberry, a typical inclusion in old American cookbooks. The three fruits are most frequently combined into a jelly, but I love to liven up this nostalgic preserve by adding shreds of quince. The perfect balance of pectin present in these fruits gives this marmalade an exquisitely soft jelly texture.

6 ounces peeled and cored quinces

3 pounds 11 ounces white cane sugar

1 pound 9 ounces crisp tart apples, quartered

1 pound 9 ounces whole quinces, cut into eighths

1 pound 6 ounces cranberries

10 ounces strained freshly squeezed lemon juice

1 to 2 ounces Calvados or quince brandy (optional)

DAY 1

First, prepare the quince shreds: Using a sharp knife, slice the peeled quince very thinly, then cut it into small matchsticks. Combine the shreds with the sugar in a wide stainless-steel kettle or sauté pan. Add 2 inches of water. Bring the mixture to a boil over high heat, then partially cover and decrease the heat to a simmer. Cook, without stirring, until the liquid has turned a rosy-tawny color and the quince shreds are translucent, 2½ to 3 hours. While the mixture cooks, check it every 20 minutes or so; if it starts bubbling a lot or looking too syrupy, add a little boiling water to thin it out. When the quince has finished cooking, cover it and let rest at room temperature overnight.

Meanwhile, prepare the mixed-fruit juice: Place the quartered apples, quince eighths, and cranberries in a medium stainless-steel kettle and add enough cold water for the fruit to bob freely. Bring to a boil over high heat, then decrease the heat to a lively simmer.

Cook the fruit, covered, for 1 hour or longer, until the apples are disintegrating and the liquid has thickened to a slightly syrupy consistency. As the fruit cooks, stir it gently every 20 minutes or so, adding a little more water if necessary. The water level should stay consistently high enough for the fruit to remain submerged as it cooks.

Strain the apple-quince-cranberry juice by pouring the fruit into a medium-fine-mesh strainer suspended over a heatproof storage container or nonreactive saucepan. Cover the entire setup well with plastic wrap and place in the refrigerator to drip overnight.

DAY 2

Place a saucer with five metal teaspoons in a flat place in your freezer for testing the marmalade later.

Remove the mixed fruit and its juice from the refrigerator and discard the fruit. Strain the juice well through a very fine-mesh strainer to remove any lingering solids.

In a large mixing bowl, combine the cooked juice with the quince shreds and their liquid. Stir in the lemon juice and Calvados. Transfer the mixture to an 11- or 12-quart copper preserving pan or a wide nonreactive kettle.

Bring the mixture to a boil over high heat and boil vigorously, skimming off any surface scum with a stainless-steel spoon. Continue to boil, stirring occasionally, until the bubbles become smaller, the jelly has acquired a glossier look, and the color has darkened slightly. Depending upon how viscous your initial juice was, this could take anywhere from 25 minutes to 1 hour. At this point, test the marmalade for doneness.

To test, carefully transfer a small representative half-spoonful of marmalade to one of your frozen spoons. Replace the spoon in the freezer for 3 to 4 minutes, then remove and carefully feel the underside of the spoon. It should be neither warm nor cold; if still warm, return it to the freezer for a moment. Nudge the marmalade gently with your finger; if it has formed a cohesive jelly, it is either done or nearly done. Tilt the spoon vertically to see whether the marmalade runs; if it does not run, and if it has thickened to a semisolid consistency, it is done. If it runs, cook it for another minute or two, stirring, and test again as needed.

Using a stainless-steel spoon, skim any remaining foam from the surface of the marmalade. Pour immediately into sterilized jars and process according to the manufacturer's instructions or as directed on page 42.

Approximate Yield: ten to eleven 8-ounce jars *Shelf Life:* 1 year

CRANBERRY-POMEGRANATE MARMALADE

Perhaps more than any other preserve, this marmalade just screams "holiday!" Year after year, it wins raves from lovers of both sweet and bitter flavors. This extremely festive marmalade is not only delicious alongside the Thanksgiving turkey; it is perfect for breakfast as well.

4½ pounds white cane sugar

1⅛ ounces powdered apple pectin

6 cups strained freshly squeezed pomegranate juice

8 ounces strained freshly squeezed lemon juice

1½ pounds cranberries

Place a saucer with five metal teaspoons in a flat place in your freezer for testing the marmalade later.

In a large mixing bowl, combine the sugar and pectin and whisk well to evenly distribute the pectin granules throughout the sugar. Place the pomegranate juice in a large bowl and slowly pour the sugar-pectin mixture over the juice, stirring as you pour to prevent the pectin from clumping. Stir in the cranberries and the lemon juice. Taste the marmalade mixture and slowly add more lemon juice if necessary. You should be able to taste the lemon juice, but it should not be overpowering. Keep adding lemon juice just until you are able to detect its tartness in the mixture. Add about 1 inch of cold water, stirring well. Transfer the mixture to an 11- or 12-quart copper preserving pan or a wide nonreactive kettle.

Bring the mixture to a boil over high heat and boil vigorously, skimming off any surface scum with a stainless-steel spoon. Continue to boil, stirring occasionally, until the bubbles become smaller, the marmalade has acquired a glossier look, and the color has darkened slightly, 40 to 60 minutes. At this point, test the marmalade for doneness.

To test, carefully transfer a small representative half-spoonful of marmalade to one of your frozen spoons. Replace the spoon in the freezer for 3 to 4 minutes, then remove and carefully feel the underside of the spoon. It should be neither warm nor cold; if still warm, return it to the freezer for a moment. Nudge the marmalade gently with your finger; if it has formed a cohesive jelly, it is either done or nearly done. Tilt the spoon vertically to see whether the marmalade runs; if it does not run, and if it has thickened to a semisolid consistency, it is done. If it runs, cook it for another minute or two, stirring, and test again as needed.

Using a stainless-steel spoon, skim any remaining foam from the surface of the marmalade. Let the marmalade rest off the heat for 5 to 10 minutes, stirring occasionally. As soon as the marmalade has thickened enough for the cranberries to remain submerged when you press down on them, do a jar test by filling 1 jar halfway with marmalade. Wait a few minutes to see if the berries float to the top or stay submerged. If they float, wait a few minutes more and try again. As soon as the marmalade has thickened enough for the cranberries to stay submerged, quickly pour the marmalade into sterilized jars and process according to the manufacturer's instructions or as directed on page 42.

Variation:
CRANBERRY-POMEGRANATE MARMALADE WITH ROSE GERANIUM

This is a decidedly floral breakfast preserve; the rose geranium's fragrance melds perfectly with the berries and pomegranates. Follow the recipe as directed. While the marmalade is coming to a boil, rinse 2 (8-inch) rose geranium sprigs under cold running water and pat them dry between two clean kitchen towels. When the marmalade has finished cooking, rub the rose geranium sprigs briefly between your fingers to release their oils, place them into the marmalade, and let them steep for a minute or two off the heat. Taste carefully and either remove the sprigs or leave them in another moment, keeping in mind that the rose geranium flavor will be slightly milder once the marmalade has cooled. When the flavor is to your liking, discard the sprigs. Pour the marmalade into sterilized jars and process as directed.

Approximate Yield: ten to eleven 8-ounce jars *Shelf Life:* 1 year

CITRON SHRED

This exquisitely fine-textured marmalade has a delicate lemony flavor with a strong hint of citronella. It makes an intriguing dessert glaze, as well as an elegant accompaniment to morning biscuits and butter.

2½ to 3 pounds very fresh Etrog citrons
1 pound 14 ounces white cane sugar
1 ounce strained freshly squeezed lemon juice

DAY 1

Using a paring knife, carefully cut a ³⁄₁₆-inch layer of rind from the citrons in long strips until you have enough to make ½ pound of rinds. Slice the rinds into very fine long shreds, place them into a small nonreactive saucepan, and cover amply with cold water. Cover tightly and let rest overnight at room temperature.

Meanwhile, cut enough of the remaining citron into ½-inch cubes to make 2 pounds of cubes. Place the cubes in a medium nonreactive saucepan. Add enough cold water for the fruit to bob freely. Cover tightly and let rest overnight at room temperature.

DAY 2

Drain the citron shreds and rinse them well under cold running water. Return them to their saucepan and cover amply with cold water. Bring to a boil over high heat, then decrease the heat and simmer for 8 minutes. Drain, discarding the liquid, and rinse the citron shreds well under cold water. Repeat this procedure twice, then taste a shred; if necessary, repeat the blanching procedure one last time to remove any lingering bitterness. Drain the citron shreds, discarding the liquid, and place them in a large heatproof storage container or nonreactive saucepan. Suspend a fine-mesh strainer over the shreds and set aside for later.

Meanwhile, prepare the citron juice: Bring the pan with the citron cubes to a boil over high heat, then decrease the heat to medium. Cook the fruit at a lively simmer, covered, for 2 hours, or until the cubes are very soft and the liquid has become slightly syrupy. As the cubes cook, press down on them gently with a spoon every 30 minutes or so, adding a little more water if necessary. The water level should stay consistently high enough for the fruit to remain submerged as it cooks.

When the citron cubes have finished cooking, strain their juice by pouring the hot fruit and liquid into the strainer suspended over the shreds. Cover the entire setup well with plastic wrap and let drip overnight at room temperature.

DAY 3

Place a saucer with five metal teaspoons in a flat place in your freezer for testing the marmalade later. Remove the plastic wrap from the citron cubes and discard the cubes.

In a large mixing bowl, combine the sugar, the cooked citron shreds and their liquid, from the citron cubes, and the lemon juice. Transfer the mixture to an 11- or 12-quart copper preserving pan or a wide stainless-steel kettle.

Bring the mixture to a boil over high heat. Cook at a rapid boil until the setting point is reached; this will take a minimum of 15 minutes, but may take longer depending on your individual stove and pan. Initially, the mixture will bubble gently; then, as more moisture cooks out of it and its sugar concentration increases, it will begin foaming. Do not stir it at all during the initial bubbling; then, once it starts to foam, stir it gently every few minutes with a heatproof rubber spatula. As it gets close to being done, stir it slowly every minute or two to prevent burning, decreasing the heat a tiny bit if necessary. The marmalade is ready for testing when its color darkens slightly and its bubbles become very small.

To test the marmalade for doneness, remove it from the heat and carefully transfer a small representative half-spoonful of marmalade to one of your frozen spoons. It should look shiny, with tiny bubbles throughout. Replace the spoon in the freezer for 3 to 4 minutes, then remove and carefully feel the underside of the spoon. It should be neither warm nor cold; if still warm, return it to the freezer for a moment. Tilt the spoon vertically to see whether the marmalade runs; if it does not run, and if its top layer has thickened to a jelly consistency, it is done. If it runs, cook it for another few minutes, stirring, and test again as needed.

When the marmalade has finished cooking, turn off the heat but do not stir. Using a stainless-steel spoon, skim off any surface foam and discard. Pour the marmalade into sterilized jars and process according to the manufacturer's instructions or as directed on page 42.

Approximate Yield: four 8-ounce jars *Shelf Life:* 2 years

TWO NAVEL ORANGE MARMALADES

Because of their natural sweetness, navel oranges are best combined with a tarter fruit; in these next two recipes, the tarter fruits are cranberries and lemons. In the first recipe, cranberries lend their pretty red color and slightly bitter flavor to the oranges; in the second, the bitterness of the lemons creates a subtle backdrop for the sweetness of the oranges. Both are best enjoyed for breakfast with some hearty toast. They also may be used on sandwiches or as a glaze for meats.

CRANBERRY-ORANGE MARMALADE

3 pounds navel oranges, halved crosswise,
each half cut lengthwise into quarters and sliced crosswise medium-thin
2¼ pounds cranberries
4 pounds white cane sugar
4 ounces strained freshly squeezed lemon juice
2 ounces gold rum (optional)

DAY 1

Place the sliced oranges in a nonreactive sauce-pan with water to reach 1 inch above the tops of the fruit. Cover tightly and let rest overnight at room temperature.

DAY 2

Bring the pan with the orange slices to a boil over high heat, then decrease the heat to medium and cook, covered, at a lively simmer for 30 to 40 minutes, or until the fruit is very tender As the fruit cooks, stir it gently every 15 minutes or so, adding a little more water if necessary. The water level should stay consistently high enough for the fruit to remain submerged as it cooks. Remove the pan from the heat, cover tightly, and let rest overnight at room temperature.

Meanwhile, prepare the cranberry juice: Place the cranberries in a medium stainless-steel kettle and fill with water to about 1 inch above the tops of the berries. Bring to a boil over high heat, then decrease the heat to a lively simmer. Simmer the fruit, covered, for 1 to 2 hours, or until the liquid has thickened to a slightly syrupy consistency. Strain the juice by pouring the hot fruit and liquid through a medium-fine-mesh strainer suspended over a heatproof storage container or nonreactive saucepan. Cover the entire setup well with plastic wrap and let drip overnight at room temperature.

DAY 3

Place a saucer with five metal teaspoons in a flat place in your freezer for testing the jam later.

Remove the plastic wrap from the cranberries and their juice and discard the berries. Strain the juice well through a very fine-mesh strainer to remove any lingering solids.

In a large mixing bowl, combine the sugar, cooked cranberry juice, lemon juice, and cooked orange slices and their liquid, stirring well. Transfer the mixture to an 11- or 12-quart copper preserving pan or a wide nonreactive kettle.

Bring the mixture to a boil over high heat. Cook at a rapid boil until the setting point is reached; this will take a minimum of 30 minutes, but may take longer depending on your individual stove and pan. Initially, the mixture will bubble gently for several minutes; then, as more moisture cooks out of it and its sugar concentration increases, it will begin foaming. Do not stir it at all during the initial bubbling; then, once it starts to foam, stir it gently every few minutes with a heatproof rubber spatula. As it gets close to being done, stir it slowly every minute or two to prevent burning, decreasing the heat a tiny bit if necessary. When nearly done, stir in the rum, if using. The marmalade is ready for testing when its color darkens slightly and its bubbles become very small.

To test the marmalade for doneness, remove it from the heat and carefully transfer a small representative half-spoonful to one of your frozen spoons. It should look shiny, with tiny bubbles throughout. Replace the spoon in the freezer for 3 to 4 minutes, then remove and carefully feel the underside of the spoon. It should be neither warm nor cold; if still warm, return it to the freezer for a moment. Tilt the spoon vertically to see whether the marmalade runs; if it does not run, and if its top layer has thickened to a jelly consistency, it is done. If it runs, cook it for another few minutes, stirring, and test again as needed.

When the marmalade has finished cooking, turn off the heat but do not stir. Using a stainless-steel spoon, skim off any surface foam and discard. Pour the marmalade into sterilized jars and process according to the manufacturer's instructions or as directed on page 42.

Approximate Yield: ten to eleven 8-ounce jars   *Shelf Life:* 2 years

NAVEL ORANGE MARMALADE

2 pounds lemons (preferably Lisbon), cut into eighths
2 pounds navel oranges, halved crosswise,
each half cut lengthwise into quarters and sliced crosswise medium-thin
3½ pounds white cane sugar
1 to 2 extra lemons, to make 3 ounces strained freshly squeezed juice

DAY 1

Place the lemon eighths in a nonreactive saucepan where they will fit snugly in a single layer. Add enough cold water for the fruit to bob freely. Cover tightly and let rest overnight at room temperature.

In a separate nonreactive saucepan, place the sliced oranges with water to reach 1 inch above the tops. Cover tightly and let rest overnight at room temperature.

DAY 2

Prepare the cooked lemon juice: Bring the pan with the lemon eighths to a boil over high heat, then decrease the heat to medium. Cook the fruit at a lively simmer, covered, for 2 to 3 hours, or until the lemons are very soft and the liquid has become slightly syrupy. As the lemons cook, press down on them gently with a spoon every 30 minutes or so, adding a little more water if necessary. The water level should stay consistently high enough for the fruit to remain submerged as it cooks.

When the lemons are finished cooking, strain their juice by pouring the hot fruit and liquid into a medium strainer or colander suspended over a heatproof storage container or nonreactive saucepan. Cover the entire setup well with plastic wrap and let drip overnight at room temperature.

Meanwhile, prepare the orange slices: Bring the pan with them to a boil over high heat, then decrease the heat to medium and cook, covered, at a lively

simmer for 30 to 40 minutes, or until the fruit is very tender. If necessary, add a little more water during the cooking; the fruit should remain submerged throughout the cooking process. When the orange slices have finished cooking, remove the pan from the heat, cover tightly, and let rest overnight at room temperature.

DAY 3

Place a saucer with five metal teaspoons in a flat place in your freezer for testing the marmalade later.

Remove the plastic wrap from the lemon eighths and their juice and discard the lemons. Strain the juice through a very fine mesh strainer to remove any lingering solids.

In a large mixing bowl, combine the sugar, cooked lemon juice, fresh lemon juice, and cooked orange slices and their liquid, stirring well. Transfer the mixture to an 11- or 12-quart copper preserving pan or a wide nonreactive kettle.

Bring the mixture to a boil over high heat. Cook at a rapid boil until the setting point is reached; this will take a minimum of 30 minutes, but may take longer depending upon your individual stove and pan. Initially, the mixture will bubble gently for several minutes; then, as more moisture cooks out of it and its sugar concentration increases, it will begin foaming. Do not stir it at all during the initial bubbling; then, once it starts to foam, stir it gently every few minutes with a heatproof rubber spatula. As it gets close to being done, stir it slowly every minute or two to prevent burning, decreasing the heat a tiny bit if necessary. The marmalade is ready for testing when its color darkens slightly and its bubbles become very small.

To test the marmalade for doneness, remove it from the heat and carefully transfer a small representative half-spoonful of marmalade to one of your frozen spoons. It should look shiny, with tiny bubbles throughout. Replace the spoon in the freezer for 3 to 4 minutes, then remove and carefully feel the underside of the spoon. It should be neither warm nor cold; if still warm, return it to the freezer for a moment. Tilt the spoon vertically to see whether the marmalade runs; if it does not run, and if its top layer has thickened to a jelly consistency, it is done. If it runs, cook it for another few minutes, stirring, and test again as needed.

When the marmalade has finished cooking, turn off the heat but do not stir. Using a stainless-steel spoon, skim off any surface foam and discard. Pour the marmalade into sterilized jars and process according to the manufacturer's instructions or as directed on page 42.

Variation:

ORANGE-VANILLA DREAM MARMALADE
The idea for this version came from a 1950s-inspired cocktail I once tasted: cream, orange, lemon, and vanilla vodka. For this nostalgic marmalade, add a small splash of vanilla vodka to the mixture after it has been bubbling for several minutes and is nearly finished cooking. Follow the rest of the recipe as directed.

Approximate Yield: nine to ten 8-ounce jars *Shelf Life:* 2 years

CANDIED ORANGE PEEL

Candying citrus peel is a similar process to making marmalade. Though orange is perhaps the most classic choice, any citrus peel may be preserved in this way; think of this recipe as a base from which to experiment. For stronger rinds, such as bergamot, you may need to blanch the fruit more than twice to remove excess bitterness; at the other end of the spectrum, the softer rinds of Meyer lemons tend to cook through quite quickly. Chopped candied peel is a fabulous addition to jams and conserves, such as Black Fig & Candied Citrus Jam (page 228).

4 sweet oranges, such as navel or Valencia

4½ cups white cane sugar, plus more for dredging

2 cups water

Halve each orange crosswise and juice it, saving the juice for another use. Place the orange halves in a medium nonreactive saucepan and cover amply with cold water. Bring to a boil over high heat. Reduce the heat to a lively simmer and cook for 10 minutes. Drain, discarding the water. Repeat this process once or twice more, depending on the thickness and bitterness of the rinds.

Return the orange halves to the saucepan and cover them with cold water. Place the pan over high heat and bring it to a boil. Turn the heat down to a lively simmer and cook, partially covered, until the orange halves are tender, 30 to 60 minutes. Drain the halves.

When the oranges are cool enough to handle, take each half and, cradling it in one hand, use a soup spoon to gently scrape its interior of excess pith and fibers. Repeat with the rest of the halves, going around each one two or three times until its interior is smooth and its rind is a uniform thickness. There should be a thin layer of white pith still attached to the rind when you are finished.

Slice each scraped orange half into ¼-inch strips and place the strips into your saucepan. Add the sugar and water; the fruit should be submerged. Bring the pan to a boil over high heat, then reduce the heat to a gentle simmer. Cook, without stirring, until the undersides of the rinds appear semitranslucent and the liquid is syrupy and forms a swell of foaming bubbles, approximately 1 hour. Turn off the heat and let the rinds and syrup cool for 30 minutes. Using a slotted spoon, remove the rinds to a wire cooling rack positioned over a tray or cookie sheet. As soon as the rinds are cool enough to handle, carefully separate them and spread them evenly over the rack.

Leave the rinds until dry to the touch, 1 to 2 days. Toss them in sugar and store in an airtight container.

Variation:
CANDIED BUDDHA'S HAND
The exquisitely flavored rind of the Buddha's Hand citron is an indispensable ingredient for Brandied Cherry Conserve (page 128) and is also delicious eaten out of hand. To make the candied citron, take one Buddha's Hand and cut it into ½-inch cubes,

discarding the small juicy portion at the center of the fruit (some Buddha's Hands have this portion, others do not). Place the cubes into a large saucepan. Add cold water to cover, bring the mixture to a simmer, and cook just until the citron is translucent, 30 to 40 minutes. Drain the citron well and return it to the saucepan. Add sugar and water to the citron in the ratio of 2¼ cups sugar to every cup of water until the fruit is well-submerged. Continue with the rest of the recipe as directed.

Approximate Yield: ¾ pound   *Shelf Life:* 6 to 12 months

part III

FRUITS FOR PRESERVING

Perhaps more than any other part of preserving, fruit inspires me most. The labor required to work with fruit, the beauty of each fruit and its individual personality, the strong connection to the land gained by working with fruit—each of these stands as a clarion call to the kitchen, a vital reason to make preserves. Eating a fruit out of hand may be a memorable, even life-altering, experience; we all have memories of fruit or fruit picking tucked away in our minds. But the intimacy gained by many years of cooking with fruit, of bending it to one's will in the preserving kitchen, is different.

Beyond the delight of savoring a luscious plum or pear out of hand lies an entire world of experience and possibility. Rarely when eating a fruit do we envision anything beyond that delicious moment; rarely do we think about the fruit's properties, about its possibilities. Thinking about how a fruit works, about how it acts when cooked, about how it will taste once it has been simmered, sliced, peeled, or combined with another fruit: these are the challenges and joys confronting the jam maker. From raw ingredients may be wrought something magical and transformative, something into which you have put part of yourself.

This section describes both individual raw fruits and the possibilities and quirks of preserving them. Each fruit presents its own challenges and, along with those, its beauty.

chapter 7

THE FRUITS

APPLE *Season: Mid-August Through December*

Perhaps more than any other fruit, apples have come perilously close to being ruined by large-scale commercial production. One hundred years ago, there were countless different cultivated apple varieties, and certain states and regions were renowned for their delicious heirlooms. Industrial production and the internationalization of the apple trade all but erased that; but now, a small group of dedicated farmers is struggling to preserve the precious varieties of the past. Heirloom varieties, such as the Gravenstein and Pink Pearl, are better known today than they were twenty years ago, and delicious apples have again become easier to find.

Apples are one of nature's great fall treats. A perfect apple should be crisp, without a trace of mealiness. It should be *flavorful*, with a perfect tart-sweet balance. Above all, it should be in season and organically grown; nothing is worse than an old apple coated in resin to prolong its shelf life. There are many excellent varieties of apple; when choosing one, by far your most important consideration should be freshness. Taste before buying, if possible. One of my favorite things at a farmers' market in early fall is to sample all the different and delicious apples: Each has its own distinct personality. When you find an apple grower you like, keep him in the back of your mind for the following year.

Apples are naturally well suited to preserving in one important respect: They contain a high amount of pectin. However, apples break down much more easily and quickly than either pears or quinces, their closest cousins. Thus, they are best either made into apple jelly or butter or paired with other fruits to make jam. Traditional apple jellies are often flavored, either with herbs (such as rose geranium) or spices. Because of their high pectin content, apples also often form the backbone of jellies featuring other fruits, such as elderberries or Concord grapes. A high-pectin "extract" of apple skins and cores is also sometimes made, and this may be added to fruits where pectin is lacking. Crabapples, which are much smaller and tarter than normal apples, are particularly high in pectin and are most often used for jelly.

Some of the apple recipes in this book specify which variety to use; others do not. Either way, the most important things to keep in mind are flavor, texture, and personal preference. As long as the apples are of high quality, varieties may always be substituted if necessary.

APRICOT *Season: May Through July*

Nothing is better than a perfectly ripe apricot straight off the tree. The Royal Blenheim, which is widely recognized as the best domestically grown apricot, is the classic heirloom variety of California: Lushly succulent and sweet, it has an unforgettable almondy fragrance. However, this splendid fruit is hard to come by, even in California. Because of its fragility, small size, and greenish color (which is considered to be less appealing to consumers), it is no longer grown by the largest farms and has been all but shut out of the mainstream market. If you are lucky enough to live in an area where this luscious apricot is found, please try it! It makes a truly spectacular jam.

Only perfectly ripe apricots should be used for jam. Apricots should be picked ripe or nearly ripe; they may be left to ripen for a few days at room temperature if necessary (spread them out on a sheet pan so they are not touching). Apricots will also ripen in the refrigerator, although it will take more time and their texture may suffer. There are numerous excellent apricot varieties. When assessing apricots, always go by taste more than appearance, and be sure to taste them before you buy them.

When making apricot jam, cut the apricots into large pieces (halves are usually best) to protect their structural integrity; if you cut them into smaller pieces, they will dissolve completely when heated. Always cook apricot jam in tiny batches to help preserve the naturally bright, buttery flavor of the fruit.

The kernels found inside apricot pits are used to make amaretti cookies, crème de noyaux liqueur, and almond extract; they have a pronounced bitter almond flavor and are an essential component of great apricot jam. Adding a few kernels to your jam pot brings out the apricot flavor perfectly.

APRIUM, PLUMCOT & PLUOT *Season: Late Spring Through Early Fall*
Apriums, plumcots, and Pluots are all plum-apricot hybrids. Apriums are 75 percent apricot and 25 percent plum. Plumcots are half apricot, half plum. Pluots are 25 percent apricot and 75 percent plum. Each has its own distinctive flavor and properties, and each makes a delicious jam.

Apriums are among the first stone fruits of early summer. They both taste and look similar to apricots, but they tend to be larger, darker in color, and richer and less buttery in flavor. Apriums acquire a gorgeous bright orange color when cooked. The best and most widely available variety is the **Honey Rich**, which ripens in early to mid-May.

Apriums combine exceptionally well with numerous other flavors. Because they are firmer in texture than their apricot relatives, it is sometimes preferable to cut them into quarters rather than halves; they may also be partially pureed prior to the final cooking. Like most other stone fruits, Apriums require only a minimum of sugar to taste their best. Also, like those of apricots, Aprium kernels make a lovely addition to Aprium jam.

Plumcots, of which **Flavorella** is the most common variety, are very tart and almost like greengages in their flavor. Flavorella plumcots are round, pale yellow–orange fruits. Their translucent skin resembles something between that of an apricot and a plum. Plumcot flesh is similar to plum flesh. Plumcots make an exceedingly tart summer jam, perfect for marmalade lovers and those who love mouth-puckering flavors.

Pluots are the most widely known of these hybrids and come in numerous varieties. The most famous are the **Flavor King** and the **Dapple Dandy**. The Flavor King is the most flavorful Pluot of all; the Dapple Dandy is famous primarily for its pretty speckled appearance. The Flavor King is a hybrid of an apricot and a Santa Rosa plum, which helps explain its delicious flavor. Pluots resemble plums in both texture and appearance, but their flavor is distinct.

Pluots are delicious on their own, but they also combine well with other fruits and flavors, such as strawberries, rose, and orange flower. Like plums, they are best macerated with sugar and lemon for one or more days in the refrigerator before being cooked. The best Pluots appear in the second half of the summer, and their season stretches into autumn. In addition to Flavor King, there are numerous other varieties, some of which are quite delicious; these include **Flavor Rosa** and **Flavor Grenade**.

BERGAMOT *Season: January and February*

Bergamot is a type of sour orange primarily known for lending Earl Grey tea its unique fragrance. The bergamot has no relation to bergamot mint, an old-fashioned garden herb. Rarely found in stores, bergamot is grown commercially almost exclusively in Calabria, Italy, but is also produced in small quantities in California. The fruit resembles a very firm, fine-textured yellow orange. Its strong flavor is sometimes likened to that of lavender. Bergamot juice is remarkably similar to lemon juice; most of a bergamot's distinctive fragrance is found in its skin.

Bergamot is exceptionally difficult to work with, which may explain why products (other than tea) made with it are so hard to come by. Bergamots often contain very small seeds scattered throughout the fruit. The flavor of straight bergamot is completely overpowering and unpalatable. Thus, to be used alone, the fruit must be sliced thinly and blanched multiple times to temper its flavor.

Bergamot Marmalade (page 50) has turned out to be one of Blue Chair Fruit's most popular marmalades; its perfect tart-sweet balance and unique flavor have made it a customer favorite. However, bergamot need not necessarily be the main feature; when used sparingly, its versatile flavor complements other citrus fruits exceptionally well.

BLACKBERRY *Season: May Through October*

Blackberries are among the best jam fruits, being both vividly flavored and relatively high in pectin. Wild blackberries have a different flavor from cultivated varieties; they are also smaller, with fewer druplets per berry, and they have a more fragile texture. Not all blackberries found growing wild are necessarily what we would call "wild" blackberries; as the blackberry plant is a very vigorous one, huge patches exist that likely originated with a small domestic seedling planted in a backyard or along a fence.

Blackberries differ from raspberries not by color (there are black raspberries!), but rather by physical structure: When you pick a blackberry, it retains its white core, whereas when you pick a raspberry, the core remains on the plant.

Blackberries vary widely in quality, and nonorganic berries are often heavily sprayed. Once you acquire a taste for blackberries, the pesticide on conventionally grown berries becomes unbearable. Cooking brings out the flavor of these chemicals; therefore, it is essential to use only the best organic or wild blackberries for preserving.

Blackberry season extends from late spring to early autumn, and each variety ripens at a different time. There are hundreds, perhaps even thousands, of blackberry varieties; here are a few of the most well known.

One of the best early varieties is the delicious olallieberry (a loganberry-youngberry cross), which appears in very late May or early June. Olallieberries are shiny, with a firm texture and smallish druplets, and they make a truly stellar jam. Another excellent early-season variety is Siskiou. In mid- to late June, marionberries appear; these large berries are prized up and down the West Coast for their rich flavor. In July, numerous other varieties come out. Then, in August, the small wild blackberries appear.

Blackberries are best cooked the same day they are picked, as they tend to lose their perfume under refrigeration. Tiny batches are best, and the berries should be cooked as briefly as possible to keep their vibrant flavor. Although blackberries combine well with numerous herbs, including lemon balm, lemon verbena, and rose geranium, they are equally delicious on their own. Because of their firm structures, blackberries should usually be cooked all at once rather than in stages; wild blackberries, which are more fragile, are the exception. Blackberries also make delicious jelly, either combined with apples or Concord grapes or on their own.

BLUEBERRY *Season: Summer*
Like apricots and Seville oranges, blueberries hold a special place in the hearts of many. In fact, for some, nothing can beat a really good blueberry jam. Blueberry jam is among the easiest jams to make; as with other berries, small batches are key. Huckleberries, the cousins of blueberries, also make fantastic jam, though in many parts of the country they are difficult to find fresh.

Unlike many other fruits, blueberries do not lend themselves to mixing. Though they may be enhanced with small flavor additions, they are best on their own, without the addition of a companion fruit. When cooked, the texture of blueberries is somewhat grainy. Blueberries lack acid; thus, a large amount of lemon juice, or lemon juice and vinegar, must be used to temper their sweetness. Traditionally, blueberry jams in the United States were heavily spiced and omitted lemon juice entirely in favor of cider vinegar. Blueberry butters, also heavily spiced, were common at one time as well. However, blueberry jams are at their best when the spice is subtle; the flavor of the berries should always be dominant.

When selecting blueberries, always look for very firm, smooth specimens. There are numerous different blueberry varieties, some wild, some not. For jam, smaller berries are generally best, as they contain a higher proportion of skin to flesh; the majority of the flavor resides in the skin. Blueberries keep well under refrigeration.

BOYSENBERRY & TAYBERRY *Season: May and June*

Boysenberries and tayberries unite the best qualities of both raspberries and blackberries into a superb flavor bomb of brightness, sweetness, and acidity. The boysenberry, a loganberry-raspberry-blackberry hybrid, is largish, with a blackish magenta color and matte appearance. Boysenberries ripen at the very end of May and beginning of June, and, though their season is quite short, it is best to wait until a week or so after they first appear to get the best fruit.

The tayberry, a relatively little-known black raspberry–loganberry cross, makes perhaps the best jam of any berry. The combination of its richness, vibrance, and bright color and flavor is unbeatable. Tayberry jam is truly dazzling.

When choosing boysenberries or tayberries, always look for firm specimens. The fruit should melt in your mouth and have a vivid flavor. Never use fruit that looks pale in color or has white "shoulders"" at the stem end; such fruit is certain to have been picked before it was fully ripe.

Like blackberries, boysenberries and tayberries should be cooked extremely briefly and in tiny batches. Because their texture is slightly more fragile than that of cultivated blackberries, it is best to cook them in two stages to preserve as much of the fruit's original integrity as possible. Tayberries need no enhancement; Boysenberries, though delicious on their own, combine particularly well with lemon verbena.

CHERRY *Season: Early Summer to Midsummer*

Cherries are stone fruits, in the same family as almonds, peaches, apricots, plums, and nectarines. Botanically speaking, plums are their closest relatives. Cherries are the densest stone fruits and tend to hold their shape when heated.

There are two main types of cherries: sweet and sour (the latter are sometimes called "pie" cherries). Sweet cherries may be either red or white. Early summer sweet varieties include the red Burlat, Brooks, and Chelan. Midsummer favorites include the red Bing and the white Rainier. Sour cherries, the most famous of which are the red Montmorency and the black Morello, appear at the end of June. The cherry season for many varieties is short, lasting only a few precious weeks at most.

Each cherry variety is distinct in color (of skin, flesh, and juice), flavor, texture, sweetness, acidity, and pectin content. Sour cherries have a different flavor than sweet cherries, and they are used almost solely for cooking.

Like other stone fruits, sweet cherries generally become less tart and more richly flavored as the summer progresses. The early-season Burlat, for example, is deliciously fresh tasting and has pale juice, while the later Bing oozes with dark red juice and a deeper flavor. A similar phenomenon may be observed with peaches, nectarines, and plums.

As with other stone fruits, white cherries tend to have a slightly less pungent flavor than their more brightly colored counterparts. White cherries may also be fleshier than red cherries, and they tend to hold their shape better when cooked. Some white varieties, such as Royal Ann, have a stronger flavor than others, such as Rainier. When selecting white cherries, the complexity of flavor is more important than sweetness.

When choosing cherries, always look for firm fruit, and try to taste the fruit prior to purchase. Their flavor may vary considerably from grower to grower; buying the most vividly flavored cherries you can find is essential. Cherries are most flavorful when they have received only a minimum of water; however, some farmers over-water them to swell them and increase their weight. Cherries should always have their stems attached when you buy them.

Cherry jam is among the most labor-intensive to make, but it is also among the most rewarding. Not merely must the cherries be pitted: For some recipes, the pits should also be cracked to expose the tiny almond-like kernel inside. Once cherry jam is made, it must be painstakingly skimmed of surface foam to ensure a perfectly clear preserve. The complex flavor and stunning color of cherry jam reward this hard work; cherry jam is a showstopper. Cherries are also very useful as an enhancement for other fruits, including plums and rhubarb, lending a special depth to these other flavors.

CITRON *Season: Fall and Winter (depending on the variety)*

Citrons are among the least known citrus fruits in the United States, though they are widely used in Italy and are the most ancient cultivated citrus fruit. As with all citrus, there are many varieties of citron; the most common in this country are the Etrog and the Buddha's Hand. Citrons are characterized by their almost complete lack of flesh and seeds: Unlike other citrus fruits, they are composed nearly entirely of pith and rind. Each variety of citron has its own distinct aroma. Because of their physical construction, citrons are a challenge, with only certain specific uses suited to their unusual characteristics.

Etrog citrons resemble large ridged lemons and have an overwhelmingly strong citronella-like aroma. Their flavor is almost soap-like, and they must be tempered by multiple blanchings in order to be palatable enough to eat. To use Etrogs in marmalade, it is best to cut them into thin matchsticks to curb their intensity. Etrog marmalade at its best is one of the most exquisite of all preserves: a golden jelly with filaments of citron swirling throughout. Its flavor is closest to that of lemon marmalade, but with a strong overtone of citronella.

Buddha's Hand citrons are the strangest looking citrus fruits in existence; they are large yellow fruits, deeply ridged, with tentacle-like "fingers" reaching away from the stem end. They have a gorgeously delicate flavor completely unlike that of Etrogs. For preserving, they are best candied and then integrated into other preserves rather than being made into a marmalade themselves; the gentleness of their flavor does not translate well into being the main feature.

When purchasing citrons, always be sure they are very fresh; otherwise, their aroma may be diminished and their pith spongy. With Buddha's Hands, inspect the fingers carefully to ensure that they are uniformly firm and free of blemishes. Scratching the skin with your fingernail is a useful way to gauge a citron's aroma. Citrons should always have a strong fresh scent.

Because of their physical characteristics, citrons are most frequently used for candying and alcohols; citron marmalade, though made in certain Mediterranean regions, is less common. A famous infused vodka is flavored with Buddha's Hand, and a citron version of the famous limoncello liqueur is sometimes made. In Italy, citron (or *cedro*, as it is known there) is made into a delicious liqueur with a flavor more similar to that of Buddha's Hand than that of Etrog. One or two citrons can lend a lovely aroma to your kitchen, and one single candied Buddha's Hand may be used to flavor many delicious jars of jam.

CRANBERRY *Season: November and December*

Cranberries are naturally well suited to preserving, both in terms of flavor and physical properties. They are sour high-pectin fruits that keep well under refrigeration. However, their flavor is extremely strong and is usually associated with savory sauces and jellies; thus, to be made successfully into sweet preserves, they are generally best combined with other fruits, as in the classic "paradise" triumvirate of cranberry, apple, and quince.

When selecting cranberries, always look for firm red fruit; if the fruit appears shriveled or pale in color, it is either past its prime or was picked green. Cranberries are among the best fall fruits, and they lend their dark red jewel-like color to the jams and marmalades made with them.

CURRANT *Season: Midsummer*

Currants are small, perfectly smooth round berries; they grow on bushes and are found primarily in cooler climates. There are three types of currants: red, white, and black. Because of their excellent flavor, tartness, and high pectin content, currants rank among the best fruits for preserving, and they are widely used by the British for jams and sauces of all types. Fresh currants are unrelated to dried currants; the latter are actually a type of small grape.

Black currants are exceedingly tart, with an unmistakably dark flavor, and are rarely eaten raw. Traditionally used for cassis liqueur, syrup, and preserves, they make excellent jelly and jam. However, they often are difficult to find in the United States.

Red and white currants are easier to find and are very similar to each other; white currants are the milder of the two. Red and white currants possess a very pure, tart, red-berry flavor; though they may be eaten raw, cooking brings out their flavor best. Red currants are traditionally used in England and France for jams and jellies, and in England also for Cumberland sauce, a sweet-savory condiment traditionally served with meats. In preserves, red currants are most commonly found either on their own or combined with raspberries. The most exquisite and famous French red currant jam, Bar-le-Duc, traditionally involves skewering each individual currant and drawing out its seeds prior to cooking; however, with a proper jelly-to-solid ratio, a beautifully textured red currant jam may be made with the seeds left in it.

Red currant jelly is among the most versatile of all preserves and is a traditional staple of the French and English pantries; it may be used with meats or as an ingredient with sweet braises, such as braised cabbage. It is also used as a dessert glaze. In addition, the sweet-tart bite and garnet color of red currant jelly render it particularly well suited to my favorite use of all: buttered morning toast.

ELDERBERRY & ELDERFLOWER *Season: Summer Through Fall*

Elderberries, like damsons, are known in England as "hedgerow" fruits; that is, they grow wild on trees in the countryside and are just as frequently gathered by individuals as grown commercially. Although there are numerous other fruits in this category, such as sloes, bullaces, and rowanberries, elderberries and damson plums are by far the most widely known in this country.

Elderberries, like other wild fruits, have a unique and instantly recognizable flavor. Also like other such fruits, they have a distinctive appearance. Elderberries are round, smooth, dusty bluish gray, and very small. They grow in clusters. Their highly tannic, wine-like flavor is unpalatable when raw; the berries must be cooked or fermented in order to be eaten. Elderberry wine is a famous backyard brew, and elderberry jelly is a favorite old-fashioned preserve.

For elderberry preserves, always use firm, unbroken berries; inspect the fruit carefully to be sure it is free of insects. Although elderberries may be kept briefly in the refrigerator, it is best to use them right away. When picking elderberries, always gather whole clusters of fruit at a time. To use the berries, rinse the clusters well under cold water and pat them dry. Then, gently pull the berries from the stems over a bowl and weigh them.

Elderberries are well suited to both sweet and savory uses, but especially to savory ones. Elderberry jelly is an excellent companion for all manner of meats and game, and it also makes an excellent dessert glaze or partner for cheese. Elderberries lack pectin and may be paired with other fruits, such as apples, which will provide pectin and mellow out their uniquely pungent flavor.

Elderflowers, the flowers of the elderberry tree, have a very delicious lychee-like perfume. They are most frequently used to flavor syrups and liqueurs. The delicate flavor of elderflower liqueur is a uniquely pleasing accompaniment to numerous fruits, including pears, nectarines, and lemons. And, of course, a few dashes of it always adds a special something to elderberry jelly, too!

FIG *Season: Summer and Fall*

Figs are one of the most ancient cultivated fruits, famous for their exceptional sweetness and beauty. For those who live where they are grown—primarily California, the Mediterranean, Turkey, and the Middle East—they are one of nature's most special treats. Because they are extremely fragile and do not ripen after picking, figs are an especially exotic treat for the rest of the world, where they are most frequently enjoyed dried or made into jam or paste. Fig jam is one of the most delicious and distinctive of all jams and is made all over the world where figs are grown.

Fig trees typically produce two crops per year: June and September. The fall crop is the more flavorful of the two. Figs come in many different varieties and are botanically distinct from other fruits. Though all figs taste somewhat similar, each variety has its own special personality. Figs may be distinguished both by color and by physical characteristics. A partial list of favorites follows.

Adriatic and Greek Royal figs are strikingly beautiful: They possess pale green skin and a cherry-colored interior. Among domestic figs, their flavor is unsurpassed. Adriatics are especially well suited to jam making because of their relatively thin skins, which soften more easily than those of some other varieties. Adriatics combine well with ginger; however, both Greek Royals and Adriatics are delicious on their own. Kadota, another green-skinned variety, is one of the most widely grown figs in California. Among green figs, though, Adriatics and Greek Royals are superior.

Brown Turkey figs are very well suited to jam making due to their exceptionally thin skins and pleasing flavor. They are purply brown in color with brown interiors.

Black Mission figs are the most common figs in California. Black Missions range in quality from bland to very flavorful, so it is important to choose well when buying or picking them. Only use perfectly ripe specimens. Black Mission figs make an excellent jam, especially when combined with citrus or other flavors. Black Missions have thicker, firmer skins than some varieties, and thus they must be cut into smaller pieces and simmered with a little water prior to cooking.

Always try to get the best figs you can find. Nothing is less inspiring than a bland fig. Picking your figs yourself or purchasing them from a top-notch farmer is essential. When ripe, figs should be tender to the touch and may have a little bead or two of liquid at the tail end. However, be wary of overripe figs, because they can start to ferment inside; when that happens, they must be discarded. When confronted with extremely soft figs, it is best to smell or taste them to determine whether they are still good. Figs keep refrigerated for a few days, but ripe ones tend to go moldy very quickly; thus, using them right away is best. To refrigerate figs, spread them out on a baking sheet so that they are not touching, then put them uncovered into the fridge.

Though commercial fig jam is often uniform in texture and very sweet, fig jam is best when it contains chunks of fruit and a low dose of sugar. Figs are extremely sweet to begin with. A little Chartreuse or Benedictine liqueur always brings out their flavor, which is also deepened by the cooking process. To make fig jam, first assess the thickness of the figs' skin; thick skin will not cook through simply by being thrown into a pan with sugar, but will need to be precooked with a little water first. Keeping in mind that your fig pieces, no matter what the thickness of their skin, will not fully disintegrate during cooking, you may cut them either smaller or larger, according to the recipe and your own personal preference. When making fig jam, some of the fruit must always be pureed in order for the jam to have a nice texture. For the best texture, the chunks of fruit should also be mashed with a potato masher during cooking.

Figs combine exceptionally well with other flavors and have a wide range of sweet and savory uses. They are famously good with cheese, and they may also be served with meats or fowl. The possibilities for fig jam are infinite; when deciding what to add to figs, if anything, always let the subtle flavor of each different variety guide you. The recipes in this book represent but a few of the many delectable possibilities.

GRAPE *Season: Late Summer Through Early Fall*

Slip-skin grapes, of which Concord is the most famous variety, are the best grapes for preserving; most other grapes lose their delicate perfume when cooked over high heat.

One of the few widely known fruits native to North America, Concord grapes grow like weeds all over New England and the Northeast, though they are also grown commercially elsewhere in the country.

Concord grapes consist of two distinct entities: a thick skin and a soft center. To use these grapes for jam, the centers must first be squeezed from the skins by hand. The centers are then cooked briefly, put through a sieve to remove their seeds, and recombined with the skins. For the best flavor, citrus or another flavoring is added to the fruit before cooking. As with all jams, only a minimum of sugar should be used in order to let the fruit's natural brilliance shine through.

When selecting grapes, always look for firm, unshriveled fruit. The fruit should be unsprayed. Always taste the fruit first; you are looking for a very strong flavor. Although it is more work, smaller grapes are best: Because there is a higher proportion of skins to centers, they will yield a more flavorful jam.

Concord grapes are very high in pectin. In addition to jam, they make an excellent jelly, and they are also delicious combined with certain other fruits, such as blackberries or apples. Concord grape preserves may also be spiced, if you like; vanilla and cinnamon are nice additions.

GRAPEFRUIT *Season: Winter*

Grapefruit, along with lemon and orange, is one of the classic fruits for English marmalade. Like these other fruits, grapefruits have very tart juice and very bitter rind. However, they differ physically from most other citrus fruits; their rind is extremely thick, and they have much thicker membranes dividing their sections. Making marmalade from grapefruits thus demands more steps than most other marmalades in order to produce a delicious result.

To make grapefruit marmalade, whether using white, pink, or ruby grapefruits, the fruit must be cut in half, and then blanched multiple times before being cooked through; otherwise, it will be too bitter. After the blanching, the halved fruit is simmered in water until tender, after which the flesh is scooped out and the interior of the rind is scraped free of excess spongy pith. Only then is the grapefruit rind sliced. This process takes time, but the end result is worth it; nothing is better than a really delicious grapefruit marmalade, and a few grapefruits will produce several jars.

When selecting grapefruits for marmalade, flavor and ripeness should be your number-one considerations; avoid any fruit that has been picked green. If you are including the grapefruit's flesh, it is best to use a seedless variety if possible. Grapefruit and lemon are natural partners; their flavors complement each other perfectly. Grapefruits are traditionally combined with lemons and oranges in Great Britain for three-fruit marmalade.

GUAVA *Season: January and February*

Guavas are tropical fruits, and they come in numerous colors and sizes. White guavas are considered the finest.

Guavas are frequently used for preserves in the tropics, where they are made into jams, jellies, and fruit butters. A guava paste, similar to membrillo or damson cheese, is also made. Guavas are well suited to preserving in two important respects: Their pectin content is very high and they have a strong flavor. However, due to the natural sweetness of guavas and the sugar required for preserving, guava preserves can often be cloyingly sweet. Thus, combining guavas with other fruits, such as citrus, produces a better result.

Guavas will not ripen after picking, so they should be perfectly ripe when you get them. They should be just the tiniest bit tender to the touch, and white guavas may begin to show hints of dark brown dots when ripe. White guavas should never appear really green; if they do, they were picked prematurely. Guavas should have a buttery texture, not a spongy or mealy one. Always try to taste your guavas before buying to be sure they will be delicious.

KUMQUAT *Season: December Through April*

Kumquats, though long considered citrus fruits, have recently been classified in a category all their own. Though they physically resemble tiny oblong oranges, they differ from oranges in that their rind is sweet and their flesh sour. Their rind is also very thin, with virtually no pith. Kumquats have an unmistakably snappy and delicious flavor. There are several varieties of kumquat, of which Nagami and Meiwa are the most common. For preserving, tarter kumquats, such as Nagamis, are best.

Kumquats may be used for a variety of preserves; they make an excellent fine-cut marmalade and also work well in jellies or jams made with other fruits. Marmalades made with kumquats may lack some of the chewiness of those made with citrus fruits, as the skin of kumquats softens considerably during cooking. Kumquats take time to prepare, and seeding them can be quite laborious. Although they keep well and usually have good flavor, always look for fresh, firm fruit when purchasing. Kumquats have a very long growing season.

There are numerous kumquat hybrids, each of which is a kumquat crossed with a citrus fruit; the most famous are mandarinquats and limequats. Limequats are exceedingly sour; both mandarinquats and limequats may be made into marmalade.

LEMON *Season: Year-round*

Of all fruits, lemons are the most essential to preserving. Nearly all jam and marmalade recipes call for lemon juice, and lemons combine well with all types of fruits. Lemons are in season year-round where they are grown, and in these areas lemon trees abound in backyards and along side streets. When choosing lemons, look for firm, unwaxed fruit with smooth skin. Leathery skin indicates the lemon is old. Oversized fruit frequently has thick pith, which often means a less juicy interior.

Although different lemons are grown all over the world, three are most widely known in the United States: Eureka, Lisbon, and Meyer. Eurekas and Lisbons are the common lemons found in every corner grocery store; they are similar to each other, though Lisbons have a cleaner flavor. Another excellent variety, Sorrento, has few seeds, thin skin, and a perfectly tart lemon flavor.

Eurekas and Lisbons have a high amount of acid. In preserving, they are used primarily for their juice, which both sharpens and balances flavor and provides the acid necessary for preserves to set. Lemon juice contains a small amount of pectin, though most of a lemon's pectin is found in its rind.

The Meyer lemon, thought to be a hybrid of a Eureka lemon and a mandarin orange, differs markedly from other varieties. Meyer lemons have thinner, more porous skin than most other lemons. They are also much less acidic. They tend to be juicier than other lemons, and they have an instantly recognizable fragrance. For these reasons, Meyer lemon juice should never be used as a replacement for Eureka or Lisbon juice in a preserve recipe.

Both Meyer lemons and common lemons make exceptionally delicious marmalade. Like many citrus fruits, Meyer lemons become juicier, sweeter, more flavorful, and darker in color the longer they hang on the tree; depending on how rich a flavor you want, you may either use younger or slightly older fruit. Like strawberries, Meyer lemons have a strong flavor and should be used carefully when combined with other fruits. They cook extremely quickly due to the porousness of their skin; keep a close eye on them as they cook. Because their skin is so permeable, it is important to use them immediately after the initial cooking. Never let Meyer lemons sit for any length of time in their water, or they will quickly turn to mush.

Common lemons, particularly Lisbons, also make stellar marmalade, and they are among the fruits most often used for this purpose in the British Isles. When selecting lemons for marmalade, look for a very clean, tart taste and firm skin; these are both indicators of freshness. Lemons usually should be blanched briefly prior to being made into marmalade; this rids their rind of some of its bitterness while preserving its clear flavor. Lemons combine very well with other citrus fruits, and the possibilities for delicious lemon marmalades are truly endless.

LIME *Season: Year-round*
There are many varieties of lime, but the Bearss, or Persian lime, is the only one widely cultivated in the United States. Bearss limes make a superior marmalade, especially in their ripe state; though they may be picked green, like all limes they turn yellow when fully ripe. Bearss limes have a smooth, tart flavor and are nearly always seedless.

When choosing limes, as with other citrus, look for firm specimens. The skin should be smooth and should have a strong aroma when scratched with a fingernail. Bearss limes, like Meyer lemons, have more porous skin than that of most other citrus fruits, and it is important not to overcook them. Their flavor complements other fruits well, as it is very tart without being bitter. Limes, like lemons, bear fruit in cycles throughout the year.

MANDARIN & TANGERINE *Season: Early Winter Through Spring*

Mandarins, a group of citrus fruits whose closest relative is the orange, include many varieties, among which are the Satsuma, Page, and Gold Nugget. The word *tangerine* as used in the United States actually refers to a subset of mandarins, generally those with many seeds and darker skin. Mandarins are distinguishable from oranges by their milder flavor (they generally have less sugar and less acid than oranges) and by their appearance (they are smaller and/or flatter). Unlike oranges, mandarins tend to have a web of fibers on the underside of their skin, and their skin is often only loosely affixed to their flesh.

Mandarins are not as well suited to preserving as many other citrus fruits. They tend to taste too sweet when made into plain marmalade. In addition, they pose a technical problem, in that the underside of their skin is often unpleasantly fibrous. However, different mandarin varieties have different characteristics, and certain ones, such as Page and Gold Nugget, can work quite well. When selecting mandarins for marmalade, always go with those whose skin adheres strongly to their flesh. You are looking for firm fruit with a vivid flavor. Mandarins may sometimes be bland or dry, so it is important to taste the fruit first if possible. The sweetest mandarins are best eaten raw and the tartest saved for preserving.

MELON *Season: Midsummer Through Late Summer*

Sweet melons are commonly used for preserving in France, though we rarely see melon jam in this country. Though perhaps not for everyone, melon jam is one of the most unusual and delicious summer jams.

For melon jam, always use melons with peachy or orange-colored flesh; honeydews are not well suited to preserving. The quality of melon jam depends entirely on that of the individual melon: It must be absolutely perfect, or your jam will suffer. This adds an element of surprise to the jam-making process, because it is impossible to be completely sure of a melon's quality before actually cutting into it. However, there are a few ways to help ensure that you will choose a winner.

Purchasing or picking your melons from a trusted farm or other source increases your likelihood of getting superior fruit. As there are numerous varieties of melon, try to speak to your farmer or grocer to find out which are currently at their peak. Smell the melon at the stem end; it should smell musky and fruity. Depending on the variety, it may also be tender at the stem end. Though melons do ripen over time, never start with a melon that was picked green; the longest a melon should need to ripen is four or five days. Once you are as sure as you can be that your melon is ready to eat and is going to be good, your only choice is to cut into it. Then, and only then, will you be completely sure of its quality.

There are two reasons melons must be perfect to make jam. First, unripe fruit tends to yield a slightly green flavor in the jam, rather than the succulent, almost peachy fruitiness you desire. If a melon is bland, it will yield a spineless jam. Second, underripe fruit will remain unpleasantly firm when cooked. Thus, for melon jam, the best thing is often to improvise; if you unexpectedly find yourself with some particularly lush and succulent fruit on hand, it's time to get out the jam pot!

Melons present a few technical difficulties in addition to the challenge of determining their quality. Melons are among the fruits lowest in pectin; they require a thickener in order to be viable. In addition, even ripe melon tends not to break down in the cooking process, and must be both mashed and partially pureed for good results. Also, melons tend to be naturally sweet, so a perfect balance of sugar and lemon is essential. Last, melons have a very high water content, which must be cooked out of them without overcooking the fruit. For all these reasons, small batches are essential for melon jam.

MULBERRY *Season: July and August*

Mulberries are among the most delicious berries in the world. They grow well in the eastern, southern, and western United States but are rarely grown here commercially because they do not keep or transport well. If you are lucky enough to live near a place where mulberries are grown, making mulberry jam may become a highlight of your year.

Unlike many berries, mulberries grow on trees, which can live for several hundred years and reach enormous heights. Mulberries are one of the oldest cultivated fruits, and they come in three colors: red, white, and black. White mulberries are small and ivory colored, sometimes with a slight tinge of mauve. They are sweet and mild in flavor. Red and black mulberries are larger and more flavorful. Black are the best: They are large, intensely flavored berries with a superficial resemblance to blackberries. Their juice stains your hands, clothes, and cutting boards; this is part of the mulberry experience! Although they should ideally be used shortly after picking, mulberries may be stored briefly in the refrigerator; to do so, spread them out in a single layer on a baking sheet or tray lined with a clean rag.

Black mulberries make a dazzling jam with a very intense dark flavor. Because they lack pectin, powdered pectin is needed to thicken the jam. Like other berries, mulberries should be cooked only briefly to keep their bright flavor. They hold their shape when cooked and must be mashed with a potato masher during cooking. Mulberries need no ornament.

NECTARINE (see also PEACH, page 344) *Season: May Through November*

Nectarines, or fuzzless peaches, are similar to peaches in most respects. Like peaches, nectarines are either yellow or white, and may be shot through with red. However, nectarines tend to be firmer than peaches and have a subtly different, tarter flavor. Unlike peaches, nectarines need not be peeled before using. Nectarines vary considerably in quality; as with peaches, always look for a strong high-acid flavor. Like peaches, nectarines combine well with almond; ginger-nectarine is another excellent combination.

ORANGE *Season: Year-round (depending on the variety)*

Oranges are among the most versatile fruits for preserving, useful both as a central ingredient and as a flavoring. Like other citrus fruits, they are high in pectin and acid. There are two main categories of orange: sour and sweet. Within these two broad groups, there are numerous different varieties. Oranges vary considerably in flavor, sweetness, acidity, quantity of seeds, and appearance. Each variety has its own distinct personality.

Winter is high season for the two main types of sour orange: Seville and bergamot. (For more information on Bergamot, see page 322.) Of these two, the Seville is the most common and is widely known as the classic fruit for Scotch and English marmalade. Seville oranges are small to medium orange fruits. Their skin is thick,

bitter, and slightly rough, and they are full of round seeds. They make a strong marmalade redolent of wintry spice, with an unmistakable sour orange flavor.

Seville oranges, like other intensely flavored fruits, may be handled in a number of ways. For hard-core marmalade lovers, nothing can beat the mouth-puckering complexity of a really good thick-cut Seville marmalade. However, Sevilles may also be made into a less intense preserve by being sliced thinly and blanched prior to cooking. Sour orange juice and rind may be used as a flavoring for cherries or other fruits. Sliced Sevilles may also be combined with other citrus fruits.

Sweet oranges may be divided into two main categories: blood oranges and other oranges. Among blood oranges, Moro, Tarocco, and Sanguinello are the most common varieties. Blood oranges tend to have few, if any, seeds. Their skin is less thick and rough than that of Seville oranges. They are characterized by their dark (sometimes very dark) red flesh and skin; the ratio of red to orange varies from fruit to fruit and variety to variety. Blood oranges range from sweet to exceedingly tart and mouth-puckering, though they are never as bitter as a true sour orange. Because of their color, they make a very pretty pinkish orange marmalade. Their distinctive flavor goes well with numerous other ingredients, such as rosemary, rose water, and bitters; because their season stretches into late spring, they may even be combined with strawberries.

Among other sweet oranges, navels and Valencias are the most common. There are many varieties of navel; Cara Cara and Washington are two of the best. Navels have a spongier skin than most other oranges, so they must be used with care. Because they are on the sweet side, it is often best to combine them with tarter fruits, such as lemon.

Valencia oranges, when they are good, are among the very best of all fruits for preserving. Sweet-tart, firm-textured, and bursting with flavor, they make an exceptionally pretty and delicious marmalade. Valencias are the perfect complement to a whole host of other fruits, including kumquats, strawberries, and elderberries. They are commonly found in supermarkets and have a very long growing season.

PEACH *Season: May Through November*
There are endless different varieties of peach, both yellow and white; some varieties may also be strongly tinged with red. Although the flavor of peaches varies considerably, white peaches generally have a more delicate flavor and fragile texture than yellow peaches. When selecting peaches, always look for fruit without any green that is slightly firm to the touch. Tasting the fruit before purchasing it is extremely helpful. For jam, what you are looking for is vividly flavored fruit with a high degree of tartness; such peaches are often referred to as "high-acid." If using non-high-acid peaches, you may need to increase the amount of lemon juice in the recipe. Once you arrive home with your peaches, place them on a baking sheet to ripen at room temperature, being sure they are not touching each other.

Peaches have a long growing season, though the season for each individual variety may be brief. They change dramatically over the course of the summer. In early May, they are small and wild looking, with a tart almondy fragrance; by the end of summer, they are extremely large, meaty, and richly flavored from their time hanging in the summer sun. The earliest peaches of summer are generally clingstone varieties; their pits must be cut from their flesh with a paring knife. The peaches of late summer are usually freestone; their pits can easily be twisted from their flesh. Unlike nectarines, all peaches must be peeled before being made into jam.

There is another very important difference between early- and late-season peaches: density. Early-season peaches have a much less dense and firm flesh; it is easy to tell when they are ripe because they become slightly soft to the touch. Late-season peaches, by contrast, are extremely firm, making it nearly impossible to tell their ripeness without cutting into them. Once an end-of-summer peach reaches the point of ripeness, it almost immediately starts to wither and turn moldy; thus, when using such peaches, always buy a few extras for cutting into to test their readiness.

Like all stone fruits, peaches have almond-like kernels in their pits. These nuts, though toxic when raw, add a delicate, heavenly fragrance to peach jams.

In addition to peach kernels, peaches boast another very special built-in ingredient: their leaves. Peach leaves are traditionally used in southern France for making *vin de pêche*, a fortified aperitif wine, and they are also an essential ingredient for late-summer peach jam. They have an almost marzipan-like fragrance; when infused into jam, they bring out all the background flavors of the peaches.

PEAR *Season: October and November*
There are numerous types of pears, all surprisingly different from one another: the buttery Comice, the sweet Bosc, the less sweet Anjou, and many more. When choosing pears for jam making, there are two primary qualities to consider: taste and texture. Many pears, while they may taste sweet and pleasing, derive their flavor more from their crunchy texture than from any deep pear essence. A sweet pear is not necessarily a flavorful one. In addition, pears may vary considerably from year to year and grower to grower. Thus, it is generally a good idea to taste the pear, if possible, before using. What you are looking for is a not-too-sweet, deep pear flavor. Always make sure your pears are perfectly ripe before using them for preserves.

The best jam pears are slightly gravelly in texture; the grainy Warren, for example, is preferable to the super-smooth Comice. Choose a pear whose texture you think will be interesting once it is cooked. Texture is one of the things that sets pears apart from other fruits; their slight "sandiness" will lend your jam character.

Despite having less pectin than quinces or apples, pears are perfectly suited to jam making in one special respect: They combine exceptionally well with many other flavors. The possibilities are endless: In addition to the traditional vanilla and ginger, many other and less expected flavorings are perfect with pears, such as rosemary, sage, cardamom, honey, and elderflower. Although we often think of pears as being less vivid than many summer fruits, the flavor of pear jam holds up remarkably well against toast or yogurt; a pear's flavor can be stronger than it seems. As pears vary considerably in sweetness, use the lemon juice quantities in this book as a guide, adding more if you deem it necessary.

Although pears may seem similar to apples at first glance, in fact they take much longer to break down during cooking than apples do. Thus, it is often necessary to puree a portion of your pear jam partway through cooking. Otherwise, you may end up with cooked chunks of pear with nothing binding them together.

Pears are not only excellent made into jam; they also make a delicious jelly, and they may even be combined with lemon to make an exceptional marmalade.

PLUM *Season: Summer Through Fall*

Though ignored by many, plums are among the most varied, versatile, and delicious fruits for preserving. Plums come in a wide array of colors and flavors. Due to their texture and pectin content, they require only a minimum of sugar relative to most other fruits, and their intrinsic tartness makes them ideally suited for preserving. Plums can be classified generally by color, texture, and flavor. The following is a partial list of my favorites.

Gages are a family of plums from England, where the greengage is a famous dessert and jam fruit. Gages tend to have a delicately flavored interior with tart skin, and they may be greenish, yellowish, or transparent with hints of pink. There are numerous varieties of gages, all of which make excellent tart jam. They are higher in pectin than many other plums and should always be cooked in small batches to prevent overcooking. They come into season in midsummer to late summer.

Santa Rosa plums, of Japanese derivation, are perhaps the most famous plums grown in the United States. There are different types of Santa Rosas, each of which ripens at a different time. Santa Rosas possess a rich flavor and are in every way the essence of plumminess. Other flavorful red plums, such as Showtime or Mariposa, may sometimes be used interchangeably with Santa Rosas in recipes. Santa Rosas are very versatile and may be combined with other fruits or flavors.

Black plums, such as Laroda or Black Splendor, are notable for their dark, rich flavor. These plums ripen in late summer or early fall and make superior jam. They may have black or yellow flesh, but their skins are always very dark. Black plums are less bright tasting than Santa Rosas, but they have an earthy depth of flavor all their own. These plums are best used alone or with only a slight flavor enhancement in order to let their excellent flavor shine its brightest.

Prune plums come in two main types: French and Italian. Both are better cooked than raw. Prune plums are instantly recognizable by their slightly oblong shape and relatively small size. Both French and Italian prune plums make excellent preserves. The flavor is concentrated almost exclusively in the skin. French prune plums are delicious with pluots or other plums, while Italian prune plums are particularly well suited to spiced preserves. They are a fall fruit, appearing at markets in September and October.

Damson plums (at right) are the "wildest" plums, belonging to a different botanical strain than all other varieties. Damsons are small and dark, with yellow flesh. They are meant for cooking and are among the firmest of all plums. Their excellent flavor is almost akin to that of dried plums and is more dense and deep than that of most other plums. Damsons are in season in September. They are higher in pectin than other plums, and in England they are made into damson "cheese," a damson butter cooked until it has lost enough moisture to form a solid mass when cool. Damsons pair deliciously with citrus, almond, tomato, and spices.

Elephant Heart plums are dear to all those who taste them. An heirloom variety with a devoted group of followers, Elephant Hearts are exquisitely beautiful fruits with a spectacular flavor. They are medium sized, with

dusty-looking, slightly speckled mauve-gray skin. Their flesh is a strikingly vivid dark cherry red color. Their flavor is unsurpassed, and, though they have less acid than some other plum varieties, they make a gorgeous jam. Elephant Hearts come into season in late summer.

All plums should be tender to the touch when ripe, though some varieties have denser flesh than others. Like other stone fruits, plums may be laid out on a baking sheet at room temperature to ripen. As with all stone fruits, they should never be picked rock hard or green.

Despite the large number of plum varieties, all plum jams are remarkably similar from a technical standpoint. Plums contain a large amount of moisture, much of which must be cooked out of them for the jam to thicken. The flavor of plum jam is best when little sugar is used; thus, the plums often may be partially pureed or mashed to help thicken the jam. Lemon juice is essential to plum jam, as it pairs naturally with the tartness of the plum's skin and accentuates the fruit's natural flavor. Plum jams vary somewhat in texture; depending upon the amount of pectin and moisture present in the raw fruit, the jam may be more or less dense. To make plum jam, the fruit is typically cut into large pieces, layered with sugar and lemon juice, and left to macerate in the refrigerator for one to several days prior to cooking.

Plums are incredibly versatile. Depending on the variety, they may be combined with other fruits, such as strawberry, rhubarb, apple, cherry, or tomato. They may also be spiced with cinnamon, clove, or cardamom. They combine well with herbs, including lavender and rosemary. They also often benefit from a splash of liquor: Plum brandy, plain brandy, or almond liqueur are natural choices. With plums, delicious variations are truly endless. The recipes in this book represent but a few of the many possibilities.

POMEGRANATE *Season: Fall*
Pomegranates are composed of numerous small white seeds, each surrounded by a juicy red sac. The seeds are divided into distinct regions by the fruit's white pith, and the whole is encased in a dark pink skin. Pomegranates are used primarily for their juice, which is best extracted by squeezing pieces of the raw fruit with a citrus press or forcing the seeds through a sieve. Pomegranate juice is a gorgeous deep magenta color and will easily stain your hands, clothes, and cutting boards.

Pomegranates, like red currants, have a distinctly tart red-fruit flavor, which may either stand on its own or provide a backdrop for other flavors. Pomegranate juice makes an excellent dark red jelly when used alone; it may also be combined with cranberry or other fruits to great effect. Because pomegranate juice lacks pectin, powdered pectin must be added in order for the juice to jell.

When selecting pomegranates, look for unbroken, smooth skin that is more pink than gray. The skin should be slightly shiny; dull, leathery, shriveled skin is a sign of old fruit. The seeds of the pomegranate should be a brilliant dark red color; extremely dark seeds may indicate old fruit, and pale seeds may indicate fruit that was picked too early.

QUINCE *Season: October and November*
For those who love quince, there are few things to match its honeyed complexity, and for those who have never tasted it, it is invariably an exciting surprise. Quinces are most similar to apples, which they somewhat

resemble in appearance, but their flavor is distinct and complex. They are exceedingly hard and are not palatable in their raw state; they must be cooked for several hours to reach the height of their flavor. Quinces are a pale yellowy green when raw, gradually turning deep red as they cook. They are among the oldest cultivated fruits, and quince preserves are a staple of several ancient cuisines, including those of Iran and Turkey. Quince paste, or membrillo, is a quince butter cooked down until it has thickened enough to be cut into slices when cool. Increasingly seen here in specialty food shops, it is found throughout the Mediterranean, where it is usually served with sheep's milk cheese.

Quinces are ideally suited to preserving. They require sugar to be palatable, being quite devoid of sweetness themselves. They possess an extremely high amount of pectin. Their strong flavor combines well with numerous spices and flavorings but is equally delicious plain. Quinces hold their shape when cooked, and for this reason they are most often either made into jelly or preserved in large pieces.

Quinces should always be picked yellow, not green; when green, their flavor has not yet fully developed. Although they keep well even at room temperature, it is best to refrigerate them for longer storage. Quinces should be peeled prior to using, unless they are being used for jelly; in this case, they may simply be cut up whole. Before cooking with quinces, be sure to rub off their furry coating under running water.

Quinces are perhaps most striking in their concentrated forms, jelly and membrillo. However, a delicious jam may also be made with them, and their juice may be used to flavor other fruits, such as rhubarb or cranberry.

RANGPUR LIME *Season: Winter and Midsummer*
Rangpur limes are not true limes, but a type of sour mandarin. Physically, they resemble small mandarins, but their skin is very porous and they are exceedingly tart. Like most citrus fruits, Rangpurs are extremely high in pectin and, like many mandarins, they have very few seeds. Rangpur lime trees produce prodigious amounts of fruit in cycles throughout the year. When selecting fruit, avoid specimens with leathery or dry skin. If possible, cut a sample in half crosswise; the fruit should be juicy and bright throughout. Refrigerate the fruit if you are unable to use it right away, and keep in mind that fresher fruit is always best.

Rangpur limes make one of the best marmalades. Their flavor is a mixture of lime, mandarin, and citron, yet different from all three. They are extremely easy to work with, and the rewards are great.

RASPBERRY *Season: June Through November*
Raspberries come in four principal colors: red, golden, white, and black. Red, golden, and white raspberries are closely related; black raspberries belong to a different botanical strain. Black raspberries possess a flavor distinct from that of other raspberries and are smaller, with more seeds and a drier texture.

Red, golden, and white raspberries may be used interchangeably for jam, though white raspberries tend to be less flavorful than their red and golden cousins. Whatever their color, no store-bought raspberry will ever compare to the ones you pick yourself. Because a perfectly ripe raspberry will last for only a few hours before it starts to wither, commercial berries are invariably picked before they have reached their highest pinnacle of

flavor. Picking one's own raspberries is a great pleasure, and making raspberry jam is one of the best ways to keep and enjoy your berries all year round. If you are unable to use your raspberries immediately, spread them on paper towels on a baking sheet and refrigerate them, uncovered, until you are ready to use them.

Unlike nearly every other fruit, red or golden raspberries do not require lemon juice to balance their flavor; in fact, red or golden raspberry jam is at its best with ample sugar and little or no lemon. Raspberry jam may be either seeded or seedless, though black raspberry jam is perhaps best with the seeds left in; black raspberries are so full of seeds that removing them would leave very little jam to enjoy. When making seeded raspberry jam, cook the berries in stages in order to preserve their delicate texture. In addition to being delicious on their own, raspberries combine exceptionally well with red currants, rose, and rose geranium.

RHUBARB *Season: Spring Through Fall*

Rhubarb is not actually a fruit, but a stem. Rhubarb plants consist of several stalks, each growing straight out of a central ground-level base, with very large poisonous dark green leaves at the ends. To pick rhubarb, grasp the stem you want, hold the surrounding stems in place at their base, and pull hard. Then, to trim the rhubarb, cut off the bottom of the stem, the leaf, and any dark green parts. Rhubarb should always be freshly trimmed just prior to using.

Rhubarb is very tart and must be sweetened prior to eating. It lacks pectin and tends to disintegrate very quickly when heated. Although delicious on its own, it is also often combined with other summer fruits, such as strawberry, raspberry, and cherry; these fruits give rhubarb jam a deeper color and an extra shot of pectin.

When preserving rhubarb, there are several things to remember. Always use very fresh, firm stalks, the reddest you can find. It is important to cut the rhubarb in long, rather than short, lengths; otherwise, your jam will have a soupy texture with no personality. When combining rhubarb with another fruit, it is often best to use a large quantity of rhubarb relative to the companion fruit, as this will give your jam a nice tartness and allow the flavor of the rhubarb to shine.

In addition to fruits, rhubarb combines well with numerous flavorings, including vanilla, ginger, rose, and rose geranium. Rhubarb also makes a stellar jelly, either on its own or combined with other fruits.

STRAWBERRY *Season: May Through November*

Strawberries have an exceptionally long growing season, and there are numerous different varieties. Strawberries combine well with other fruits, such as rhubarb, plums, and Pluots, as well as with a wide array of herbs and flavorings. Their juice also may be added to citrus fruits to make some surprising and truly delicious marmalades. The flavor of strawberries tends to dominate; when combining them with other fruits, it is important to be careful with the amounts to let the other fruits shine through.

Like other berries, strawberries will not ripen after picking, so choosing good berries at the outset is very important. When selecting strawberries, always look for bright or dark red fruit with just the slightest hint of tenderness. Pull up the leaves to examine the "shoulders" of the fruit; they should be red, not white. Strawberries can go bad very quickly; to avoid spoiled-tasting jam, discard any blemished or soft berries and also any berries touching them. Always use the most flavorful berries you can find.

For preserves, use medium to large berries; they are quicker to hull and will give more texture to your finished product. As with other berries, using unsprayed fruit is essential; industrially grown strawberries have more pesticide on them than just about any other fruit.

It may be challenging to choose between the many different varieties of strawberry; tasting the different berries and getting to know your local growers is very helpful. Two of the most common varieties in California are Seascape and Chandler, both of which make a fine jam, though Seascapes vary considerably in size and quality and are sometimes frustratingly small. I prefer Chandlers; they are my favorite strawberry for spring and make a beautifully clean-tasting bright red jam. My other favorite varieties are Aroma and Albion, espe-

cially Aroma. This wonderful berry possesses everything the perfect jam berry should have: velvety texture, medium-large size, dark red color, and excellent flavor. Albions have many of these same attributes, although they are sometimes just a shade less vividly flavored. As with any fruit, growing conditions, specifically sunlight and rain, strongly affect each berry's size and flavor. One of summer's great pleasures is to taste different varieties from different growers, one after the other; the variations among them may amaze you!

TOMATO *Season: Summer Through Fall*

Tomatoes are perhaps the most surprising of all jam fruits, but tomato preserves have a long history both in Europe and in the United States. Classic American tomato preserves include tomato jam and tomato marmalade, both traditionally heavily spiced with cinnamon and cloves. Tomato preserves are extremely delicious and a lot of fun to make, because the flavor of tomatoes becomes so much sweeter and deeper during cooking.

Both green (unripe) and ripe tomatoes may be used for preserves, though not interchangeably. For ripe tomatoes, look for vividly flavored, firm, luscious fruit. Dry-farmed tomatoes, preferably from a very sunny area, are best; because they have received less water than other tomatoes, their sugars are more concentrated. There are numerous good tomato varieties. The best for preserving are small to medium red ones, such as Early Girl. Tomatoes are relatively low in pectin and high in acid.

Tomatoes should never be refrigerated prior to being combined with sugar. They must always be peeled before being made into preserves, and this should be done over a bowl to catch the juice. Tomatoes do not fully break down during cooking, but starting with large chunks is still best; this will lend your jam or marmalade more character. Tomatoes are startlingly versatile; they combine well with stone fruits, spices, and citrus, to name but a few possibilities. When used in jams, their texture somewhat resembles that of plums, while in marmalades, they may become almost candied in texture. Tomato preserves are especially delicious with cheese and are excellent served on sourdough, cornbread, or English muffins.

ACKNOWLEDGMENTS

I would especially like to thank:

Erin McKinney, whose unexampled kindness and support have been a beacon of light in my life these past two years. From the bottom of my heart, thank you!

Luz Lopez, left-hand woman extraordinaire: This book would never have happened without you. I'm going to miss you so much!

Sara Remington, whose gorgeous photos have brought this book to life. You are truly one in a million, and I have loved every moment of our work together.

Ethel Brennan, whose excitement, expertise, and fabulous eye brought so much to this book; and Kami Bremyer, for the generous use of her beautiful linens and dishes.

Francesca Bautista, whose designs are a continual source of joy and inspiration; Blue Chair would not be Blue Chair without you.

Jane Dystel, my fantastic agent: I really admire you, and I am so glad to have the chance to work with you; you make me want to do my best!

Jean Lucas, my editor: I feel so fortunate to work with you. Thank you for your warmth, humor, intelligence, and dedication.

Kirsty Melville, for your support and belief in this project. I feel so lucky to have you behind me.

John Carroll, Carol Coe, and Dave Shaw at Andrews McMeel, for making the publishing process go so smoothly. Thank you!

Valerie Cimino and Ann Cahn, for your hard work and razor-sharp eye for detail. Thank you for your invaluable copyediting and proofreading!

Jennifer Baum and Chris Langley at Bullfrog and Baum and Tammie Barker and Amy Worley at Andrews McMeel, for your extraordinary efforts on behalf of this book.

Jan Newberry and Anne Saunders, for generously offering your time, support, and excellent recipe feedback!

Flo Braker, Lance Velasquez, Peter Perez, Charlie Hallowell, and Claude Millman, for lending me a helping hand just when I needed it most. Thank you!

The Blue Chair Fruit team, past and present: Your hard work, humor, and dedication are what allowed me to write this book. I would like to extend a special thanks to Stephen Brown and David Routman. Thank you!

My deepest thanks also to:

The Loewen family and Blossom Bluff Orchards; Willow Haven Farm; Dirty Girl Produce; Lucero Organic Farms; Guru Ram Das Orchards; Kaki Farm; Happy Quail Farms; Will Brokaw; Poli Yerena; Scott Vermeire; Bill Fujimoto; Chuy and Martin at Monterey Market; Deborah O'Grady and Eloise; Alice Erb; Elena Eger and Marc and Naomi Beyeler; Georgeanne Brennan and Jim Schrupp; Tse-Sung Woo and Nirmala Ramalingam; Slow Food Alameda; Melanie Eisman; Chris Willging and Miles Finnegan; Yvette Molina and Josh Ross; The Pasta Shop; Rainbow Grocery; BiRite Market; Urban Village Farmers' Market Association; John Challk, Lorena Jones; Miriam Godderich; and all my wonderful clients, past and present. Special thanks also to the late Tom Duffy: You helped me more than you could know, and I will never forget your early support of my preserves.

I would also like to thank my wonderful parents for their support and proofreading, and my husband Mark, for believing in Blue Chair from the very start.

BIBLIOGRAPHY

Davidson, Alan.
The Penguin Companion to Food. New York: Penguin,
2002.

Grigson, Jane.
Jane Grigson's Fruit Book. New York: Atheneum,
1982.

Madison, Deborah.
The Savory Way. New York: Bantam Books,
1990.

Medrich, Alice.
Pure Dessert. New York: Artisan,
2007.

Waters, Alice.
Chez Panisse Fruit. New York: HarperCollins,
2002.

Wilson, C. Anne.
The Book of Marmalade. New York: St. Martin's,
1985.

SOURCES

Blue Chair Fruit Company
www.bluechairfruit.com
510 459 6135

Beautiful jam labels for home preserving, Blue Chair Fruit T-shirts, Blue Chair Fruit aprons, and gift-wrapped autographed copies of this book, in addition to a wide array of organic jams and marmalades. You can also join our mailing list and view our schedule of upcoming classes.

Canning Pantry
www.canningpantry.com
435 245 6776

Mason jars, various types of cherry pitters and apple peelers, and many other useful items.

Market Hall Foods
www.markethallfoods.com
888 952 4005

Chestnut honey, pinecone bud syrup, and muscovado sugar.

Melissa Guerra
www.melissaguerra.com
877 875 2665

Piloncillo and chestnut honey.

Metro Kitchen
www.metrokitchen.com
888 892 9911

Mauviel hammered copper preserving pans and high-quality knives.

Pacific Gourmet
www.pacgourmet.com
888 652 9252

A superb wholesale source for powdered apple pectin, spices, extracts, and obscure ingredients. They are located in San Francisco but ship nationwide.

Penzeys Spices
www.penzeys.com
800 741 7787

High-quality spices, including vanilla beans, Ceylon cinnamon, blade mace, and Turkish bay leaves. They also carry excellent almond and vanilla extracts.

Sur La Table
www.surlatable.com
800 243 0852

A great source for electronic kitchen scales, heatproof gloves, heatproof rubber spatulas, and other kitchen needs

The Sausage Maker
www.sausagemaker.com
888 490 8525

The Sausage Maker makes our favorite cherry pitter (shown on page 132). It's expensive, but if you are planning to pit a large number of cherries on a regular basis, it's worth it.

The Spice House
www.SpiceHouse.com
847 328 3711

Very good Mexican vanilla extract, in addition to a wide range of herbs and spices.

INDEX